Hands-On Enterprise Application Development with Python

Design data-intensive Application with Python 3

Saurabh Badhwar

BIRMINGHAM - MUMBAI

Hands-On Enterprise Application Development with Python

Commissioning Editor: Aaron Lazar
Acquisition Editor: Chaitanya Nair
Content Development Editor: Manjusha Mantri
Technical Editor: Ashi Singh
Copy Editor: Safis Editing
Project Coordinator: Prajakta Naik
Proofreader: Safis Editing
Indexer: Mariammal Chettiyar
Graphics: Jisha Chirayil
Production Coordinator: Jyoti Chauhan

First edition: December 2018

Production reference: 1271218

Published by Packt Publishing Ltd.
Livery Place
35 Livery Street
Birmingham
B3 2PB, UK.

ISBN 978-1-78953-236-4

www.packtpub.com

`mapt.io`

Mapt is an online digital library that gives you full access to over 5,000 books and videos, as well as industry leading tools to help you plan your personal development and advance your career. For more information, please visit our website.

Why subscribe?

- Spend less time learning and more time coding with practical eBooks and Videos from over 4,000 industry professionals

- Improve your learning with Skill Plans built especially for you

- Get a free eBook or video every month

- Mapt is fully searchable

- Copy and paste, print, and bookmark content

Packt.com

Did you know that Packt offers eBook versions of every book published, with PDF and ePub files available? You can upgrade to the eBook version at `www.Packt.com` and as a print book customer, you are entitled to a discount on the eBook copy. Get in touch with us at `customercare@packtpub.com` for more details.

At `www.Packt.com`, you can also read a collection of free technical articles, sign up for a range of free newsletters, and receive exclusive discounts and offers on Packt books and eBooks.

Contributors

About the author

Saurabh Badhwar is a developer and open source enthusiast who is passionate about improving software performance and scalability. He has been actively contributing to Mozilla Servo and Fedora Project in the fields of release engineering, quality assurance, and community building. He has given talks at various community organized events and universities to onboard and engage new members in the community. Saurabh is currently exploring the microservices architecture and has given various talks on it. His most recent talk on the microservices architecture happened at DevconfCZ 2018. Currently, Saurabh works as an Associate Software Engineer, Performance and Scale Engineering at Red Hat.

About the reviewer

Zhuo Qingliang (also known online as KDr2) works at Beijing Paoding Tech (PAI), a start-up fintech company in China that is dedicated to improving the financial industry by using artificial intelligence technologies. He has over 10 years of experience in Linux, C, C++, Java, Python, and Perl development. He is interested in programming, consulting, and contributing to the open source community.

Packt is searching for authors like you

If you're interested in becoming an author for Packt, please visit `authors.packtpub.com` and apply today. We have worked with thousands of developers and tech professionals, just like you, to help them share their insight with the global tech community. You can make a general application, apply for a specific hot topic that we are recruiting an author for, or submit your own idea.

Table of Contents

Preface

Python is a dynamically typed, interpreted language that facilitates the rapid building of applications in various areas of software development, including AI, desktop, and web applications.

With recent advancements in the Python ecosystem and the availability of a huge number of libraries that support high re-usability and enable the compilation of modular code, Python can be used to build applications that can solve an organization's problems. These applications can be developed in short timeframes and, if developed carefully, can allow them to be scaled in a manner that solves the needs of an organization.

Python version 3.7 brings with it several improvements and new features that make application development a breeze. Along with new features, improvements in the language's performance make it a good choice for building scalable, mission-critical applications powered by a choice of different runtimes based on the organization's needs.

Who this book is for

An enterprise application is a critical application that aims to solve the specific business needs of an organization. The requirements of an enterprise application differ greatly from those that are usually needed by an individual. These applications are supposed to provide high performance and scalability to enable the increasing everyday needs of an organization.

Keeping this in mind, this book is intended for developers who have an intermediate knowledge of coding in Python and are willing to dive deeper into building applications that can be scaled up, based on the needs of the organization. The book provides several examples that can be executed on Python 3.7 running on Linux-based distributions, but which also work on other operating systems.

To make the best use of this book, you must have a basic understanding of fundamental operating system concepts, such as process management and multithreading. Beyond this, a basic working knowledge of database systems may be beneficial, although not mandatory.

Developers who are familiar with the different aspects of building applications in Python can get to learn about the tools and techniques that can help them build scalable applications and provide them with an idea of the enterprise application development approach.

What this book covers

This book contains 16 chapters organized into roughly 4 parts: an introduction to Python in enterprises; the testing, performance, and security of enterprise applications; the shift toward microservices; and enterprise application integration.

The first part covers the utilization of Python in enterprise application development and deals with the various aspects related to building a performant and scalable application with Python. This first part consists of seven chapters.

Chapter 1, *Using Python for Enterprise Application Development*, introduces the capabilities of Python that make it a rich language when it comes to developing enterprise applications and provides information about the changes that have happened in the Python ecosystem and how they have helped in boosting the utilization of Python within the community.

Chapter 2, *Design Patterns – Making a Choice*, explains the importance of design patterns in the development of applications and covers some of the commonly used design patterns in application development and how they can be implemented in Python. This chapter also provides guidance on how to choose which design patterns to use while developing the application.

Chapter 3, *Building for Large-Scale Data Operations*, covers how to build enterprise applications that can handle a large number of concurrent data operations while maintaining the consistency of data. This chapter takes a look at how the data models are developed to allow for scalability and performance and then goes on to provide information about how to make database operations efficient.

Chapter 4, *Dealing with Concurrency*, introduces us to the different ways in which we can improve the ability of our application to deal with concurrent workloads. For this, the chapter introduces us to various techniques in Python related to the implementation of multiprocessing and multithreading and how we can use them to boost the concurrency-managing capability of the application.

Chapter 5, *Building for Large-Scale Request Handling,* introduces us to the ways in which we can make our application scale well when it comes to a high number of concurrent users while keeping the response times adequate. We will also cover the different techniques related to maximizing the output from multithreading, utilizing asynchronous operations, and so on.

Chapter 6, *Building BugZot,* makes use of what we have learned in the preceding chapters to come up with an example application known as BugZot, which provides our dummy organization, Omega Corporation, with a bug tracking system. While building this application, we get to implement the techniques related to building efficient database models, implementing concurrency, and handling the uploading of large files.

Chapter 7, *Building Optimized Frontends*, takes us through the importance of building application frontends that are responsive and light on resources. This chapter covers various techniques related to the optimization of web-based frontends and how to provide an experience that keeps the user engaged with the application.

With this, we enter the second part of the book, which consists of three chapters aimed at improving the delivery aspects of the application.

Chapter 8, *Writing Testable Code,* focuses on the points related to the importance of writing code that can be tested easily and how it helps in delivering applications that are stable and robust when deployed in production. This chapter introduces us to a Python-based testing framework that can be used to write unit tests and integration tests and also covers the aspects of automated testing of the code.

Chapter 9, *Profiling Application for Performance*, introduces us to the tools and techniques that we, as developers, can use to build performance profiling into the core of the application to understand the performance implications of running the applications and allow us to uncover bottlenecks in production.

Chapter 10, *Securing Your Applications,* covers the different attack vectors that are used by attackers to compromise enterprise data security and then helps us to understand the basics of how we can avoid introducing vulnerabilities into our applications.

The third part of the book includes the following chapters that cover the architecture of application development.

Chapter 11, *Taking the Microservices Approach*, takes us on a journey of developing applications based on microservice architecture. In this chapter, we will take a look at what exactly microservice architecture is and the advantages it provides. We will then move on to understanding the different components that power microservice architecture and conclude by building a small application based on microservice principles.

Chapter 12, *Testing and Tracing in Microservices*, goes into how the move to microservices has changed the way we approach application testing, which now comprises the interaction of several small services instead of large components. We take a look at additional steps that might be required in making sure the applications work in the manner they are expected to, before we dive into another concept that allows us to trace the flow of the request in our application as it passes through different services.

Chapter 13, *Going Serverless*, introduces us to yet another method of building our applications where we, as developers, do not need to care about where the application will run and how it will scale. In this chapter, we will learn about how we can divide our application into functions that can run without our supervision and execute based on a set of events.

Chapter 14, *Deploying to the Cloud*, introduces us to the different cloud deployment strategies and how they can help us while also providing us with guidance about which type of cloud deployment to choose, based on the requirements of the organization.

The fourth and final part of the book includes the following chapters, which introduce us to the need to integrate different applications inside the enterprise.

Chapter 15, *Enterprise Application Integration and their Patterns*, takes us through an introduction to why enterprise application integration is necessary and how it was achieved in days gone by, before diving into the concepts of using middleware and an enterprise service bus. This chapter concludes with a discussion of various EAI patterns that are in use.

Chapter 16, *Microservices and Enterprise Application Integration*, takes us through the differences that the move toward microservices has introduced to the EAI landscape. In this chapter, we will take a look at how the modern concepts of microservices have changed how application integration was achieved in the past and how we can plan ahead for integrating different applications in this modern age.

To get the most out of this book

Other than being familiar with programming in general, no particular specialist knowledge is expected in order to be able to take advantage of this book.

Odoo is built using Python, so it is a good idea to have a sound knowledge of the language. We also choose to run Odoo in an Ubuntu host (a popular cloud hosting option) and will do some work on the command line, so some familiarity will be beneficial.

To get the most out of this book, we recommend that you find complementary readings on the Python programming language, Ubuntu/Debian Linux operating system, and the PostgreSQL database.

Although we will run Odoo in an Ubuntu host, we will also provide guidance on how to set up our development environment in a Windows system with the help of VirtualBox. Of course, working from an Ubuntu/Debian system is also a possibility.

All the required software is freely available, and instructions on where to find it will be given.

Download the example code files

You can download the example code files for this book from your account at `www.packt.com`. If you purchased this book elsewhere, you can visit `www.packt.com/support` and register to have the files emailed directly to you.

You can download the code files by following these steps:

1. Log in or register at `www.packt.com`.
2. Select the **SUPPORT** tab.
3. Click on **Code Downloads & Errata**.
4. Enter the name of the book in the **Search** box and follow the onscreen instructions.

Once the file is downloaded, please make sure that you unzip or extract the folder using the latest version of:

- WinRAR/7-Zip for Windows
- Zipeg/iZip/UnRarX for Mac
- 7-Zip/PeaZip for Linux

The code bundle for the book is also hosted on GitHub at `https://github.com/PacktPublishing/Hands-On-Enterprise-Application-Development-with-Python`. We also have other code bundles from our rich catalog of books and videos available at `https://github.com/PacktPublishing/`. Check them out!

Conventions used

There are a number of text conventions used throughout this book.

`CodeInText`: Indicates code words in text, database table names, folder names, filenames, file extensions, pathnames, dummy URLs, user input, and Twitter handles. Here is an example: "Beyond these three packages, the reader will also require the `sqlalchemy` package, which provides the ORM we will be using throughout the chapter, and `psycopg2`, which provides `postgres` database bindings to allow `sqlalchemy` to connect to `postgres`."

A block of code is set as follows:

```
username = request.args.get('username')
email = request.args.get('email')
password = request.args.get('password')
user_record = User(username=username, email=email, password=password)
```

When we wish to draw your attention to a particular part of a code block, the relevant lines or items are set in bold:

```
username = request.args.get('username')
email = request.args.get('email')
password = request.args.get('password')
user_record = User(username=username, email=email, password=password)
```

Any command-line input or output is written as follows:

```
mkdir ch3 && cd ch3
virtualenv --python=python3 .
source bin/activate
pip install sqlalchemy psycopg2
```

Bold: Indicates a new term, an important word, or words that you see on screen. For example, words in menus or dialog boxes appear in the text like this. Here is an example: "In the web client, access the **Apps** top menu and select the **Update Apps List** menu option."

Warnings or important notes appear like this.

 Tips and tricks appear like this.

Get in touch

Feedback from our readers is always welcome.

General feedback: Email `customercare@packtpub.com` and mention the book title in the subject of your message. If you have questions about any aspect of this book, please email us at `customercare@packtpub.com`.

Errata: Although we have taken every care to ensure the accuracy of our content, mistakes do happen. If you have found a mistake in this book, we would be grateful if you would report this to us. Please visit `www.packt.com/submit-errata`, selecting your book, clicking on the Errata Submission Form link, and entering the details.

Piracy: If you come across any illegal copies of our works in any form on the internet, we would be grateful if you would provide us with the location address or website name. Please contact us at `copyright@packt.com` with a link to the material.

If you are interested in becoming an author: If there is a topic that you have expertise in, and you are interested in either writing or contributing to a book, please visit `authors.packt.com`.

Reviews

Please leave a review. Once you have read and used this book, why not leave a review on the site that you purchased it from? Potential readers can then see and use your unbiased opinion to make purchase decisions, we at Packt can understand what you think about our products, and our authors can see your feedback on their book. Thank you!

For more information about Packt, please visit `packt.com`.

Using Python for Enterprise 1

Python has been around in the world of programming for more than two decades now, and over the years, the language has seen a number of refinements, a growing community, and a lot of production-ready and well-supported libraries. But is Python ready to make a dent in the world of enterprise application development, which has been long dominated by the likes of C++, Java, and .NET, the so-called **enterprise-grade languages**?

Over the course of this chapter, we will see how Python has evolved over the years and how it is ready to become a serious competitor in the world of enterprise application development.

This chapter will cover the following topics:

- Recent developments in Python to enable its growth in enterprise application development
- The special use cases where Python shines
- The differences between enterprise and general-purpose software
- The requirements for developing an enterprise application

Technical requirements

The code listings in this book can be found under chapter01 directory at https://github.com/PacktPublishing/Hands-On-Enterprise-Application-Development-with-Python.

The code samples can be cloned by running the following command:

```
git clone
https://github.com/PacktPublishing/Hands-On-Enterprise-Application-Developm
ent-with-Python
```

The instructions to run the code can be found under the README file in the individual chapter directories.

The code has been tested to run on a system that is running Fedora 28 and Python version 3.6.5, but it should be able to run on any system running Python 3.6.5.

Recent developments in Python

Python is a dynamically typed, interpreted language that was initially well suited for scripting tasks that are boring and repetitive day-to-day tasks. But as the years progressed, the language gained a number of new features and the huge backing of its community, which propelled its development to make it a language that is now well suited to performing tasks that range from very simple applications, such as web scraping, to analyzing large amounts of data for training machine learning models that themselves are written in Python. Let's take a look at some of the major things that have changed over the years and see what the latest release of Python, Python 3, brings to the table.

Dropping backward compatibility

Python as a language has evolved a lot over the years, but despite this fact, a program written in Python 1.0 will still be able to run in Python 2.7, which is a version that was released 19 years after Python 1.0.

Though a great benefit for the developers of Python applications, this backward compatibility of the language is also a major hurdle in the growth and development of major improvements in the language specification, since a great amount of the older code base will break if major changes are made to the language specification.

With the release of Python 3, this chain of backward compatibility was broken. The language in version 3 dropped the support for programs that were written in earlier versions in favor of allowing a larger set of long-overdue improvements to the language. However, this decision disappointed quite a lot of developers in the community.

It's all Unicode

In the days of Python 2, the text data type `str` was used to support ASCII data, and for Unicode data, the language provided a `unicode` data type. When someone wanted to deal with a particular encoding, they took a string and encoded it into the required encoding scheme.

Also, the language inherently supported an implicit conversion of the string type to the `unicode` type. This is shown in the following code snippet:

```
str1 = 'Hello'
type(str1)          # type(str1) => 'str'
str2 = u'World'
type(str2)          # type(str2) => 'unicode'
str3 = str1 + str2
type(str3)          # type(str3) => 'unicode'
```

This used to work, because here, Python would implicitly decode the byte string str1 into Unicode using the default encoding and then perform a concatenation. One thing to note here is that if this str1 string contained any non-ASCII characters, then this concatenation would have failed in Python, raising a UnicodeDecodeError.

With the arrival of Python 3, the data types that dealt with text changed. Now, the default data type str which was used to store text supports Unicode. With this, Python 3 also introduced a binary data type, called bytes, which can be used to store binary data. These two types, str and bytes, are incompatible and no implicit conversion between them will happen, and any attempt to do so will give rise to TypeError, as shown in the following code:

```
str1 = 'I am a unicode string'
type(str1) # type(str1) => 'str'
str2 = b"And I can't be concatenated to a byte string"
type(str2) # type(str2) => 'bytes'
str3 = str1 + str2
---------------------------------------------------------
Traceback (most recent call last):
File "<stdin>", line 1, in <module>
TypeError: can't concat str to bytes
```

As we can see, an attempt to concatenate a unicode type string with a byte type string failed with TypeError. Although an implicit conversion of a string to a byte or a byte to a string is not possible, we do have methods that allow us to encode a string into a bytes type and decode a bytes type to a string. Look at the following code:

```
str1 = '₹100'
str1.encode('utf-8')
#b'\xe2\x82\xb9100'
b'\xe2\x82\xb9100'.decode('utf-8')
# '₹100'
```

This clear distinction between a string type and binary type with restrictions on implicit conversion allows for more robust code and fewer errors. But these changes also mean that any code that used to deal with the handling of Unicode in Python 2 will need to be rewritten in Python 3 because of the backward incompatibility.

Here, you should focus on the encoding and decoding format used to convert `string` to `bytes` and vice versa. Choosing a different formatting for encoding and decoding can result in the loss of important information, and can result in corrupt data.

Support for type hinting

Python is a dynamically typed language, and hence the type of a variable is evaluated at runtime by the interpreter once a value has been assigned to the variable, as shown in the following code:

```
a = 10
type(a)          # type(a) => 'int'
a = "Joe"
type(a)          # type(a) => 'str'
```

Though dynamic interpretation of the type of a variable can be handy while writing small programs where the code base can be easily tracked, the feature of the language can also become a big problem when working with very large code bases, which spawn a lot of modules, and where keeping track of the type of a particular variable can become a challenge and silly mistakes related to the use of incompatible types can happen easily. Look at the following code:

```
def get_name_string(name):
    return name['first_name'] + name['last_name']

username = "Joe Cruze"

print(get_name_string(username))
```

Let's see what happens if we try to execute the preceding program:

```
Traceback (most recent call last):
  File "<stdin>", line 1, in <module>
  File "<stdin>", line 2, in get_name_string
TypeError: string indices must be integers
```

The program exited with a `TypeError` because we passed a `string` type to the `get_name_string()` method and then tried to access the keys inside a string, which is not the correct solution.

With the release of Python 3.5, the community added support for type hinting that was built into the language. This was not an effort to enforce a method, but was rather provided to support the users who may want to use modules that can catch errors that are related to a variable changing its type in between the execution flow.

The general syntax to mark the type of a variable is as follows:

```
<variable>: <type> = <value>
```

To mark the types in a method, the following syntax can be used:

```
def method_name(parameter: type) -> return_type:
    # method body
```

One of the examples of how to use type hinting in the program code is shown in the following code:

```
from typing import Dict

def get_name_string(name: Dict[str, str]) -> str:
    return name['first_name'] + name['last_name']

username = "Joe Cruze"

print(get_name_string(username))
```

When the preceding code is written in an IDE, the IDE can use these type hints to mark the possible violations of the type change of variable in the code base, which can prove out to be really handy by helping to avoid errors that are related to an incorrect type change when dealing with large code bases.

An important point that needs to be reiterated here is that using type hinting does not guarantee that the interpreter will raise an error if you pass a parameter with an incorrect type to the method. The type hinting support is not enforceable and should only be used either with other tools that can help check type violations or with IDEs to support the development process.

Where Python shines

Every language has been developed to solve a certain type of problem that developers face while trying to build software for a specific domain. Python, being a dynamically typed, interpreted language, also has a set of use cases where it excels.

These use cases involve the automation of repetitive and boring tasks, quick prototyping of applications, and small applications focusing on accomplishing a specific goal, such as the installation of software, the setting up of a development environment, performing cleanup, and so on.

But is that all? Is Python good only for doing small tasks? The answer to this is no. Python as a language is much more powerful and can easily accomplish a large amount of increasingly complex tasks, such as running a website that scales to cope with millions of users using it in a very short span of time, processing large sets of incoming files, or training a machine learning model for an image-recognition system.

We are talking about achieving increasingly complex tasks using Python, but isn't Python slow compared to our traditional compile-time languages, such as C++, Java, and .NET? Well, that completely depends upon the context in which a person wants to use Python. If your aim is to run a Python program on an embedded device with only a limited amount of processing power, then yes, Python might be inadequate because of the sheer extra load that its interpreter will have on the processing environment. But if you are planning to use Python to run a web application on decently configured modern hardware, you might never experience any slowdowns while using Python. Rather, you might well feel a bit more productive while using it because of the sheer simplicity of its syntax and the ease of performing operations without writing hundreds of lines to achieve simple tasks.

So, let's see how Python fares in the enterprise environment.

The requirements of enterprise IT

Enterprise IT is complex, and an application that needs to be built for the enterprise will differ a lot from one that is built for a regular consumer. There are several factors that need to be kept in mind before developing an application for enterprise users. Let's take a look at what makes enterprise IT applications different from regular consumer offerings, as shown in the following list:

- **Business oriented**: Unlike an application that is built to solve the problems of individual users, an enterprise application is built to meet the specific needs of an organization. This requires the application to conform to the business practices of the organization, their rules, and the workflow they use.

- **Robustness at scale**: Most enterprises usually consist of thousands of employees who depend upon the internal applications to work and collaborate with each other. These kinds of use cases generate a large amount of data in various ways, and an application built for enterprise should be robust enough to handle thousands of users at the same time while also being able to crunch through a large amount of data that is distributed over a large network of nodes. During this time, the application should provide adequate mechanisms to deal with unexpected events that may happen for various reasons, such as attempts to breach security, the failure of nodes, power failure, and so on.
- **Long-term support**: An enterprise application needs to provide long-term support because enterprises usually don't want to move to newer applications as frequently as a regular consumer does. This happens because most enterprise applications are developed to integrate with the workflow of the organizations, and frequently changing an application will not only increase ownership costs for the enterprise, but will also cause a major disruption in the workflow for the employees of the organization.
- **Ability to integrate**: Most of the applications that are built for the enterprise won't be running as standalone applications. They will frequently need to interface with the other applications inside the organization. This gives rise to the need to provide a mechanism for easy integration of the application with others in the organization.

Python in the enterprise ecosystem

Python has been present in the enterprise ecosystem in quite a few forms; be it the automation of boring and repetitive tasks, being used as a glue between two layers of a product, or being used for building quick and easy-to-use clients for big server backends, the language has seen an increasing amount of adoption for various use cases. But what makes Python ready for the development of large enterprise applications? Let's take a look:

- **Ability to build quick prototypes**: The syntax of Python is very simple, and a lot of things can be achieved with very few lines of code. This allows developers to quickly develop and iterate over the prototypes of an application. In addition to this, these prototypes do not always need to be thrown away, and if the development is properly planned, they can act as a good base to build the final application upon.

- With the ability to quickly prototype an application, an enterprise software developer can see exactly how the requirements align in the application and how the application is performing. With this information, the stakeholders of the application can more accurately define the path for the application development, thereby avoiding midcycle architectural changes because something didn't work out the way it was expected to.

- **A mature ecosystem**: The mature ecosystem is one of the features of Python that deserve a lot of attention. The number of external libraries in Python has been growing at a rapid pace. For most of the tasks that need to be achieved in an application, such as two-factor authentication, testing code, running production web servers, integrating with message buses, and so on, you can easily look for a library with quite decent support.

This proves to be of great help, since it reduces the amount of code duplication and increases the reusability of the components. With the help of tools such as `pip`, it is very easy to get the required library added to your project, and with the support of tools such as `virtualenv`, you can easily segregate a lot of different projects on the same system without creating a dependency mess.

For example, if someone wants to build a simple web application, they can probably just use Flask, which is a microframework for developing web applications, and go ahead with the development of the web application without having to worry about the underlying complexities of dealing with the sockets, manipulating data on them. All they will require is a few lines of code to get a simple application up and running, as shown in the following code:

```
from flask import Flask
app = Flask(__name__)

@app.route('/', methods=["GET"])
def hello():
    return "Hello, this is a simple Flask application"

if name == '__main__':
    app.run(host='127.0.0.1', port=5000)
```

Now, as soon as someone calls the preceding script, they will have a `flask` HTTP application up and running. All that remains to be done here is to fire up a browser and navigate to `http://localhost:5000`. Then we will see Flask serving a web application without any sweat. All of this is made possible in under 10 lines of code.

With a lot of external libraries providing support for a lot of tasks, an enterprise developer can easily enable support for new features in the application without having to write everything from scratch, thereby reducing the chance of possible bugs and non-standardized interfaces creeping into the application.

- **Community Support:** The Python language is not owned by any particular corporate entity, and is completely supported by a huge community backing that decides the future of the standard. This ensures that the language will continue to see support for quite a long time, and won't become obsolete any time soon. This is of great importance to organizations, since they want long-term support for the applications they run.

Given all of the preceding benefits of Python, developer productivity will get a boost when using the language while also reducing the total cost of ownership for the software if decisions are made in a well-planned way. These decisions involve how the application architecture will be laid out and which external libraries to use or to develop in-house. So yes, Python is indeed now ready to be used in the mainstream world of enterprise application development.

Introducing BugZot – a RESTful bug tracker

As we progress through the chapters in this book, we will need some way to implement what we have learned.

Imagine that you work for an organization known as **Omega Corporation**, which is a market leader for selling software products to companies and individuals. Omega Corporation needs a system through which it can track the bugs in its products. After a lot of brainstorming, they initiate a project codenamed BugZot, which will be their tool to track the bugs in their products.

Let's take a look at what Omega Corporation wants to achieve with project BugZot:

- **Ability for users to report bugs in products**: The users, be they internal or external, should be able to file bugs against a particular product of the organization, and while filing these bugs, the users should be able to select the release version of the product they are filing bugs against so as to provide increased granularity.

- **Ability to control who can see the bug details**: Since the application allows both internal and external users to file bugs, it is possible that internal users, such as quality engineers or internal IT teams, may file bugs against a product that has not yet been made available to the customers. This will mean that BugZot should be able to hide the details about the bugs that have a confidential status.

- **Providing support for role-based permissions**: BugZot should be able to support the concept of roles and permissions so that an unauthorized person cannot change the details of a particular bug. For example, we might not want an external customer to come and change the target release version for a bug, which is a task that should be done by product management.

- **Support for file uploads**: When a bug is filed, usually an error report or a log file from the product greatly helps to drill down to the root cause. This will mean that BugZot should be able to deal with file uploads and link the uploaded files to their respective bugs.

- **Search functionality**: A person using BugZot should be able to search for the bugs that are filed into the system based upon certain filter criteria, such as the identity of the user who filed the bugs, the current status of the bug, filing bugs against, and so on.

- **Integration with email**: When a bug changes state—for example, if a bug is moved from NEW to ASSIGNED—there should be an email notifying the people associated with the bug. This will require BugZot to provide integration with the email service provider of Omega Corporation.

- **Ease of integration**: Omega Corporation plans to extend the usage of BugZot at a later time by integrating BugZot with the various other internal applications they have. For this, BugZot should provide an easy way to achieve this integration.

Throughout the course of this book, we will be learning various concepts in Python and applying them to build BugZot, the bug-tracking system for Omega Corporation.

Gathering requirements before development

Gathering the software requirements before starting the development of an enterprise application can be a tedious task, and a failure to do so adequately can have severe consequences, such as increased costs due to delays that are caused by identifying requirements later in the development cycle of the application. Applications that lack the important features to improve the business process workflow will lead users to stop using the application in the worst case.

The requirement-gathering process is complex and tedious, and can take months to complete in an organization. Covering all the steps involved in the process is beyond the scope of this book. This section tries to give a brief description about some of the important steps in the process of gathering software requirements.

Asking for the user requirements

For an application inside an organization, there might be various users who are stakeholders, and can define the requirements of the application. These users can be broadly split into two categories:

- **The workforce**: These are the users who usually use the application to achieve a certain set of tasks. They are not concerned with all the features provided by the application, but rather what they focus upon is how well the application fits into their individual workflows. These users can provide requirements specific to what they work on, but may not be able to provide ideas about what they might require in the future, or what the other teams may require.

- **The management**: The management consists of people who understand the business process of the organization and have a much broader view of what the application should be able to do. These users may not be able to define the requirements of a particular use case, but can provide requirements considering what the application should do now and what future features might be needed.

Involving both kinds of stakeholders in the requirement-gathering process is important, and something that will define how well the enterprise application meets the demands of its users.

Categorizing the requirements

Once the users have been surveyed for what they would like to have in the application, the next step is to categorize these requirements. Broadly, the requirements can be categorized into two parts:

- **Functional requirements**: These are the requirements that define the features and functionality of the application. For example, BugZot has the following functional requirements:

    - Providing functionality for filing bugs by internal and external users
    - Providing support for roles and permissions
    - Providing functionality for dealing with file uploads
    - Integrating with the email system to send emails when a bug changes its status, and much more

- **Nonfunctional requirements**: These are those sets of requirements that do not affect the functionality of the software, but rather are implicit or explicit characteristics based on the functional requirements. For example, in BugZot, the following may be defined as some of the nonfunctional requirements:

- The application should provide security against common web attack vectors, such as XSS and CSRF
- The operational costs for the application should not exceed $N\%$ of the total budget
- The application should be able to generate backups in case a recovery is needed after a crash

Prioritizing the requirements

Once the requirements are identified and categorized into functional and nonfunctional requirements, they then need to be prioritized according to their importance in the application. If this prioritization is not performed, it will lead to increased costs of development, delayed deadlines, and reduced productivity in the organization. Broadly, we can classify the requirements under the following categories:

- **Must have**: These are those requirements that are critical to the success of the application and that must be present in the application when it ships.
- **Should have**: These are those requirements that will enhance the functionality of the application but that need some further discussion about whether they should be added to the application.
- **Could have**: These are those requirements that are mostly enhancements, and the presence or absence of which won't affect the functionality of the application. These requirements can be taken care of in later updates to the application.
- **Wish list**: These are those requirements that are considered features that can be added at some later point in time, but which are not mission critical to the application. These features can be reviewed later for inclusion in the application update cycle.

Generating the software requirement specification document

Once the requirements have been identified, grouped, and prioritized, a document known as the software requirement specification is generated. This document describes the intended purpose, requirements, and nature of the software that needs to be developed.

The **software requirement specification** (**SRS**) will describe the following information:

- The intended purpose of the applications
- The conventions that are used in the document that are specific to the business process of the organization
- The features of the application
- The user classes who will be using the application
- The environment in which the application will operate
- The functional and nonfunctional requirements of the application

Once the SRS has been generated, it is sent for review and further negotiations. Once they are successfully completed, the application moves into the design phase, where an application mock-up is devised.

Summary

In this chapter, we briefly covered the changing programming landscape and explored how the Python ecosystem has changed over the years. We looked at how Python, given the fact that it allows quick prototyping, and has a vast array of well-supported libraries and an open community, is quickly rising to become the main choice for the development of large-scale applications in enterprises that require long-term support and easy integration with existing systems.

We then went on to introduce the demo application, BugZot, that we will be building throughout the course of this book, and defined the functionalities that will be required from the application.

The last section of the chapter covered the requirement-gathering process for developing an enterprise application in a brief, looking at the different stakeholders, such as the hands-on users and the management users, and categorizing the requirements into functional and nonfunctional requirements. We also looked at the importance of prioritizing the requirements.

With the basic knowledge of the environment with which we are going to work on during the course of the book, we are now ready to take a deep dive into the first important aspect of the Enterprise application development which deals with how we layout the code base of our application in production which involves, how a particular set of objects are created and utilized in the application while focusing on the increased re-usability of the modules. The next chapter focuses on this important aspect which is also known as the Design patterns and cover the different types of patterns and how they can be used during the development of your application.

Questions

1. Is it possible to perform operations such as concatenation on a `str` type and a `byte` type in Python 3?
2. Is the type hinting support introduced in Python 3 enforcing or not?
3. Beyond functional and nonfunctional requirements, are there any other kinds of requirements that also might need to be documented into the software requirement specification?

4. What are the major categories in which the prioritization of requirements can be done?

5. What are the next steps to take once the software requirement specification document has been generated?

Further reading

If you would like to go through the basics of Python programming once again before diving into the world of enterprise application development, Packt has a very good book that you can be refer to. You can get it at the following link:

- https://www.packtpub.com/application-development/learn-python-programming-second-edition

Design Patterns – Making a Choice

2

When a software application development project is taken up, it is essentially thought of as a problem that requires a solution. When we start to develop the application, we start developing a solution specific to the given problem. Eventually, this solution may start getting reused in problems of a similar kind, and becomes a standard solution for solving such problems. As time passes, we see that a lot of problems that display the same pattern. Once we modify our standard solution to work on this observed pattern, we come up with a **design pattern**. Design patterns are no joke; they take years to produce, after being tried and tested for solving a great number of problems with a similar pattern.

The design patterns not only define the way in which we architect our software application, they also provide knowledge about what worked and what did not, while trying to solve a particular type of problem. There are times when no particular design pattern might suit the needs of a particular application and the developers are left with no choice but to come up with something unique.

Are there some existing standard design patterns that can be used for a particular type of problem? How can we decide which design pattern to use for our problem? Can we deflect from a particular design pattern and use them while working on our solution? We will try to answer these questions as we progress through the chapter.

By the end of this chapter, you will know about the following:

- Design patterns and their classification
- The object-oriented nature of Python, and how we can use it to implement some common design patterns
- Use cases where a particular pattern may be used

Technical Requirements

The code listings in this book can be found under `chapter02` directory at `https://github.com/PacktPublishing/Hands-On-Enterprise-Application-Development-with-Python`.

The code samples can be cloned by running the following command:

```
git clone
https://github.com/PacktPublishing/Hands-On-Enterprise-Application-Developm
ent-with-Python
```

The instructions to run the code samples can be found under the `README.md` file present inside the chapter directory.

Design patterns

A design pattern defines a way in which we can organize our solution to a given problem. It does not define algorithms that can be used to solve the problem, but rather provides an abstraction about how, for example, the code should be organized, what classes need to be defined, what their granularity will be, and how the different objects will be created.

The design patterns have gained a lot of traction, and the book *Design Patterns: Elements of Reusable Object-Oriented Software,* though published in 1994, still serves as a de facto reference when trying to understand design patterns.

A design pattern will usually consist of the following elements:

- **A problem statement**: A problem statement describes what we want to solve and hence also defines the design patterns we can use. The problem statement will tell us about the scope of the design that we are planning to pursue, the constraints that we may need to take care of, and at times how the different components will communicate with each other in the application.
- **The solution**: A solution describes the design that makes up for the problem. It goes into detail about how the class hierarchies should be formed, how the objects will be formed, the relationship between the objects, and how the communication will take place between the different components. The solution will be an abstract design, not specifying the details of the implementation. This makes the solution generic, to be applied to a class of problems, without caring about what algorithms should be used to solve a particular problem.

- **The consequences**: In the world of software development, nothing comes for free. Everything has a cost, and we trade off one thing for another. What matters is whether the trade-off is justifiable or not. The same applies to the choice of design patterns, which come with consequences of their own. Most of the time, these consequences are in the terms of space and time trade-offs, and form an important part of evaluating alternative options if a particular design choice is not justifying the cost of trade-offs. Sometimes, the consequences may also define the implementation barriers of a language, and can often impact the reusability and flexibility of an application.

The choice of a design pattern is not something that is common for every set of problems. What pattern will be used to solve the problem will be based upon several factors, such as the interpretation of the problem by the developers, any restraints on the programming language that need to be used, the deadlines associated with the project, and so on.

Classification of design patterns

In the book *Design Patterns: Elements of Reusable Object-Oriented Software*, the design patterns have been classified into three major categories:

- **Creational patterns**: These patterns define how the objects can be created so that your code can be made independent of which objects are present, and hence decouples it from the impact that may happen when new objects are introduced into the code base. This requires the isolation of the object creation logic from the code base. The patterns, such as Singleton and Factory, come under the category of creational patterns.
- **Structural patterns**: Unlike creational patterns, which deal with how the objects are created, the structural patterns are often used to describe the composition of how the individual classes and objects will make up a larger structure. The structural patterns, instead of focusing on how to compose an interface or implementation, will rather focus on how to compose objects to realize new functionality. Patterns, such as proxy pattern, come under this category.
- **Behavioral patterns**: Behavioral patterns are used to describe the algorithms and the responsibility an object will fulfill. These patterns also define the way the communication happens between the different objects, and shift your focus on how the different objects are interconnected. Chain of Responsibility, Observer, and Visitor patterns are a few examples of the patterns that come under the category of behavioral patterns.

The different patterns do not mark the choice that only a single pattern can be used in the development of the application. Rather there are times when these patterns can be in conjunction with one another, because a particular pattern complements the functionality of another pattern. Which patterns to use will depend completely upon what the application demands. Let's take a look at what may define the choice of a design pattern.

Defining the choice of design patterns

When choosing a design pattern, we may want a certain set of characteristics that the design pattern should fulfill. Let's take a look at what these characteristics may consist of if we were to use Python to implement our design pattern:

- **Principle of least astonishment**: The Zen of Python says that the principle of least astonishment should be followed. That means that a design pattern being used should not surprise its user in terms of the behavior it is expected to show.
- **Reduced coupling**: Coupling is defined as the degree to which the different components inside a software are interdependent on each other. A software with a high degree of coupling may be very hard to maintain, since a change to one component may require a change to a lot of other components. Coupling as an effect cannot be completely removed from the software, but the choice of design pattern should be made such that the degree of coupling can be minimized in the development process.
- **Focus on simplicity**: Starting to develop a software with a design principle that is too generalized can do more harm than good. It may introduce a lot of unwanted functionality into the code base, which is used very sparingly or not used at all. The choice of design pattern should be made to focus more on providing a simple solution to the stated problem, rather than with a focus on how many common types of problems a particular design pattern can solve.
- **Avoid duplication**: A good choice of design pattern will help the developer to avoid duplicating the code logic and keep it in one place, from where the different components of the system can access it. The reduction in duplication of logic will not only save development time, but will also make the maintenance process easy, where the change in the logic will need to be done only at a single point, and not in multiple parts of the code base.

Object-oriented Python

Object-oriented programming (**OOP**) refers to the organization of code in a format where we are not concerned with the organization of methods, but rather we are concerned with the objects, their properties, and their behavior.

An object may represent any logical entity, such as an animal, vehicle, and furniture, and will contain properties and behaviors describing them.

The basic building block of an OOP-based language is the **class** that often groups the logically related entities together into a single unit. When we need to work with this unit, we create a new instance of this unit known as the class object, and manipulate the object using the public interfaces exposed by the object.

Object-oriented programming in Python differs quite a lot from what a person might see in C++ or Java, and these differences also affect the way in which we implement the different design patterns in Python. Let's take a look at how Python's object-oriented model can affect the implementation of different design patterns, and what other functionality the language provides to ease out on some of the tasks.

The basic OOP principles

A language cannot be considered an object-oriented language merely based on the fact that it supports classes and objects. The language will also need to support a set of different functionalities, such as encapsulation, polymorphism, composition, and inheritance, to be considered an object-oriented langauge. Python in this regard supports a lot of OOP-based concepts, but does it a bit differently due to its loosely typed nature. Let's take a look at how these features differ in Python.

Encapsulation

Encapsulation is a term that is used to refer to the ability of a class to restrict the access to its members only through the public interfaces exposed by the object. The concept of encapsulation helps us in just working on the details about what we want to do with the object and not about how the object will deal with the changes internally.

In Python, the encapsulation is not strictly enforced, in that we do not have the support of access modifiers, such as private, public, and protected, which can be used to strictly control the access to a particular member inside a class.

However, Python does support encapsulation with the help of name mangling, which can be used to restrict direct access to a particular property of a class by prefixing the property name with __(double underscores). The following code snippet shows an example of this:

```
class PyOOP:
    __name = None
    def __init__(self, name):
        self.__name = name

    def get_name():
        return self.__name

pobj = PyOOP('Joe')
print(pobj.__name)

Traceback (most recent call last):
  File "<stdin>", line 1, in <module>
AttributeError: 'PyOOP' object has no attribute '__name'
```

As we can see from the preceding code example, an attempt to access the __name property of PyOOP object raised an AttributeError because the property was identified as private in the class.

Composition

Composition is a property that is used to express a relationship between the different objects. The way this relationship is expressed in composition is by making an object an attribute of another object.

Python supports the concept of composition by allowing the programmer to build objects that can then be made part of other objects. For example, let's take a look at the following code snippet:

```
class MessageHandler:
    __message_type = ['Error', 'Information', 'Warning', 'Debug']
    def __init__(self, date_format):
        self.date_format = date_format
    def new_message(message, message_code, message_type='Information'):
        if message_type not in self.__message_type:
            raise Exception("Unable to handle the message type")
        msg = "[{}] {}: {}".format(message_type, message_code, message)
        return msg

class WatchDog:
```

```
def __init__(self, message_handler, debug=False):
    self.message_handler = message_handler
    self.debug = debug

  def new_message(message, message_code, message_type):
    try:
      msg = self.message_handler.new_message(message, message_code,
message_type)
    except Exception:
      print("Unable to handle the message type")
    return msg

message_handler = MessageHandler('%Y-%m-%d')
watchdog = WatchDog(message_handler)
```

As we can see from the example, we have made the message_handler object an attribute of the watchdog object. This marks one of the ways through which we can achieve composition in Python.

Inheritance

Inheritance is a way through which we create hierarchies in the objects, going from the most general to the most specific. A class that usually forms the base for another class is also known as a base class, whereas a class that inherits from a base class is known as a child class. For example, if a class B derives from class A, then we will say that class B is a child class of class A.

Just like C++, Python supports the concept of both multiple and multilevel inheritance, but does not support the use of access modifiers while inheriting in a class that C++ supports.

Let's take a look at how inheritance can be achieved in Python by trying to model how a new request will look in our BugZot application. The following snippet gives us a small example about the concept of inheritance:

```
class Request:
  def __init__(self, title, description, is_private=False):
    self.title = title
    self.description = description
    self.is_private = is_private
  def get_request():
    request_data = {
      'title': self.title,
      'description': self.description,
      'is_private': self.is_private
    }
```

```
        return request_data

  class Bug(Request):
    def __init__(self, title, description, affected_release, severity,
  is_private):
      self.affected_release = affected_release
      self.severity = severity
      super().__init__(title, description, is_private)

    def get_bug():
      bug_data = {
        'title': self.title,
        'description': self.description,
        'severity': self.severity,
        'affected_release': self.affected_release,
        'is_private': self.is_private}
      return bug_data
```

As we can see from the example, we just used inheritance while creating the `Bug` class by making the `Bug` class derived from the request class. In OOP terminology, the `Bug` class will be called the child of the `Request` class. When an object of the `Bug` class is created, it calls the constructor of the `Bug` class, followed by the constructor of the Request class.

In Python, all the classes inherit from the `object` class:

```
req = Request('Missing access modifier support in class inheritance', 'We
are lacking the support for using access modifiers in class inheritance',
False)
isinstance(req, object)
>>> True
```

Multiple inheritance in Python

Let's take a look at an abstract example of how we can implement multiple inheritance in Python, as can be seen in the code snippet that follows:

```
class A:
    def __init__(self):
        print("Class A")

class B:
    def __init__(self):
        print("Class B")

class C(A,B):
    def __init__(self):
        print("Class C")
```

The example shows how we can get multiple inheritance to work in Python. One interesting thing here is to understand how the method resolution order works in Python when we use multiple inheritance. So, let's take a look.

Method resolution order in multiple inheritance

So, based on the previous example, what happens if we create an object of the C class?

```
>>> Cobj = C()
Class C
```

As we can see, only the derived class constructor was called here. So what if we wanted to call the parent class constructor also? For that, we will require the help of the super() call inside our class C constructor. To see it in action, let's modify the implementation of C a little bit:

```
>>> class C(A,B):
...    def __init__(self):
...       print("C")
...       super().__init__()
>>> Cobj = C()
C
A
```

As soon as we created the object of the derived class, we can see that the derived class constructor was called first, followed by the constructor of the first inherited class. The super() call automatically resolved to the first inherited class.

So, what if we wanted to call the constructors of all the classes in order? For that, we could have added a super call to all the classes:

```
class A:
  def __init__(self):
    print("Class A")
    super().__init__()

class B:
  def __init__(self):
    print("Class B")
    super().__init__()

class C(A,B):
  def __init__(self):
    print("Class C")
    super().__init__()
>>> Cobj = C()
```

```
C
A
B
```

When we created an object of C, we can see that all the constructors are called in the order of how they were inherited. The first call went to the derived class constructor, followed by the call to constructor A, which came first in the inheritance chain, and then the call was made to constructor B.

Here in this example, everything seems to be fine because none of the constructors take any parameters in their initialization call. As soon as the constructors start taking some parameters in the initialization call, things start to get complicated. Now we need to make sure every constructor accepts all the parameters. Now, if we implement this approach, we have tightly coupled all the classes, which in itself defeats the purpose of inheritance where one class is supposed to do only one thing. To deal with these kinds of problems, we can use something known as a **mixin**.

Utilizing mixins

Mixins is a concept that is present in every object-oriented language, and can be used to implement object classes that can be reused again and again in different places of the code. Projects such as Django web framework provide a lot of pre-built mixins, which can be used to achieve a certain set of functionality (for example, object manipulation, rendering of forms, and so on) in the custom classes we implement for our applications.

So, are mixins some special feature of the language? The answer to this is no, they are not some special feature, but rather are small classes that are not built to be turned into independent objects. Instead, they are built to provide some specified extra functionality to a class through the support of multiple inheritance.

Going back to our sample application, BugZot, we will need a way to return the data from multiple objects in JSON format. Now, we have two options; we can build the functionality of returning JSON data at the level of individual methods, or we can build a mixin that can be reused again and again in multiple classes:

```
Import json
class JSONMixin:
  def return_json(self, data):
    try:
      json_data = json.dumps(data)
    except TypeError:
      print("Unable to parse the data into JSON")
    return json_data
```

Now, let's imagine, if we wanted our bug class that we implemented in the example while trying to understand inheritance. All we needed to do was to just inherit `JSONMixin` in the `Bug` class:

```
class Bug(Request, JSONMixin):
   ...
```

And, by simply inheriting the class, we got the required functionality.

Abstract base classes

In OOP, abstract base classes are those classes that contain just the method declarations and not their implementations. These classes are not supposed to have independent objects, but rather are built to act as base classes. The classes that derive from the abstract base classes are required to provide implementation for the methods declared in the abstract classes.

In Python, although you can build abstract classes by not providing the implementation for the declared methods, the language in itself does not enforce that concept of derived classes to provide the implementation for the method. So, the following example will run perfectly fine if executed in Python:

```
class AbstractUser:
  def return_data(self):
    pass
class User(AbstractUser):
  def __init__(self, username):
    self.username = username
    self.user_data = {}
  def return_username(self):
    return self.username
aUser = AbstractUser()
user = user('joe')
>>> aUser
<__main__.AbstractUser object at 0x7eff33fe3d68>
>>> user
<__main__.User object at 0x7eff3055b748>
```

As we can see, the program executed perfectly, even though we did not provide an implementation of the `return_data` method in the user class.

To work around this problem, Python provides a module called `abc`, which refers to Abstract Base Class. Let's take a look at how we can use this module to implement abstract base classes in Python:

```python
from abc import ABC, abstractmethod
class AbstractUser(ABC):
  @abstractmethod
  def return_data(self):
    pass

class User(AbstractUser):
  def __init__(self, username):
    self.username = username
    self.user_data = {}
  def return_username(self):
    return self.username
  def return_data(self)
    return self.user_data
```

In this example, the `AbstractUser` class derives from the `abc` class, which is the base class for defining the abstract base classes in Python. The `@abstractmethod` decorator marks a method as abstract and enforces that the derived class should provide an implementation for the method. So, let's take a look at what happens if we try to initialize an object of `AbstractUser` class:

```
>>> aUser = AbstractUser()
TypeError: Can't instantiate abstract class AbstractUser with abstract
methods return_data
```

An attempt to do so ends up with Python raising a `TypeError`.

So, we can see from the preceding example that using the `abc` module, we can put some enforcement on derived classes to provide an implementation for abstract methods in a class.

The implementation of an abstract base classes provide a template which can be implemented by the child classes while making sure that the child classes must implement the functionality declared inside the base class they are deriving from.

Metaclasses

Python provides a lot of features, some of which are directly visible to us, such as list comprehensions, dynamic type evaluation, and so on, and some of them not so directly. In Python, a lot of things can be considered magic, happening behind the scenes. One of them is the concept of metaclasses.

In Python, everything is an object, be it a method or a class. Even inside Python, classes are considered to be first-class objects that can be passed on to methods, assigned to variables, and so on.

But, as the concept of OOP states, every object denotes an instance of a class. So, if our classes are objects, then they should also be instances of some class. So, which class is that? The answer to this question is the `type` class. Every class in Python is an instance of the `type` class.

This can be verified quite easily, as shown in the following snippet:

```
class A:
  def __init__(self):
    print("Hello there from class A")

>>>isinstance(A, type)
True
```

These classes, whose object is a class, are known as metaclasses.

In Python, we don't often use metaclasses directly, because most of the time the problems we are trying to solve with the help of metaclasses can usually be solved through the use of some other simple solutions. But the metaclasses do provide us with a lot of power to how we create our classes. Let's first take a look at how we can create our own metaclasses by designing a `LoggerMeta` class, which will enforce the instance class to provide a valid handler method for different log methods prefixed by `HANDLER_`:

```
class LoggerMeta(type):
  def __init__(cls, name, base, dct):
    for k in dct.keys():
      if k.startswith('HANDLER_'):
        if not callable(dct[k]):
          raise AttributeError("{} is not callable".format(k))
    super().__init__(name, base, dct)


def error_handler():
  print("error")
def warning_handler():
```

```
    print("warning")


class Log(metaclass=LoggerMeta):
  HANDLER_ERROR = error_handler
  HANDLER_WARN = warning_handler
  HANDLER_INFO = 'info_handler'

  def __init__(self):
    print("Logger class")
```

In this example, we have defined a `metaclass` named `LoggerMeta` by inheriting from the type class. (For defining any metaclass, we need to either inherit from the type class or any other metaclass. The concept of inheritance is applicable even during the `metaclass` creation.) Once we have declared our `metaclass`, we provide a definition for the __init__ magic method in the `metaclass`. The __init__ magic method of the metaclass takes in the class object, the name of the new class to be created, a list of base classes the new class will derive from, and a dictionary containing the properties of the new class that is used to initialize the new class.

Inside the __init__ method, we have provided an implementation for verifying if the class properties whose name starts with `HANDLER_` have a valid handler assigned to them or not. In case the handler assigned to the property is not callable, we raise an `AttributeError` and prevent the creation of the class. And at the end of the __init__ method, we return the call results of a base class __init__ method.

In the next example, we create two simple methods that will act as our handlers for dealing with error type messages and warning type messages.

Moving on in the example, we define a class log whose metaclass is `LoggerMeta`. This class contains a few properties, such as `HANDLER_ERROR`, `HANDLER_WARN`, `HANDLER_INFO` and the magic method __init__.

Now, let's see what happens if we try to execute the provided example:

```
python3 metaclass_example.py
Traceback (most recent call last):
  File "<stdin>", line 1, in <module>
  File "<stdin>", line 6, in __init__
AttributeError: HANDLER_INFO is not callable
```

As we can see from the output, as soon as the definition of class log was parsed by the interpreter to create the class, the metaclass __init__ method was called, which validated the properties of the class and raised an `AttributeError`.

The metaclasses in Python provide us with a lot of power at our disposal and enable us to do a lot of things magically, for example, generating class properties based on the name of the methods, and keeping track of how many instances of a class have been initialized.

With all the things we have learned about OOP and metaclasses in Python, let's now move on to using them to implement some of the design patterns in Python, and learning about how to decide upon the choice of the design pattern to use.

The Singleton pattern

The Singleton pattern is one of the patterns that finds its place in the book by *Gang of Four*, and which can have various uses where all we want is a class to have a single instance throughout an application.

The Singleton pattern enforces that a class will have only one instance that will be used by any of the components/modules inside an application. This kind of enforcement can be useful when we want to control the access to a resource using only one object. These type of resources can be log files, databases, crash-handling mechanisms, and so on.

In most of the OOP-based languages, to implement the Singleton pattern, the first step is to make the class constructor private and then use a static method inside a class to return the same instance whenever some part of the code needs to use the functionality of the class. In Python, we do not have the functionality of having a private constructor, so, how can we implement the Singleton pattern?

The answer to this question lies with the use of metaclasses. We can use metaclasses to implement the Singleton pattern. Let's take a look at how we can implement the Singleton pattern by using metaclasses.

For an example, let's take our BugZot application. In our BugZot application, we will require the functionality that the different modules should be able to access the database for a various set of reasons, such as writing a new record for a bug, fetching the bug records, creation of new users, and modification of user permissions. Now, this can be done in two ways; either we can create a database class and allow the modules to instantiate a unique database class object by themselves and use it, or we can instantiate the database class object once the application starts and, whenever some module tries to instantiate the database class object for their own use, we can provide the same object that we instantiated. In the first approach, we will unnecessarily create a lot of objects wasting the precious database connection resources, while also causing an unnecessary increase in memory usage, due to an increased number of objects. So, let's take a look at how we can implement the Singleton pattern here to solve our problem.

Let's first create a file, `Singleton.py`, under the meta directory of our application. This file will hold the implementation for our Singleton metaclass, which we will be using to create Singleton classes later in our application whenever we require them:

```
class SingletonMeta(type):
  _instance_registry = {}    #Build an instance registry which tracks the
different class objects
  def __call__(cls, *args, **kwargs):
    if cls not in cls._instance_registry:    # check, if the class has
already been instantiated
      cls._instance_registry[cls] = super().__init__(*args, **kwargs)
    return cls._instance_registry[cls]
```

In this example, we provided a definition for our Singleton metaclass, which derives from the type metaclass.

Inside the class, we first initialize a dictionary, which will hold the records of the objects of individual classes that use the Singleton class as their metaclass. The next thing we declare in our metaclass is the __call__ magic method, which takes class name, its arguments, and keyword arguments as parameters. Before discussing what exactly the __call__ magic method does, let's first see what we are doing inside the method.

Once this method is executed, we first check if we already have an initialized object of the class by checking for the records under the _instance_registry dictionary. If we don't find the instance of the class already initialized, we initialize a new instance of the class and save it in the dictionary. Following that, we return the initialized instance.

What this means in a practical scenario is, when the class is first initialized, a new instance will be created, a record of it will be stored in the _instance_registry dictionary, and then the instance will be returned. Any further attempt to create a new instance will always end up with returning the same object. And that is what the Singleton pattern aims to achieve.

The __call__ magic method

The __call__ magic method is special in context to Python metaclasses. Unlike the __init__ method, which gets called when we create a new class from our metaclass, the __call__ method is called when the object of the initialized class is created. To better understand this, let's try to run the following example:

```
class ExampleMeta(type):
  def __init__(cls, name, bases, dct):
    print("__init__ called")
    return super().__init__(name, bases, dct)
  def __call__(cls, *args, **kwargs):
    print("__call__ called")
    return super().__call__(*args, **kwargs)
class Example(metaclass=Example):
  def __init__(self):
    print("Example class")
__init__ called
>>> obj = Example()
__call__ called
```

From this example, it is clear that the __init__ method is called once the interpreter has completed the initialization of a class based on the metaclass and the __call__ method is called when the object of the class is created.

Now, with this understanding in place, let's build our database connection class, which will provide the hold of our database operations. In this example, we will just focus on the initialization part of the class, while providing the complete class implementation details in the later chapters.

Now, under the bugzot directory, let's create a file named database.py which will hold our database class:

```
from bugzot.meta import Singleton

class Database(metaclass=Singleton):
    def __init__(self, hostname, port, username, password, dbname, **kwargs):
        """Initialize the databases
        Initializes the database class, establishing a connection with the
database and providing
        the functionality to call the database.
        :params hostname: The hostname on which the database server runs
        :parms port: The port on which database is listening
        :params username: The username to connect to database
        :params password: The password to connect to the database
        :params dbname: The name of the database to connect to
        """
        self.uri = build_uri(hostname, port, username, password, dbname)
        #self.db = connect_db()
        self.db_opts = kwargs
        #self.set_db_opts()

    def connect_db(self):
        """Establish a connection with the database."""
```

```
    pass
  def set_db_opts(self):
    """Setup the database connection options."""
    pass
```

In this example, we have defined the database class that will help us establish a connection to the database. The different thing about this class is, whenever we try to create a new instance of this class, it will always return the same object. For example, let's try to see what happens if we create two different objects of this same class:

```
dbobj1 = Database("example.com", 5432, "joe", "changeme", "testdb")
dbobj2 = Database("example.com", 5432, "joe", "changeme", "testdb")
>>> dbobj1
<__main__.Database object at 0x7fb6d754a7b8>
>>> dbobj2
<__main__.Database object at 0x7fb6d754a7b8>
```

In this example, we can see that the same instance of the database object was returned when we tried to instantiate a new object of the class.

Now, let's take a look at one other interesting pattern, known as the **Factory** pattern.

The Factory pattern

During the development of large applications, there are certain cases where we might want to initialize a class dynamically, based upon the user input or some other dynamic factor. To achieve this, either we can initialize all the possible objects during the class instantiation and return the one that is required based on the inputs from the environment, or we can altogether defer the creation of class objects until an input has been received.

The Factory pattern is the solution to the latter case, where we develop a special method inside a class, which will be responsible for initializing the objects dynamically, based on the input from the environment.

Now, let's see how we can implement the Factory pattern in Python in a simplistic way, and then we will see how we can use the dynamic nature of Python to make our Factory class more dynamic.

So, let's take an example of an HTML Form Component, which needs to be rendered on a web page. Let's see how we can deal with this using Python classes and the Factory pattern:

```
from abc import ABC, abstractmethod
class HTMLFormEntity(ABC):
  def __init__(self, id, name):
```

```
        self.id = id
        self.name = name
    @abstractmethod
    def render(self):
        pass

class Button(HTMLFormEntity):
    def __init__(self, id, name):
        super().__init__(id, name)
        self.type = "button"
    def render(self):
        html = "<input id={idx} name={name} type={itype} />"
        return html.format(idx=self.id, name=self.name, itype=self.type)

class Text(HTMLFormEntity):
    def __init__(self, id, name):
        super().__init__(id, name)
        self.type = "text"
    def render(self):
        html = "<input id={idx} name={name} type={itype} />"
        return html.format(idx=self.id, name=self.name, itype=self.type)

class HTMLForm(HTMLFormEntity):
    __elements = {
    "button": Button,
    "text": Text
    }
    def __init__(self, id, name, action, method):
        super().__init__(id, name)
        self.action = action
        self.method = method
        self.elements = []
    def add_entity(self, entity_type, id, name):
        if entity_type in self.__elements.keys():
            self.elements.append(self.__elements[entity_type](id, name))
    def render(self):
        # render method body
```

In this example, we can see how we implement the Factory pattern in our `HtmlForm` class. The class contains a mapping of classes that we may want to dynamically instantiate. Inside the `HtmlForm` class, the `add_entity` method acts as our factory method, which checks if the object being asked for inclusion in our form is present inside the dictionary of possible elements we can instantiate or not, and then, if it is present, it is instantiated and added to the list of elements that need to be rendered, when the form is rendered.

Now, this approach has one drawback. Whenever we want to support a new HTML Form element, we will have to modify our `HtmlForm` class to add a mapping for the element. This process is cumbersome, and there should be a better way to deal with this situation. So let's take a look at how we can exploit the dynamic nature of Python to make our `add_entity` method more dynamic.

Let's re-implement our `HtmlForm` class to be a bit more dynamic here:

```python
from importlib import import_module

class HTMLForm(HTMLFormEntity):
    def __init__(self, id, name, action, method):
        super().__init__(id, name)
        self.action = action
        self.method = method
        self.elements = []
    def add_entity(self, entity_type, id, name):
        module_name = entity_type
        class_name = module_name.capitalize()
        module = import_module('.'+module_name, package="bugzot")
        class = getattr(module, class_name)
        self.elements.append(class(id, name))
    def render(self):
        # render method implementation
```

In this example, we modified the implementation of our `add_entity` method that now does not need to know which classes can be dynamically instantiated. To do this, we used the `importlib` library from Python. The `import_module` method from the `importlib` can be used to dynamically import the modules from our application, and then we can retrieve the classes from the imported module. Once the class is imported, all we need to do is to instantiate an object from the class, and then add it to our list of elements that need to be rendered.

This kind of approach not only makes the implementation of the Factory method simple, but also helps the developer to allow for the addition of new modules easily, without modifying the factory class.

We have now seen how the Factory pattern works, but what are some of the possible use cases where the Factory pattern can be of help? These include the following:

- When we don't know which of the classes need to be instantiated in advance.
- When future changes are required in the application, the Factory pattern can help in keeping the object creation logic segregated from how the class implementation has been done.

Now, let's take a look at one of the most common design patterns, the **Model-View-Controller** (**MVC**) pattern, which is used in many applications and a lot of web frameworks.

The Model-View-Controller pattern

Let's start the discussion about the MVC pattern with a diagram:

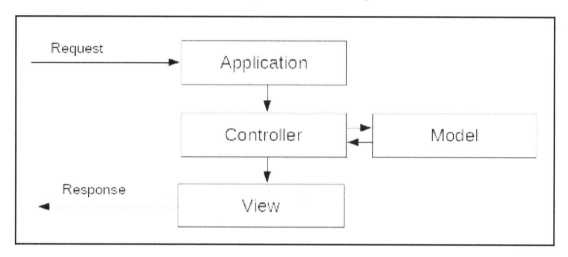

The diagram shows the flow of a request in an **Application** using the MVC pattern. When a user makes a new **Request**, the **Request** is intercepted by the **Application**, which then forwards the **Request** to the appropriate **Controller** for that **Request**. Once the **Request** is received by the **Controller**, it then interacts with the model, which performs some business logic based on the **Request** received by it. This could involve the updating of databases, or fetching some data. Once the business logic is executed by the **Model**, the **Controller** executes the **View** with any data that needs to be passed to the **View**, which then displays the **Response** for the **Request**.

Although we will be implementing the MVC pattern later in the book, when we develop our BugZot application, let's take a look at the different components in the MVC pattern, and what roles they play.

Controller

The controller acts as an intermediary between the model and the view. When a request is first made to the application, the controller intercepts the request and, based on that, decides which model and views need to be called. Once this is decided, the controller then executes the model to run the business logic, retrieving the data from the model. Once the data has been retrieved and model execution has been finished, the controller then executes the view with the data that is gathered from the model. Once the view execution is finished, the user sees a response from the view.

In a brief, the controller is responsible for doing the following operations:

- Intercepting the requests made to the application, and executing the required models and views based on that
- Manipulating the view when the model changes
- Manipulating the model based on interaction of the user with the view

Model

The model is the place where the business logic of the application lives. Many a time, developers confuse a model with a database, which may be true for some web applications, but is otherwise not if considered in general.

The role of the model is to deal with the data, provide access to it, and allow for modifications as they are requested. This includes retrieving data from the database or filesystem, adding new data to it, and modifying the existing data when updates are required.

A model is not concerned with how the data stored should be presented to the user or another component of the application, and hence decouples the presentation logic from the business logic. The model also doesn't change its schema frequently, and is more or less consistent throughout the application life cycle.

So, in brief, the model is responsible for performing the following roles:

- Provide methods to access the data stored in the application
- Decouple the presentation logic from business logic
- Provide persistence to the data being stored in the application
- Provide a consistent interface to deal with the data

View

The view is responsible for presenting the data to the user, or presenting an interface to the user through which they can manipulate the data stored in the model. The view in MVC is usually dynamic and changes frequently based on the changes that happen in the model. A view can also be considered to contain just the presentation logic for the application, without having consideration for how the data will be stored by the application and how it will be retrieved. Often, a view can be used to cache the presentation state to accelerate the display of the data.

So, in brief, here are the functions performed by the view:

- Provide the presentation logic for the application to display the data stored in the application
- Provide the user with an interface to modify the model
- Optionally provide an ability to cache the view state to accelerate the display of the interfaces

As we can see, in the MVC model, every single component performs its own set of functions and does not duplicate the functionality. This translates into the application, with reduced coupling on a macro scale. Such an implementation makes the task of making the changes in the application less daunting, since a team dealing with the presentation of the data does not need to worry about making changes to the way the application stores and retrieves the data from the underlying storage, and a team dealing with the functionality of how the application deals with the data does not have to worry about how the data will be presented to the user.

The clear separation of interfaces also allows for a way to improve the testing process of the application, where tests can be clearly written to target the individual components.

So, let's take a look at some of the advantages of using the MVC pattern in application development:

- It provides clear separation of the presentation logic and the business logic
- It improves code reuse when multiple interfaces need to deal with the same backend model
- It provides improved ability for unit testing, due to its decoupled user interface and data model
- It provides improved development workflow, since changes to the view do not affect the model, or the other way around

The MVC pattern finds quite a lot of use in the development of web applications, as well as applications that provide a GUI, where the separation of the UI logic from the data-handling logic can prove to be of great help. Python web frameworks, such as Django, provide a working example of an MVC pattern, where their application structure enforces the use of an MVC pattern by clearly creating boundaries between where the business logic lives and where the presentation logic lives.

Summary

In this chapter, we went through the concept of design patterns and how they can help us solve some of the commonly encountered problems in designing our applications. We then went through how to decide upon which design pattern to use, and if it is compulsory to choose one of the patterns that has already been defined. Moving further in the chapter, we explored some of the object-oriented capabilities of Python as a language, and also explored some examples of implementing abstract classes and metaclasses in Python, and how we can use them to build other classes and modify their behavior.

Equipped with the knowledge of object-oriented Python, we moved on to implement some of the common design patterns, such as the Singleton and Factory patterns in Python, and also explored the MVC pattern, learning about what problems they try to solve.

Now with the knowledge of design patterns with us, it is time for us to understand how we can make the process of handling the data inside our application efficient. The next chapter takes us through the journey of exploring the different techniques that will help us in efficiently handling the database operations that are going to take place inside our applications.

Questions

1. How can we implement the chain of responsibility pattern in Python, and what are some of the possible use cases where it can be used?
2. What are the differences between the `__new__` method and the `__init__` method?
3. How can we implement an abstract class using the ABCMeta class as the metaclass for the abstract class?

3
Building for Large-Scale Database Operations

In the area of enterprise software development, developers have always built applications that deal with large amounts of data. In the early days of computing, systems used to span rooms bigger than the ones we currently live in, and data was stored in a flat file format, whereas today, systems have shrunk so much that in the same sized room that used to store a single system, we can now have thousands of systems running, each coordinating with the others, providing us with machines that can crunch data at the speed of light. Over time, the way data is stored has also evolved from using flat files to sophisticated database management systems.

With enterprises growing in size and their ever-expanding operations due to emerging fields, the amount data that needs to be processed by enterprise applications is also growing, and this makes it important to understand how to build our applications to deal with large-scale database-related operations. Though building for large-scale database operations can never be a one-approach-fits-all solution, we'll cover some points that are common to building applications that can scale easily to handle the increase in data, the requirements of schema modification, increasing application complexity, and so on.

Although there are multiple types of databases, such as SQL, NoSQL, and Graph, that can be used to store application data, depending what kind of application is required by the enterprise, this chapter focuses on the use of relational database management systems using SQL, due to their vast popularity and their ability to handle a large amount of use cases.

By the end of this chapter, you will have learned about the following:

- Using **Object Relational Mappers** (**ORMs**) and the benefits they provide
- Structuring database models for efficiency and ease of modification
- Focusing on maintaining database consistency

- The differences between eager loading and lazy loading
- Taking advantage of caching to speed up queries

Technical requirements

The code listings in this book can be found under `chapter03` directory at `https://github.com/PacktPublishing/Hands-On-Enterprise-Application-Development-with-Python`.

The code samples can be cloned by running the following command:

```
git clone
https://github.com/PacktPublishing/Hands-On-Enterprise-Application-Developm
ent-with-Python
```

The code samples provided in this chapter require you to have the following system packages installed and configured on their systems:

- `python-devel`
- PostgreSQL
- Python – `virtualenv`

Beyond these three packages, you will also require the `sqlalchemy` package, which provides the ORM we will be using throughout the chapter, and `psycopg2`, which provides `postgres` database bindings to allow `sqlalchemy` to connect to `postgres`.

Database and object relational mappers

As we discussed in the previous chapters, Python provides us with a lot of object-oriented capabilities, and allows us to map our use cases in terms of classes and objects. Now, when we can map our problem set into a class and its objects, why shouldn't we also map our database tables as objects, where a particular class represents a table, and its objects represent the rows in the table. Going down this route helps us to maintain not only the consistency of how we write our code, but also how we model our problem.

The frameworks that provide the functionality through which we can map our databases to objects are known as ORMs and they help us to visualize our database as a set of classes and objects.

In the Python landscape, it is quite common to see ORMs. For example, a popular Python web framework, Django, provides its own ORM solution. Then, there is SQLAlchemy, which provides a fully-fledged ORM solution and database toolkit supporting a wide variety of relational databases.

But to convince developers to use ORM frameworks, there should be better advantages than merely saying that they are able to map your database into classes and objects, and provide you with an object-oriented interface to access the database. Let's take a look at a few of the advantages the use of ORMs brings to the table:

- **Abstraction from the vendor-specific SQL**: The relational database space is full of choices, with several companies marketing their products. Each of these products can have differences in how to achieve a certain functionality through the use of SQL. Sometimes, some of the databases may implement some SQL keywords that are not yet supported in other databases. For developers, this can become a problem if they need to support multiple databases with a disjointed set of functionality. Since ORMs already know how to deal with these differences in databases, they help the developer alleviate the problem of supporting multiple databases. Most of the time, when using an ORM, all the developer has to do is modify a database connection Uniform Resource Identifier (**URI**) and they are ready to work with a new database in their application.
- **Reduces the need for repetitive SQL**: When writing an application, there are quite a lot of places where the data needs to be retrieved from the same tables using similar queries. This will cause a lot of repetitive SQL being written in a lot of places, not only giving rise to quite a lot of poorly formatted code, but also opening doors for errors to creep in due to an improperly constructed SQL query (humans are quite vulnerable to losing their focus when doing repetitive work, so won't this apply to developers also?). ORM solutions help by reducing the need for writing SQL to achieve the same results, by providing abstractions over SQL commands and generating SQL on the fly, based on how we call the different methods.
- **Increased application maintainability**: Since ORMs allow you to define a database model once and reuse it throughout the application by instantiating the classes, it allows you to make changes in one place, which are then reflected across the whole application. This makes the task of maintaining the application a bit less tiresome, (at least the parts related to the handling of the database).

- **Increased productivity**: This in itself is not a feature but a side effect of the points mentioned previously. With the use of ORM solutions, developers are now a bit more relaxed about always thinking about SQL queries, or trying to follow a particular design pattern. They can now just focus on how to best architect their applications. This significantly improves developers' productivity, and allows them to get more done and improve the utilization of their time.

In this chapter, we will focus on how we can utilize ORMs to best develop our enterprise applications so that they can easily interact with databases and handle large-scale database operations efficiently. For the sake of keeping the chapter simple, we will stick with the use of SQLAlchemy, which markets itself as an SQL toolkit, and an ORM solution for Python, and provides a lot of bindings for different frameworks in the Python landscape. It is being used by some quite large-scale projects, such as OpenStack, the Fedora Project, and Reddit.

Setting up SQLAlchemy

Before we dive into how to create optimal database models for your application to promote efficient large-scale database operations, we will first need to set up our ORM solution. Since we are going to use SQLAlchemy here, let's see how we can set it up in our development environment.

For SQLAlchemy to work, you should have a database management system setup, either on your system or a remote machine, that you can connect to. A container with an exposed port will also get the work done for us. To keep the examples simple, we assume the reader is using PostgreSQL as their database solution here, and is knowledgeable about how the PostgreSQL setup works. Now, let's see how we can set up SQLAlchemy:

```
mkdir ch3 && cd ch3
virtualenv --python=python3 .
source bin/activate
pip install sqlalchemy psycopg2
```

Let me explain what we did here. We first created a directory for this chapter and then initialized a Python 3-based virtual environment inside the directory. The next thing we did was to activate that virtual environment. This allows us to keep the changes the Python packages make segregated into one place so that they don't affect the whole system (which is the preferred way and prevents you from getting any surprises due to broken dependencies for other Python projects that may be living on your system).

Once our virtual environment is activated, we move on and install the Python SQLAlchemy library and the `pyscopg2` Python package, which provides Python bindings for PostgreSQL in Python, and which is also a requirement for connecting to a PostgreSQL database using SQLAlchemy.

Now, with the SQLAlchemy setup complete, we are ready to dive into the world of database modeling with ORM solutions.

Building optimal database models

The first step to achieve any efficient access to your database is to build an optimal model for your database. If a model is not optimal, the rest of the techniques to speed up access to the database will make very little difference.

But before we dive into how we can build an optimal model for the database, let's first see how we can actually build any model for our database using SQLAlchemy.

For this example, let's imagine we want to build a model to represent a user in our BugZot application. In our BugZot application, a user will be required to provide the following fields:

- First name and last name
- Username
- Email address
- Password

Additionally, our BugZot application also needs to maintain some more information about the user, such as their membership level in the system, the privileges the user is entitled to, whether the user account is active or not, and the activation key that is sent to the user to activate their account.

Now, let's see what happens if we try to model our user table with these requirements using SQLAlchemy. The following code depicts how we build a user model in SQLAlchemy:

```
from sqlalchemy.ext.declarative import declarative_base
from sqlalchemy import Boolean, Date, Integer, String, Column
from datetime import datetime

# Initialize the declarative base model
Base = declarative_base()
```

```
# Construct our User model
class User(Base):
  __tablename__ = 'users'

  id = Column(Integer, primary_key=True, autoincrement=True)
  first_name = Column(String, nullable=False)
  last_name = Column(String, nullable=False)
  username = Column(String(length=25), unique=True, nullable=False)
  email = Column(String(length=255), unique=True, nullable=False)
  password = Column(String(length=255), nullable=False)
  date_joined = Column(Date, default=datetime.now())
  user_role = Column(String, nullable=False)
  user_role_permissions = Column(Integer, nullable=False)
  account_active = Column(Boolean, default=False)
  activation_key = Column(String(length=32))

  def __repr__(self):
  return "<User {}>".format(self.username)
```

This example shows how we can build a model using SQLAlchemy. Now, let's take a look at what we did in the code sample.

In the starting part of the code sample, we first imported the `declarative_base` method that is responsible for providing the base class for our models.

The `Base = declarative_base()` line assigns the base model to our base variable.

The next thing we did was to include the different datatypes from SQLAlchemy that we will be using in our definition of the model.

The final import imports the Python `datetime` library that we will be using in our database model.

Now, without considering how our code will populate the different fields of the database model, let's take a look at how we designed our user model.

The first step of designing the model was to define a class user that acts as our model class. This class derives from the base model that we initialized earlier in our code.

The `__tablename__ = 'users'` line defines the name that should be given to the table when this database model is realized inside the database.

Following on from there, we start to define the columns our table will consist of. To define the column, we use a `key=value` type approach, where the key defines the name of the column, and the value defines the attributes of the column.

For example, to define the column id, which should be of integer type and should act as a primary key for table users, we define it like this:

```
id = Column(Integer, primary_key=True, autoincrement=True)
```

We can now see how simple it is. We did not have to write any SQL to define our column. Similarly, it is quite easy to enforce that a particular field should have a unique value and cannot have null as a value by just passing `unique=True` and `nullable=False` parameters to the column constructor, as can be taken as an example from the following line:

```
username = Column(String(length=25), unique=True, nullable=False)
```

After we have defined all the columns, we provide the definition for the __repr__ method. The __repr__ method is a magic method that is called by the internal `repr()` Python method to provide the representation of the object, such as when a user issues `print(userobj)`.

This completes our definition of our user model using SQLAlchemy. It was simple, wasn't it? We did not have to write any SQL; we just quickly added the columns to a class and left everything else for SQLAlchemy to deal with. Now, while all of this was quite fun and easy to achieve, we made some mistakes, which doesn't seem to have caused any harm now, but will prove to be costly as our application scales up. Let's take a look at these mistakes.

Issues with our model definition

While SQLAlchemy provided us with a lot of abstraction to easily define our user model, it also makes it easy for us to make some mistakes, which can prove to be costly once the application use scales up and the enterprise grows. Let's take a look at some of the mistakes that we have made while defining this model:

- **Vulnerability to changes**: The current definition of our user model makes it very hard to make changes to the model once the application scales up. Let's take the example of the organization deciding to provide users with more permissions on a bug report. In terms of SQL, to achieve the effect, we will need to write a query that will traverse through all the records and has `user_role` as the user and update the `user_role_permissions` column for them. This would be absolutely fine if we had only a few hundred users, but the problem would start to creep up on us if the database contains the records of thousands of users in an organization. We would immediately start to see our application slow down because updates would take a long time. This problem will be amplified if we had to modify the permissions of more than one `user_role`.

- **High repetitiveness**: In our model, we have to provide the values for `user_role` and `user_role_permissions` for every other record that we insert. This creates a lot of repetitive storage of data and unnecessarily increases the storage size of the records in our database. This kind of mistake doesn't show up early in the application's use, but shows up when the application grows in use. All of a sudden, you will see issues such as spikes in memory and increased disk usage.
- **Prone to inconsistencies**: As humans, no matter what we do, we cannot completely eliminate the possibility of making errors. If the same error happens in the logic that feeds in the data to our user model, and is detected late, it doesn't take a lot of guesswork to estimate that a lot of the records in our user table would then have inconsistent data. For example, in a particular code commit, we accidentally renamed the administrator role admin; now we have a huge amount of records that have administrator privileges but with two different role names, which we now need to support in our application.

Now we know about the issues our current model causes us, it's time to take a look at how to build models that are not prone to these issues, and can scale easily as our application expands.

Optimizing our models

Before we discuss how to build optimal models, we first need to understand the characteristics that need to be present in an optimal model. Let's take a look at the following:

- **Easy to adapt**: An optimal model should be easy to adapt according to the changing needs of the application as its user base grows. This means changing a particular model should not require changes all across the application, and should be high in cohesion.
- **Maximizes the throughput on a host**: Every host has a different architecture, and a data model should be able to exploit the underlying host resources in a manner that maximizes its throughput. This can be made possible by using the correct data storage engine for a particular architecture and use case, or running the database across a cluster of machines to increase the parallel execution capabilities.

- **Efficient storage**: A database model should also be considerate of the storage it may use as the data being stored inside it grows. This can be done by carefully choosing data types. For example, just to represent a column that can have only two values, true or false, an integer type would be overkill, wasting a lot of disk space, as the number of records in the database grows. A nominal data type for such a column could be Boolean, which doesn't takes that much space internally.
- **Easy to tune**: An efficient model will carefully index the columns that can speed up the processing of queries against a particular table. This results in an improved response time for the database, and having happy users who don't get frustrated because your application takes up to 20 minutes to return 10,000 records from the database.

To achieve these goals, we now need to simplify our models, and use the concept of relationships that relational databases provide. Let's now start re-factoring our user model to make it a bit more optimal.

To achieve this, first we need to break it down from one large model to multiple small models, which live independently in our code base and don't have everything coupled so hard. Let's get started.

The first thing that we will move out of the model is how we deal with roles and permissions. Since roles and their permissions are not something that will differ too much from user to user (for sure not every user will have a unique role, and not every role can have a varying set of permissions), we can move these fields to a different model, known as permissions. The following code illustrates this:

```
class Role(Base):
    __tablename__ = 'roles'

    id = Column(Integer, primary_key=True, autoincrement=True)
    role_name = Column(String(length=25), nullable=False, unique=True)
    role_permissions = Column(Integer, nullable=False)

    def __repr__(self):
    return "<Role {}>".format(role_name)
```

Now, we have the roles decoupled from the user model. This makes it easy for us to make a modification to the provided roles without causing much of an issue. These modifications may include renaming a role or changing the permissions for an existing role. All we do is make a modification in a single place and it can be reflected for all the users that have the same role. Let's see how we can do this with the help of relations in **Relational Database Management System (RDBMS)** in our user model.

The following code example shows how to achieve the relation between the role model and the user model:

```
class User(Base):
    __tablename__ = 'users'

    id = Column(Integer, primary_key=True, autoincrement=True)
    first_name = Column(String, nullable=False)
    last_name = Column(String, nullable=False)
    username = Column(String(length=25), unique=True, nullable=False)
    email = Column(String(length=255), unique=True, nullable=False)
    password = Column(String(length=255), nullable=False)
    date_joined = Column(Date, default=datetime.now())
    user_role = Column(Integer, ForeignKey("roles.id"))
    account_active = Column(Boolean, default=False)
    activation_key = Column(String(length=32))

    def __repr__(self):
        return "<User {}>".format(self.username)
```

In this code example, we modified the `user_role` to be an integer, and stored a value that is present in the `roles` model. Any attempt to insert a value into this field that is not present in the roles model will raise an SQL exception that the operation is not permitted.

Now, continuing with the same example, let's think about the `activation_key` column of the user model. We might not need an activation key once the user has activated their account. This provides us with an opportunity to perform one more optimization in our user model. We can move this activation key out of the user model and store it in a separate model. Once the user has successfully activated their account, the record can be safely deleted without the risk of the user model being modified. So, let's develop the model for the activation key. The following code sample illustrates what we want to do:

```
class ActivationKey(Base):
    __tablename__ = 'activation_keys'

    id = Column(Integer, primary_key=True, autoincrement=True)
    user_id = Column(Integer, ForeignKey("users.id"))
    activation_key = Column(String(length=32), nullable=False)

    def __repr__(self):
        return "<ActivationKey {}>".format(self.id)
```

In this example, we implemented the `ActivationKey` model. Since every activation key belongs to a unique user, we need to store which user has which activation key. We achieve this by introducing a foreign key to the user model's `id` field.

Now, we can safely remove the `activation_key` column from our user model without causing any trouble.

Taking advantage of indexes

Indexes are something that can provide a huge amount of performance advantages if done on fields that are good candidates for being indexed. But indexes can also prove to be of no use or can even harm database performance if the columns that are being indexed are not selected with care. For example, indexing every single column inside a table may not prove to be of any advantage and will unnecessarily eat up disk space, while also making database operations slow.

So, before jumping into how to index a particular field using the ORM we have taken up as an example here, let's first clarify what exactly an index is in this context of databases, (without diving too deeply into how exactly they work), which data structure is used to store indexes, and what algorithms a database uses to query indexes.

Indexes are a copy of selected columns that are stored in special data structures by the database to improve the efficiency of looking for a record inside a database. When looking through an index, a database does not need to traverse through all the records inside a table before it finds a matching record. All a database does here is quickly look into the index and find out whether a particular value is present or not. If present, it just returns the row corresponding to the value. This process can really speed up the performance of a database, sometimes, even by 100 times, if done efficiently.

Now, how do we add indexes to the models that we have already built? Well, it's a very easy task. But first, let's identify which fields we should index.

In our `Roles` model, we will be mostly querying through the `id` role, which we can find in the `user` model. Also, since there won't be too many roles, we can simply ignore indexing any other field inside the role model, because it won't necessarily impact the performance of the database. The same is valid for the activation keys model too, and hence we can also ignore adding indexes to the model.

Now, looking at the user model, we can assume that a search might be made more frequently based upon the `id` of the user, their `username`, and their `email` ID. Also, the user model is a model that will eventually grow considerably in size, and any improvements we can get in terms of data retrieval here will provide a lot of benefits in terms of overall response times for the application.

So, let's add an index to these fields. The following code snippet shows how this can be achieved:

```
username = Column(String(length=25), unique=True, nullable=False,
index=True)
email = Column(String(length=255), unique=True, nullable=False, index=True)
```

Yes, it was that simple. That's what using an ORM provides us with in terms of increased productivity, while hiding the underlying differences different databases have in terms of creating indexes.

Now, with an understanding of how to optimize models, let's take a look at how we can maintain the consistency of database when a lot of database queries are being executed by the application in parallel.

Maintaining database consistency

Databases usually have a lot of operations happening in parallel throughout the life of an application after it has been deployed. These operations can be as simple as retrieval of information from the database, or can be operations that modify the state of the database by inserting new records, updating existing ones, or deleting others. Most of the databases that are currently being used in production by large organizations have been built with quite a lot of resilience, in terms of dealing with errors and crashes that can happen in the environment to disturb the normal functioning of a database. These methods prevent the corruption of data and downtime.

But this does not relieve the application developer completely of the fact that they still need to be careful about maintaining the consistency of the data inside the database. Let's try to understand this situation.

In an enterprise-grade application, there will be a number of database queries running in parallel at any given point in time. These queries arise from the use of applications from a number of users or internal application maintenance jobs. One major fact or in this is that, not all of the queries can be successfully executed. This could be due to several reasons, such as data in the query not conforming to the schema, an incorrect data type being provided for a column value, and violations of constraints. When this happens, the database engine just blocks the query from executing and returns an error for the query. This is absolutely fine as our incorrect query didn't make any incorrect changes to the database. But the situation gets tricky when this query is part of a larger set of operations creating a new resource in the database. Now we need to make sure that the changes made by other queries before the failed query are reverted.

This kind of behavior can still be fixed with some hard work by the developer of the application by tracking the SQL queries and reverting their changes manually when things go bananas in between.

But what if the database engine crashes due to an error in between, while one of the queries was executing. Now we are in a situation where we cannot predict the state of the database, and dealing with these kinds of situations can become really tiresome, and can be a task that halts the operations of the whole organization for a long time until database consistency is validated. So, what we can do? Is there some way through which we can prevent these types of issues from arising? The answer is a big yes. Let's take a look.

Utilizing transactions to maintain consistency

A transaction in a relational database provides us with the power to solve the issues that we have just discussed. In terms of a relational database, a transaction can be considered an envelope consisting of multiple database queries that are either executed as one task or are completely reverted if any of them fails. We can also consider a transaction an atomic unit in terms of database's operations, where even a single failure will revert the whole transaction. But, isn't this exactly what we require to solve the issue with our database consistency?

Now, let's take a look at how our ORM solution can help us to implement transactional support.

To understand this, let's take an example. Our BugZot application has been newly developed and will be replacing an existing application, which the Omega Corporation was using previously. The IT team has provided us with a CSV dump (hail the great CSV) of the user records, which they expect us to restore in our new application.

One of the engineers in the BugZot team went creative and developed a script in Python that parses the provided CSV file and returns a dictionary that can be mapped to one of our models (role, user, ActivationKeys), and has asked us to use these dictionaries to start loading the data into our new database schema. So, let's take a look at how we can do this while leveraging transactions in our ORM. The following code snippet takes a look at this example:

```
from sqlalchemy import create_engine
from sqlalchemy.orm import sessionmaker
from .models import Role, User, ActivationKey

db_engine = create_engine("postgresql://bugzot:alphonso@localhost/bugzot")

Session = sessionmaker(bind=db_engine)
```

```
def load_data(db_record):
  role = get_role(db_record)
  user = get_user(db_record)
  activation_key = get_activation_key(db_record)
  db_session = Session()
  db_session.add(role)
  db_session.add(user)
  db_session.add(activation_key)
  try:
    db_session.commit()
  except:
    db_session.rollback()
    raise
  finally:
    db_session.close()

#Call to the load_data method
```

In this example, we utilized sessions to implement a transaction through SQLAlchemy. Now let's take a look at this and understand what we did.

In the first two lines, we imported the `create_engine` and `sessionmaker` objects from `sqlalchemy`. The `create_engine` object is used to create a new connection to the database by providing the object with the database connection URI.

The `sessionmaker` object is used to initialize a database session object, which can be used to further initialize new transactions.

In the next line, we created a new connection to the database engine by providing the URI of the database engine:

```
db_engine = create_engine("postgresql://bugzot:alphonso@localhost/bugzot")
```

Once the database engine had been created, we then initialized a session by calling the `sessionmaker` object with the engine parameter whose value is equivalent to the one we initialized in the previous step:

```
Session = sessionmaker(bind=db_engine)
```

Next, we define our `load_data` method, which takes as a parameter a dictionary that represents a single user data record. The method parses the dictionary and creates three different model objects, a role, a user, and an `activation_key`.

The next thing we do is add these models to the session one by one:

```
db_session.add(role)
db_session.add(user)
db_session.add(activation_key)
```

Now, once the data has been added to the session, we are all set to write this data to our database. To do this, we call the `commit()` method from the session object. The `commit` method obtains a connection to the database, starts a transaction, runs the queries, and closes the transaction.

Since, as we know, any inconsistency in any of the models described can cause the transaction to be aborted, we wrap our `commit()` call in a `try-except` block. If the `commit()` method raises an exception, we roll back the whole session, effectively undoing all the changes that we made to the database.

Once all of this is done, we call the `close()` method of session in the final block to clean up any of the resources that may be remaining.

 When we create a new session object, no connection to the database has been established yet, and no database state has been initialized by the session object. Once we call the `query()` method from the session or `commit()` method, a new connection to the database is established, and transactional state is initialized.

Transactions provide us with a lot of power to keep our database in a consistent state.If case the database server experiences a crash while a transaction is happening, we can have a certain amount of assurance that no changes will have been made to the final database state attributed to the atomic nature of a transaction.

Now, let's take a look at one of the important aspects of how relationship loading works in SQLAlchemy, and how we can optimize our data access patterns.

Understanding lazy loading versus eager loading

When we make a query to load the data from a database, there is a huge possibility that this operation might define the response time of the applications we build. This happens mainly when there is a lot of data that needs to be loaded and the application waits on the database to return all those rows and columns back to it.

Such operations may take some time, ranging from a few milliseconds to more than 10 seconds, depending on how much data is being queried from the database. The question here is, can we optimize this to improve the response times of our application?

The answer to this lies in the use of SQL relationships and ORM layer loading techniques. While relationships can help us to define how the two models relate to each other, loading techniques define how relationships are retrieved by the ORM. When a lot of data needs to be loaded, this can prove to be of great help, by not only providing a mechanism through which we can defer the loading of data of the relationships until they are required, but by also saving quite a lot in terms of memory footprint of the application. So, let's take a look at these techniques.

Using relationships

With relational database management systems in picture, we can now define how two models relate to each other. The databases support the modeling of different kinds of relationships between the two models, such as:

- **One to One Relationships**: These are the kind of relationships where a record from one model relates to only one record from another model. For example, a user in our user model has only one activation key mapped to it from our ActivationKey model. This is a one to one relationship.
- **One to Many Relationships**: These are the kind of relationships where a record from one model maps to multiple records from another model. For example, if we have a model named Bug, describing the bug entries, then we can say, a user record from our user model can map to a number of records in our Bug model, since the same user can file multiple bugs. This is a one-to-many relationship.
- **Many to Many Relationships**: These are the kind of relationships where a record from one model can map to more than one record from another model, which can indeed map back to multiple records in the first model. For example, a user record from our user model can be mapped to many bug records from our bug assignee model, and a record from our bug assignee model can map to multiple user records from our user model. This is a many to many relationship.

There are a few more relationships that can be expressed in a relational database management system, such as self-referencing relationships, but covering all of them is beyond the scope of this book.

Now, if we think back to the example of the optimized models we built for representing our users, we may recall that we utilized a foreign key relationship between our role model and user model, and also in our user model and activation key model.

Now let's try to imagine this. When we want to access the role data of a user, how do we do it? The following snippet gives an example of how we can do this:

```
Session = sessionmaker(bind=engine)
db_session = Session()
user_record = db_session.query(User).first()
role_id = user_record.role_id
role = db_session.query(Role).filter_by(id=role_id)
```

In this example, we first initialized the database session to perform the queries on the database. The next thing we did was to get the first user record from the user model. Our user model maps to the role model through the use of `role_id`, which is a foreign key to the `id` field inside the role model.

This allows us to query the information about the role by using its role id. Once we get the role id of the user from the user model, we can then issue a query to the role model to fetch the required record from it.

Now, there should be an easy way to achieve this effect, where we don't have to issue these two queries ourselves. Can our ORM help us somehow?

Yes, we can make our ORM solution do this work for us. But for that to work, we need to create a relationship between our role model and user model. So, let's redefine our user model to express this relation. The following code snippet shows this:

```
class User(Base):
    __tablename__ = 'users'

    id = Column(Integer, primary_key=True, autoincrement=True)
    first_name = Column(String, nullable=False)
    last_name = Column(String, nullable=False)
    username = Column(String(length=25), unique=True, nullable=False)
    email = Column(String(length=255), unique=True, nullable=False)
    password = Column(String(length=255), nullable=False)
    date_joined = Column(Date, default=datetime.now())
    user_role = Column(Integer, ForeignKey("roles.id"))
    role = relationship("Role")
    account_active = Column(Boolean, default=False)
    activation_key = Column(String(length=32))

    def __repr__(self):
        return "<User {}>".format(self.username)
```

In this code snippet, we added a new field named role. This field maps a relationship from our user record to a record in the role model. The filtering happens automatically based on the `user_role` column, which has a foreign key mapped to the `id` field of the role model.

Now, going back to the example where we queried our user model to fetch the user record, and then fetching our role record for the user, we can re-write it as shown in the following code snippet:

```
Session = sessionmaker(bind=engine)
db_session = Session()
user_record = db_session.query(User).first()
role = user_record.role
```

And there we go, we did not have to first retrieve the `role_id` key and then query the role model manually to fetch the role information about the user.

But, the interesting story is happening behind the scenes. To achieve this effect, what SQLAlchemy did was to utilize lazy loading techniques. When we queried our user model to fetch the record of one user, SQLAlchemy did retrieve the record for the user, but never made an effort to retrieve the record of the role to which the user was associated. We can poke around the fields that are present in `user_record` by running the following command:

```
dir(user_record.user_role)
```

By doing so, we would have seen that the `role` field was present. But until this time, the role field simply held an instance of the SQLAlchemy `query` object. This object just contains the query that will be used to fetch the role data of the associated role from the role model but does not contain any real data as of yet. This won't happen until we call the following code:

```
role = user_record.role
```

The query object from the role field in our `user_record` is executed and the role field is populated with some real data.

This technique is called lazy loading, as we will see in the next section.

Lazy loading

A lot of ORM layers, as well as SQLAlchemy, try to make the effort to delay the loading of data for as long as possible. Usually, data is loaded only when the object is actually accessed by the application. This technique of delaying the loading of data until there is an attempt to access that data is known as lazy loading.

This technique is really helpful for reducing the response times of an application, since the entire data is not loaded in one go but is instead loaded on demand. This optimization comes at the expense of running a few more SQL queries, which will retrieve the actual data as the request is made. But is there some way we can have explicit control over this technique?

The answer to this will differ for every ORM solution, but quite a lot of them actually allow you to enable or disable lazy loading behavior. So, how do we control this in SQLAlchemy?

Taking a look at the user model modification we made in the previous section, we can explicitly tell SQLAlchemy to lazy load the data from our role model by adding an extra attribute in our role field, as can be seen in the following snippet:

```
role = relationship("Role", lazy_load='select')
```

This extra `lazy_load` attribute defines the technique SQLAlchemy uses to load the data from our role model. The following example shows the flow of a request during a lazy load:

```
>>> Session = sessionmaker(bind=engine)
>>> db_session = Session()
>>> user_record = db_session.query(User).first()
INFO sqlalchemy.engine.base.Engine SELECT users.username AS users_username,
users.id AS users_id, users.role_id AS users_role_id
FROM users
 LIMIT %(param_1)s
INFO sqlalchemy.engine.base.Engine {'param_1': 1}
>>> role = user_record.role
INFO sqlalchemy.engine.base.Engine SELECT roles.id AS roles_id,
roles.role_name AS roles_role_name, roles.role_permissions AS
roles_role_permissions
FROM roles
WHERE roles.id = %(param_1)s
INFO sqlalchemy.engine.base.Engine {'param_1': 1}
```

As we can see from this example, SQLAlchemy dosen't make an attempt to load the data of the role model until and unless we try to access it. As soon as we try accessing the data from the role model, SQLAlchemy makes a SELECT query to the database, fetches the results in the object, and returns the populated object, which we can use now.

In contrast to the technique of loading data on demand, we can also ask SQLAlchemy to load all the data as soon as the first request is made. This can save us waiting those few extra milliseconds that the application will wait until the ORM layer fetches the data on demand from the database.

This technique is called **eager loading**, as we will explain in the upcoming section.

Eager loading

There are situations when we want the data of the object we want to be loaded along with the relationships our object maps to. This is a valid use case, such as when the developer is sure they will be accessing the data of the relationship, no matter the situation.

In these kinds of use cases, there is no point wasting time while the ORM layers load the relationships on demand. This technique of loading the object data along with the data of the associated objects to which our main object is related is known as eager loading.

SQLAlchemy provides an easy way to achieve this behavior. Remember the `lazy_load` attribute we specified in the previous section? Yes, that's all you need to switch from lazy load behavior to eager load behavior.

For example, let's consider our user model only. If we wanted to make our roles relation use the eager loading technique, all we would need to do is modify the `lazy_load` attribute and set it to `joined`, as can be seen in the following snippet:

```
role = relationship("Role", lazy_load='joined')
```

Setting `lazy_load` to `joined`, will cause SQLAlchemy to emit a `JOIN` statement to load the data of our user object and the related data from the associated `role` object, as can be seen from the following example:

```
>>> Session = sessionmaker(bind=engine)
>>> db_session = Session()
>>> user_record = db_session.query(User).first()
sqlalchemy.engine.base.Engine BEGIN (implicit)
sqlalchemy.engine.base.Engine SELECT users.username AS users_username,
users.id AS users_id, users.role_id AS users_role_id, roles_1.id AS
roles_1_id, roles_1.role_name AS roles_1_role_name,
roles_1.role_permissions AS roles_1_role_permissions
FROM users LEFT OUTER JOIN roles AS roles_1 ON roles_1.id = users.role_id
INFO sqlalchemy.engine.base.Engine {}
```

As you can see from this example, SQLAlchemy used a `LEFT OUTER JOIN` to eager load the user object as well as the associated role object.

There is another way through which SQLAlchemy can eager load the results. This technique involves SQLAlchemy emitting successive `SELECT` statements to load the data and then joining the results to form one complex result object.

This behavior is also easy to achieve and requires the setting of `lazy_load='subquery'`.

So, with all this knowledge , how can we optimize our data loading techniques so that our application will work easily when dealing with large-scale data? Let's take a look in the next section.

Optimizing data loading

One of the boosts that we can give to our application's performance is by optimizing the way it loads data from the database. This is not something that is complex to implement, and ORM solutions make it much simpler to get all of this up and running.

Optimizing data loading just has a few rules. So, let's take a look at what these are, and how they can prove to be advantageous:

- **Defer the loading of data that can be skipped**: When we know that we won't require all the data that we are fetching from the database, we can safely defer the loading of that data by utilizing the lazy loading technique. For example, if we wanted to send a mail to all those users of our BugZot application who have more then 10 bugs pending against them and who are not an administrator, we could just defer the loading of the role's relationship. Considering a big database with a lot of users, this can help to significantly reduce the response time of the application, as well as its overall memory footprint, at the expense of a few extra queries, which might be a desirable trade-off to make.

- **Load data early if it is going to be used**: In complete contrast to the first point, if we know that the application will use data, no matter the situation, then it makes complete sense to load it in one shot rather than emitting extra queries to load data on demand. For example, if we wanted to promote all the administrators to super administrators, we know we will be accessing the role field of all the users. Then, it doesn't makes sense to make the application lazy load the roles field. We can simply ask the application to eager load the required data so that the application doesn't wait for the data to get loaded on demand. This type of optimization comes at the cost of increased memory usage and slow initial response times, but provides the advantage of fast execution, once all the data has been loaded.

- **Do not load data that won't be required**: There are times when some of the relationships an object maps to are not required at all during processing. In these kinds of situations, we can save a lot of memory and time by simply not loading those relationship objects at all. This can be fairly easily achieved in SQLAlchemy by simply setting `lazy_load='noload'`. One example of such a use case is where loading of the relation is not required when all we want to do is to update the `last_active` time of the user in the database. In this case, we know that we are not required to validate anything related to the role of the user, and hence we can skip the loading of the role altogether.

Achieving these effects clearly cannot be done if the loading technique is embedded in the model definition altogether. So, SQLAlchemy does provide another way to achieve these effects through the use of different methods, named, aptly, based on the technique they use to load the data from the database, for example, `lazyload()` for lazy loading, `joinedload()` for joined eager loading, `subqueryload()` for subquery eager loading, and `noload()` for no loading, which we will explain in later chapters, including how they can be used in a real application.

Now that we're familiar with loading techniques and how we can use them to our advantage, now let's take a look at one of the final topics of this chapter, where we will see how we can utilize caching to speed up our application response times, as well as saving the effort of querying our database again and again, which will indeed help us during times when the application is performing a lot of data-intensive operations.

Utilizing caching

In most enterprise applications, data that has been accessed once is used again and again. This could be in different requests, or could be because the requests are operating on the same set of data.

In these kinds of scenarios, it would be a huge waste of resources if we tried to access the same data again and again from the database, causing the application to make a lot of queries to the database, resulting in high database loads and poor response times.

The ORM layers we use provide some degree of caching to already accessed data, but still, most of the control resides in the hands of the application developer, who can use his wisdom to make the application performant by analyzing which data will be used again and again, and providing mechanisms for caching it.

Let's take a look at some the caching techniques and see how they can help us to make our application performant in terms of data access.

Caching at the database level

Databases are quite a complex piece of software. Not only do they store our data efficiently, they provide us with mechanisms to retrieve that data with the same efficiency as well. This involves quite a lot of complex logic going on behind the scenes.

One of the advantages of using an ORM is the caching the database can perform at the query level. Since databases are supposed to return data in the fastest manner possible, database systems usually cache queries that are performed again and again. This caching happens at the query parsing level so that some time can be saved by not parsing the same query again and again when it is done on the database.

This kind of caching boosts response times since quite a lot of effort is saved parsing queries.

Caching at the block level

Now, let's take a look at the kind of caching we can use at the application level, which can prove to be a major help.

To understand the concept of caching at the application block level, let's take a look at the following simple code snippet:

```
for name in ['super_admin', 'admin', 'user']:
  if db_session.query(User).first().role.role_name == name:
    print("True")
```

From what we can assume, this could have done a query once and then retrieved the data from the database, and then will have used it again and again to compare it with the name variable. But let's take a look at the output of the preceding code:

```
INFO sqlalchemy.engine.base.Engine SELECT users.username AS users_username,
users.id AS users_id, users.role_id AS users_role_id
FROM users
 LIMIT %(param_1)s
INFO sqlalchemy.engine.base.Engine {'param_1': 1}
True
sqlalchemy.engine.base.Engine SELECT users.username AS users_username,
users.id AS users_id, users.role_id AS users_role_id
FROM users
 LIMIT %(param_1)s
sqlalchemy.engine.base.Engine {'param_1': 1}
sqlalchemy.engine.base.Engine SELECT users.username AS users_username,
users.id AS users_id, users.role_id AS users_role_id
```

```
FROM users
 LIMIT %(param_1)s
sqlalchemy.engine.base.Engine {'param_1': 1}
sqlalchemy.engine.base.Engine SELECT users.username AS users_username,
users.id AS users_id, users.role_id AS users_role_id
FROM users
 LIMIT %(param_1)s
INFO sqlalchemy.engine.base.Engine {'param_1': 1}
```

From this output, we can see that the ORM layer didn't cache the query and act as a simple object, but rather executed four queries to fetch the data again and again.

Although this mistake was made intentionally, it shows the side effects of not caching data at the block level, and how costly it would be if this code was to iterate over a lot of records. Although this mistake was costly, it can be avoided quite easily with the use of block-level caching. The following code snippet modifies the preceding example to use block-level caching:

```
user = db_session.query(User).first()
user_role = user.role.role_name
for name in ['super_admin', 'admin', 'user']:
  if user_role == name:
    print("True")
```

When run, this code just executes one query to fetch data from the database, and then uses the same data again and again to compare it without issuing a query to the database.

A simple implementation of a block-level variable to cache the data helped us to reduce the load on the database considerably, while also improving the response of the application.

Using user-level caching

User-level caching is another level of caching that can prove to be of quite a lot of use. Imagine querying the personal details of the user from the database every time the user moves from one page to another. This would not only be inefficient, but would also penalize during high-load situations, when the response times of the database could be so high that a request could just time out and the user would not be able to log in to the application until the overall load reduced.

So, is there anything that can help here?

The answer to this is user-level caching. When we know that some data is specific to the user and is not critical to security, we can simply load it once from the database and save it on the user side. This can be achieved by implementing cookies or creating temporary files on the client side. These cookies or temporary files store non-confidential data about the user, such as user ID or username, or other non-important data, such as the name of the user.

Whenever the application wants to load this data, instead of going to the database directly, it first checks whether the user has this data available at their end. If the data is found, then the data is loaded from there. If the data is not found on the user side, the request is made to the database, and the data is loaded from there, before being finally cached on the client side.

This kind of technique helps a lot when trying to reduce the impact of data loading that is specific to users and does not need to be refreshed from the database frequently.

There are much more sophisticated techniques for caching data by using key-value caching mechanisms, as we will see in later chapters, such as implementing in-memory caches using tools such as memcached, which can prove to be of great help when dealing with huge amounts of data. However, this is beyond the scope of this book, due to the complexity of the topics involved, which can span several hundreds of pages.

Summary

In this chapter, we learned about how to build database models that can help us make our application performant when dealing with data on a large scale. We saw how optimizing a model can be the first stage of optimization, and how it can help us make our application more maintenance-friendly, by reducing coupling across database models. We then moved on to cover how indexes can be useful for making accessing data inside the database faster, by indexing columns that are more frequently accessed.

We later covered one of the important aspects of maintaining the consistency of the database, through the use of transactions.

The final part of the chapter covered data loading techniques, such as lazy loading, eager loading, and no loading, which can help us reduce the time it usually takes to load the data from the database, and process it before it is presented to the user. We also covered a little bit about how the caching of this data at different levels can help to reduce the load from the application and the database, resulting in improved response times from the database, even in situations with a heavy load.

Questions

1. What is the benefit of normalizing database tables?
2. What is the difference between lazy loading through `select` versus lazy loading through `joined`?
3. How can we maintain the integrity of data while running database update queries?
4. What are the different levels of caching data from a database?

4
Dealing with Concurrency

As we saw in the previous chapter, when working on any large-scale enterprise application, we deal with a lot of data. This data is processed in a synchronous manner and the results are sent only after the data processing for a particular process is complete. This kind of model is absolutely fine when the data being processed in individual requests is not large. But consider a situation where a lot of data needs to be processed before a response is generated. What happens then? The answer is, slow application response times.

We need a better solution. A solution that will allow us to process data in parallel, resulting in faster application responses. But how do we achieve this? The answer to the question is **concurrency**.

This chapter will introduce techniques of employing concurrency in your applications and how it can be leveraged to reduce the response times of your application.

During the course of the chapter, we will see how we can spawn multiple processes to deal with heavy workloads, or utilize threading to hand off blocking, unrelated tasks so as to return the actual results early.

In this chapter, you will learn about the following topics:

- Launching and working with multiple processes
- Establishing communication between multiple processes
- Taking a multithreaded approach in an application
- The limitations of a multithreaded approach
- Avoiding common problems with concurrency

Technical requirements

The code listings in this book can be found under `chapter04` directory at `https://github.com/PacktPublishing/Hands-On-Enterprise-Application-Development-with-Python`.

The code samples can be cloned by running the following command:

```
git clone
https://github.com/PacktPublishing/Hands-On-Enterprise-Application-Developm
ent-with-Python
```

The code samples mentioned in the chapter require Python 3.6 and above to run. A virtual environment is a preferred option to keep the dependencies segregated from the system.

The need for concurrency

Most of the time, when we are building fairly simple applications, we do not require concurrency. Simple, sequential programming works just fine, in which one step executes after the completion of another. But as application use cases become more and more complex, and there are an increased number of tasks that can easily be pushed into the background to improve the application's user experience, we end up revolving around the concept of concurrency.

Concurrency is a different beast in itself and makes the task of programming much more complex. But regardless of the added complexity, concurrency also brings a lot of features to improve the user experience of applications.

Before we dive into the question of why we may require the support of concurrency in our enterprise applications, let's first look at a simple example in which we will see concurrency used in our day-to-day lives.

Concurrency in GUI applications

The hardware we have become accustomed to using has became more and more powerful with each passing year. Today, even the CPUs inside our smartphones have quad-core or octa-core configurations. These configurations allow the running of multiple processes or threads in parallel. Not exploiting the power of concurrency would be a waste of the hardware improvements mentioned previously. Today, when we open applications on our smartphones, most of them have two or more threads running, though we are unaware of that most of the time.

Let's consider a fairly simple example of opening up a photo gallery application on our device. As soon as we open the photo gallery, an application process is started. This process is responsible for loading up the GUI of the application. The GUI runs in the main thread and allows us to interact with the application. Now, this application also spawns another background thread, which is responsible for traversing through the filesystem of the OS and loading up the thumbnails of the photos. This loading up of thumbnails from the filesystem can be a tedious task and may take some time, depending on how many thumbnails need to be loaded.

Though we do notice that the thumbnails are slowly loading, throughout this whole time, our application GUI remains responsive and we can interact with it, see the progress, and so on. All of this is made possible through the use of concurrent programming.

Imagine if concurrency hadn't been used here. The application would have been loading the thumbnails in the main thread itself. This would have caused the GUI to become unresponsive until the main thread finished loading the thumbnails. Not only would this have been very unintuitive, it also would have caused a bad user experience, which we avoided with the help of concurrent programming.

Now we have a fair idea of how concurrent programming can prove to be of great use, let's see how it can help us with the design and development of enterprise applications and what can be achieved with it.

Concurrency in enterprise applications

Enterprise applications are large and usually deal with a lot of user-initiated actions such as data retrieval, updates, and so on. Now, let's take a short example scenario for our BugZot application, where a user may submit a graphic attachment along with their bug report. This is actually quite a common process when filing a bug that may affect the application UI or that displays an error on the UI. Now, every user may submit an image, which may differ in quality and hence their sizes may vary. This may involve images that are very small in size and images that may have very large sizes and high resolutions. As an application developer, you may know that storing an image with 100% quality can, at times, not only waste the storage quota of the application but may also cause the rendering of the bug report to be slow, if, every time, the full resolution image needs to be downloaded by the client from the server.

One of the possible workarounds to this situation is to process images once they are uploaded and store them in a resolution that we determine to be a good trade-off between quality and performance. Now, image processing is a CPU-intensive task and can take quite some time, depending on the resolution of the uploaded image. If we process this in a sequential manner, we may end up with a small problem. Until the image has been converted to a specific resolution, the user-created bug report will not be submitted to the bug database. This is something that will cause a long wait time during heavy loads, while also causing users an increased level of frustration.

Now, to solve this issue, we can use concurrency. Once we have the image attached to the bug uploaded and validated as an image, we may offload the post-processing of the image to a separate background thread or a processing queue and can successfully submit bug to the application database. This is possible because the bug report capturing is a task that does not depend on the image post-processing task, and hence both can be executed in parallel. This allows for improved response times and also a greater set of optimizations as our bug reporting application becomes more and more complex.

This is just one of the example scenarios but is not the only one that may benefit from the use of concurrency in application programming. There are many more such scenarios, such as the deletion of a user account, which may warrant the removal of database records for that user, or sending account activation emails when a new user registers.

Now, let's see how we can implement the concept of concurrent programming with the use of Python as the language of choice for our application development.

Concurrent programming with Python

Python provides a number of ways through which parallelism or concurrency can be achieved. All of these methods have their own pros and cons, and differ fundamentally in terms of how they are implemented, and a choice needs to be made about which method to use when, keeping the use case in mind.

One of the methods provided by Python for implementing concurrency is performed at the thread level by allowing the application to launch multiple threads, each executing a job. These threads provide an easy-to-use concurrency mechanism and execute inside a single Python interpreter process, and hence are lightweight.

Another mechanism for achieving parallelism is through the use of multiple processes in place of multiple threads. With this approach, every process performs a separate task inside its own separate Python interpreter process. This approach provides some workarounds to the problems that a multithreaded Python program may face in the presence of the **Global Interpreter Lock (GIL)**, which we will discuss in later sections of the chapter, but may also add to the additional overhead of managing multiple processes and increased memory usage.

So, first let's take a look at how we can achieve concurrency with the use of threads and discuss the benefits and drawbacks they come packaged with.

Concurrency with multithreading

In most modern processor systems, the use of multithreading is commonplace. With CPUs coming with more than one core and technologies such as hyper-threading, which allows a single core to run multiple threads at the same time, application developers do not waste a single chance to exploit the advantages provided by these technologies.

Python as a programming language supports the implementation of multithreading through the use of a threading module that allows developers to exploit thread-level parallelism in the application.

The following example showcases how a simple program can be built using the threading module in Python:

```python
# simple_multithreading.py
import threading

class SimpleThread(threading.Thread):
    def __init__(self, exec_target, exec_args):
        threading.Thread.__init__(self, target=exec_target,
args=exec_args)

def count_printer(counter):
    for i in range(counter, 0, -1):
        print(i)

count_thread1 = SimpleThread(exec_target=count_printer, exec_args=(5,))
count_thread2 = SimpleThread(exec_target=count_printer, exec_args=(3,))
print("Starting thread 1")
count_thread1.start()
print("Starting thread 2")
count_thread2.start()
count_thread1.join()
```

```
count_thread2.join()
print("Exiting")
```

This example showcases a simple use of Python's object-oriented programming style and threading module, through which we created a simple multithreaded program that prints numbers using more than one thread.

To achieve this, we first imported the Python 3 threading module into our program. Once the module was imported, we defined a new class, named SimpleThread, which inherits from the threading.Thread class.

To create a simple thread-based class, the minimum we have to do is to define an __init__ method for the child class.

In the __init__ method of our SimpleThread class, we ask for two parameters: exec_target, which defines the callable method that our class should run inside a thread; and exec_args, which is a tuple of arguments that will be passed to the target method.

Inside the __init__ method, all we do is call the __init__ method of the Thread class and provide it with the values for the target parameter, which asks for a callable target and the values for the args parameter, which asks for the value of arguments that need to be passed to the target.

Next, we define the count_printer method, which we will use as a target method while creating objects of our SimpleThread class.

Now, we create two objects of the SimpleThread class, representative of the two threads that we want to run. Once these objects have been created, we call the start() method of the Thread class to start the threads.

The join() method waits for the thread to complete execution and exit and then returns, effectively causing our program to wait till both the threads have completed their execution.

Now, let's see what happens when we run our program:

```
python simple_multithreading.py
Starting thread 1
5
4
3
Starting thread 2
2
3
```

```
1
2
1
Exiting
```

As we can see, it is quite simple to implement a program with multithreading in Python. But simplicity and concurrency are two roads that never intersect.

The previous example was a very simple example of implementing threading where only a loop runs and prints the numbers onscreen. But most real-life applications use threads to do much more than simply printing a natural number series. These programs may involve performing long blocking I/O operations, where they may read a file and then process it or wait on a database to send the information back for a request.

Let's take a look at the following program, which takes multiple JSON files as input and converts them to YAML format, and writes them to a single YAML file on disk for a hypothetical purpose:

```python
# json_to_yaml.py
import threading
import json
import yaml

class JSONConverter(threading.Thread):
        def __init__(self, json_file, yaml_file):
                threading.Thread.__init__(self)
                self.json_file = json_file
                self.yaml_file = yaml_file

        def run(self):
                print("Starting read for {}".format(self.json_file))
                self.json_reader = open(self.json_file, 'r')
                self.json = json.load(self.json_reader)
                self.json_reader.close()
                print("Read completed for {}".format(self.json_file))
                print("Writing {} to YAML".format(self.json_file))
                self.yaml_writer = open(self.yaml_file, 'a+')
                yaml.dump(self.json, self.yaml_writer)
                self.yaml_writer.close()
                print("Conversion completed for {}".format(self.json_file))

files = ['file1.json', 'file2.json', 'file3.json']

conversion_threads = []

for file in files:
        converter = JSONConverter(file, 'converted.yaml')
```

```
        conversion_threads.append(converter)
        converter.start()

for cthread in conversion_threads:
        cthread.join()

print("Exiting")
```

Let's just see what happens when we run this program:

```
python json_to_yaml.py
Starting read for file1.json
Starting read for file2.json
Starting read for file3.json
Read completed for file1.json
Writing file1.json to YAML
Read completed for file2.json
Read completed for file3.json
Writing file2.json to YAML
Writing file3.json to YAML
Conversion completed for file1.json
Conversion completed for file3.json
Conversion completed for file2.json
Exiting
```

As you can see, we cannot predict the reading and writing order of the program. Just imagine a situation where the Python interpreter thought it was time to switch over control from the thread that was in the middle of the process of writing the contents of file1.json to the thread that was writing the contents of file2.json. In such a scenario, we would have been left with a corrupt converted.yaml output file that would have contents intermingled from different JSON files. This is just one example of how multithreading can wreak havoc if proper care has not been taken when implementing the program.

Now, the question is, how can we avoid such scenarios?

Thread synchronization

As we explored in the previous section, although threads can be implemented quite easily in Python, they do come with their own gotchas, which need to be taken care of when trying to write an application that is being targeted for production use cases. If these gotchas are not taken care of at the time of application development, they will produce hard-to-debug behaviors, which concurrent programs are quite famous for.

So, let's try to find out how we can work around the problem we discussed in the previous section. If we think hard, we can categorize the problem as a problem with the synchronization of multiple threads. The optimal behavior for the application would be to synchronize the writes to the file in such a way that only one thread is able to write to the file at any given point in time. This would enforce that no thread can start a write operation until one of the already-executing threads has completed its writes.

To implement such synchronization, we can leverage the power of locking. Locks provide a simple way to implement synchronization. For example, a thread that is going to start its write operation will first acquire a lock. If lock acquisition is successful, the thread can then progress to perform its write operation. Now, if a context switch happens in between and another thread is about to start a write operation, it will block, since the lock has already been taken. This will prevent the thread from writing the data in between an already-running write operation.

In Python multithreading, we can implement locks through the use of the `threading.Lock` class. The class provides two methods that facilitate the acquisition and release of locks. The `acquire()` method is called by the thread when it wants to acquire a lock before executing an operation. Once the lock is acquired, the thread continues with the execution of the operation. As soon as the operations of the threads are finished, the thread calls the `release()` method to release the lock such that the lock can be acquired by another thread that may be waiting for it.

Let's see how we can use locks to synchronize the threaded operations in our JSON to YAML converter example. The following code sample showcases the use of locks:

```python
import threading
import json
import yaml

class JSONConverter(threading.Thread):
        def __init__(self, json_file, yaml_file, lock):
                threading.Thread.__init__(self)
                self.json_file = json_file
                self.yaml_file = yaml_file
    self.lock = lock

    def run(self):
            print("Starting read for {}".format(self.json_file))
            self.json_reader = open(self.json_file, 'r')
            self.json = json.load(self.json_reader)
            self.json_reader.close()
            print("Read completed for {}".format(self.json_file))
            print("Writing {} to YAML".format(self.json_file))
    self.lock.acquire() # We acquire a lock before writing
```

```
            self.yaml_writer = open(self.yaml_file, 'a+')
            yaml.dump(self.json, self.yaml_writer)
            self.yaml_writer.close()
            self.lock.release() # Release the lock once our writes are
done
            print("Conversion completed for {}".format(self.json_file))

files = ['file1.json', 'file2.json', 'file3.json']
write_lock = threading.Lock()
conversion_threads = []

for file in files:
        converter = JSONConverter(file, 'converted.yaml', write_lock)
        conversion_threads.append(converter)
        converter.start()

for cthread in conversion_threads:
        cthread.join()

print("Exiting")
```

In this example, we first create a `lock` variable by creating an instance of the `threading.Lock` class. This instance is then passed to all our threads that need to be synchronized. When a thread has to do a write operation, it first proceeds by acquiring a lock and then starting the writes. Once these writes are completed, the thread releases the lock for acquisition by the other threads.

 If a thread acquires a lock but forgets to release it, the program may get into a state of deadlock since no other thread will be able to proceed. Proper caution should be taken so that the acquired locks are released once the thread finishes its operations, to avoid deadlocks.

Re-entrant locks

Beyond the `threading.Lock` class, which provides the general locking mechanism for multithreading, where a lock can only be acquired once until it is released, Python also provides another locking mechanism that might be useful for programs that implement recursive operations. This lock, known as a re-entrant lock and implemented using the `threading.RLock` class, can be used by recursive functions. The class provides similar methods to those provided by the lock class: `acquire()` and `release()`, which are to acquire and release the taken locks, respectively. The only difference occurs when a recursive function calls `acquire()` multiple times across the call stack. When the same function calls the acquire method again and again, a new lock is given to the function. To release this lock, the function needs to call the release method.

One interesting thing to note here is that the lock will be fully released only at the final `release()` method call made by the recursive method. If some other thread tries to acquire a lock before the final `release()` call is made, the thread will block on execution and will wait until the lock is freed up from the previously executing thread.

Condition variables

Let's imagine that somehow, we had a way through which we could tell our `Thread-1` to wait until `Thread-2` has made some data available for consumption. This is exactly what condition variables allow us to do. They allow us to synchronize two threads that depend on a shared resource. To understand more about this, let's take a look at the following code sample, which creates two threads, one that feeds in the email ID and another thread that is responsible for sending the emails:

```python
# condition_variable.py
import threading

class EmailQueue(threading.Thread):

    def __init__(self, email_queue, max_items, condition_var):
        threading.Thread.__init__(self)
        self.email_queue = email_queue
        self.max_items = max_items
        self.condition_var = condition_var
        self.email_recipients = []

    def add_recipient(self, email):
        self.email_recipients.append(email)

    def run(self):
        while True:
            self.condition_var.acquire()
            if len(self.email_queue) == self.max_items:
                print("E-mail queue is full. Entering wait state...")
                self.condition_var.wait()
                print("Received consume signal. Populating queue...")
            while len(self.email_queue) < self.max_items:
                if len(self.email_recipients) == 0:
                    break
                email = self.email_recipients.pop()
                self.email_queue.append(email)
                self.condition_var.notify()
            self.condition_var.release()

class EmailSender(threading.Thread):
```

```python
    def __init__(self, email_queue, condition_var):
        threading.Thread.__init__(self)
        self.email_queue = email_queue
        self.condition_var = condition_var

    def run(self):
        while True:
            self.condition_var.acquire()
            if len(self.email_queue) == 0:
                print("E-mail queue is empty. Entering wait state...")
                self.condition_var.wait()
                print("E-mail queue populated. Resuming operations...")
            while len(self.email_queue) is not 0:
                email = self.email_queue.pop()
                print("Sending email to {}".format(email))
            self.condition_var.notify()
            self.condition_var.release()

queue = []
MAX_QUEUE_SIZE = 100
condition_var = threading.Condition()

email_queue = EmailQueue(queue, MAX_QUEUE_SIZE, condition_var)
email_sender = EmailSender(queue, condition_var)
email_queue.start()
email_sender.start()
email_queue.add_recipient("joe@example.com")
```

In this code example, we defined two classes, namely, EmailQueue, which plays the role of producer and populates the email queue with email addresses on which the email needs to be sent. Then there is another class, EmailSender, which plays the role of the consumer and consumes the email addresses from the email queue and sends a mail to them.

Now, inside the __init__ method of EmailQueue, we take in a Python list that we will use as a queue as a parameter, a variable defining how many items the list should hold at most, and a condition variable.

Next, we have a method, add_recipient, which appends a new email ID inside an internal data structure of the EmailQueue to hold the email addresses temporarily until they are added to the sending queue.

Now, let's move inside the run() method where the actual magic happens. First, we start an infinite loop to keep the thread in always running mode. Next, we acquire a lock by calling the acquire() method of the condition variable. We do this so as to prevent any kind of corruption of our data structures if the thread switches the context at an unexpected time.

Once we have acquired the lock, we then check whether our email queue is full or not. If it is full, we print a message and make a call to the `wait()` method of the condition variable. The call to the `wait()` method releases the lock acquired by the condition variable and makes the thread enter a blocking state. This blocking state will be over only when a `notify()` method is called on the condition variable. Now, when the thread receives a signal through `notify()`, it continues its operations, in which it first checks whether it has some data in the internal queue. If it finds some data in the internal queue, then it populates the email queue with that data and calls the `notify()` method of the conditional variable to inform the `EmailSender` consumer thread. Now, let's take a look at the `EmailSender` class.

Without going through every single line here, let's keep our focus on the `run()` method of the `EmailSender` class. Since this thread needs to always be running, we first start an infinite loop to do that. Then, the next thing we do is, acquire a lock on the shared condition variable. Once we have acquired the lock, we are now ready to manipulate the shared `email_queue` data structure. So, the first thing our consumer does is, check whether the email queue is empty or not. If it finds the queue to be empty, our consumer will call the `wait()` method of the condition variable, effectively causing it to release the lock and go into a blocking state until there is some data inside the email queue. This causes the transfer of control to the `EmailQueue` class, which is responsible for populating the queue.

Now, once the email queue has some email IDs in it, the consumer will start sending the mails. Once it exhausts the queue, it signals the `EmailSender` class about that by calling the condition variables `notify` method. This will allow the `EmailSender` to continue its operation of populating the email queue.

Let's take a look at what happens when we try to execute the previous example program:

```
python condition_variable.py
E-mail queue is empty. Entering wait state...
E-mail queue populated. Resuming operations...
Sending email to joe@example.com
E-mail queue is empty. Entering wait state...
```

With this example, we now have an understanding of how condition variables can be used in Python to solve producer-consumer problems. With this knowledge in mind, now let's take a look at some of the issues that can may arise when performing multithreading in our applications.

Common pitfalls with multithreading

Multithreading provides a lot of benefits but also comes with some pitfalls. These pitfalls, if not avoided, can prove to be a painful experience when the application goes into production. These pitfalls usually result in unexpected behaviors that may take place only once in a while, or may occur on every execution of a particular module. The painful thing about this is it is really hard to debug these problems when they are caused by the execution of multiple threads, since it is quite hard to predict when a particular thread will execute. So, it makes it worthwhile to discuss why these common pitfalls occur and how they can be avoided during the development stage itself.

Some of the common reasons for unexpected behaviors in multithreaded applications are race conditions and deadlocks. Let's take a look at them individually and understand why they happen and how can they be avoided.

Race conditions

In the context of multithreading, a race condition is a situation where two or more threads try to modify a shared data structure at the same time, but due to the way the threads are scheduled and executed, the shared data structure is modified in a way that leaves it in an inconsistent state.

Is this statement confusing? No worries, let's try to understand it with an example:

Consider our previous example of the JSON to YAML converter problem. Now, let's assume that we did not use locks when we were writing the converted YAML output to the file. Now consider this: we have two threads, named `writer-1` and `writer-2` which are responsible for writing to the common YAML file. Now, imagine both the `writer-1` and `writer-2`, threads have started their operations of writing to the file and, with the way the operating system scheduled the threads to execute, `writer-1` starts writing to the file. Now, while the `writer-1` thread was writing to the file, the operating system decided that the thread finished its quota of time and swaps that thread with the `writer-2` thread. Now, one thing to note here is that the `writer-1` thread had not completed writing all the data when it was swapped. Now, the `writer-2` thread starts executing and completes writing of data in the YAML file. Upon completion of the `writer-2` thread, the OS then starts executing the `writer-1` thread again which starts to write the remaining data again to the YAML file and then finishes.

Now, when we open the YAML file, what we see is a file with data mingled up from two writer threads, and hence, leaves our file in an inconsistent state. A problem such as what happened between the `writer-1` and `writer-2` threads is known as a race condition.

Race conditions come under the category of problems that are very hard to debug, since the order in which the threads will execute depends on machine to machine and OS to OS. So, a problem that may occur on one deployment may not occur on another deployment.

So, how do we avoid race conditions? Well, we already have the answers to the question and we have just recently used them. So, let's take a look at some of the ways in which race conditions can be prevented:

- **Utilizing locks in critical regions**: Critical regions refer to those areas of code where a shared variable is being modified by a thread. To prevent race conditions from happening in critical regions, we can use locks. A lock essentially causes all the threads to block except the thread that holds the lock. All the other threads that need to modify the shared resource will execute only when the thread that is currently holding the lock releases it. Some of the categories of locks that can be used are mutex locks, which can only be held by a single thread at a time; re-entrant locks, which allow a recursive function to take multiple locks on the same shared resource; and condition objects, which can be used to synchronize execution in producer-consumer type environments.
- **Utilizing thread-safe data structures**: One other way of preventing race conditions is by using thread-safe data structures. A thread-safe data structure is one that will automatically manage the modifications being made to it by multiple threads and will serialize their operations. One of the thread-safe shared data structures that is provided by Python is a queue. A queue can be used easily when the operation involves multiple threads.

Now, we have an idea about what race conditions are, how they happen, and how they can be avoided. With this in mind, let's take a look at one of the other pitfalls that can arise due to the way we prevent race conditions from happening.

Deadlocks

A deadlock is a situation when two or more threads are blocked forever because they depend on each other or a resource that never gets freed up. Let's try to understand how a deadlock occurs by taking a simple example:

Consider our previous example of the JSON to YAML converter. Now, let's assume we had used locks in our threads such that when a thread starts to write to the file, it first takes a mutex lock on the file. Now, until this mutex lock is freed up by the thread, other thread cannot execute.

So, let's imagine the same situation with two threads, `writer-1` and `writer-2`, which are trying to write to the common output file. Now, when `writer-1` starts to execute, it first acquires a lock on the file and starts its operation. Now, during the execution of `writer-1`, a context switch occurs and control transfers to `writer-2`. Now, `writer-2` tries to acquire the lock but enters a blocking state, since `writer-1` is currently holding the lock. The control transfers back to the `writer-1` thread and it completes its execution, writing all its data. But due to a bug, the `writer-1` thread does not release the acquired lock, even though it has completed execution.

This causes the `writer-2` thread to stay in the blocking state, since the lock was never freed. A situation such as that experienced by the `writer-2` thread, where it stays in a blocking state, is also known as a deadlock.

Deadlocks can happen when an acquired lock is not freed up properly or if a thread doesn't have a mechanism to time out if lock acquisition takes a long time. So, let's see some of the ways through which we can avoid deadlocks occurring:

- **Taking care to release the acquired locks**: If the programmer is careful about releasing the acquired locks by a thread, then deadlocks can be avoided quite easily. This can be achieved by calling the associated release call of an acquired lock and implementing proper thread cleanup mechanisms if the thread terminates abruptly during its execution.
- **Specifying lock acquisition timeout**: One other way to prevent deadlocks is to specify a timeout value for which a particular thread will wait to acquire the lock. If this timeout value is exceeded, the acquisition operations execution will fail with an exception. In Python, the timeout value for a lock acquisition can be provided as a parameter to the `acquire()` method. This can be specified as: `acquire(timeout=10)`. Here, the timeout parameter specifies the time in seconds for which the acquire operation will wait for the lock to be acquired and will fail if the lock is not acquired during the specified duration, essentially avoiding the thread being in a blocked state forever.

With this, we now have knowledge about two common pitfalls that can happen in multithreaded applications and how they can be avoided. Now, let's take the opportunity to discuss a common design pitfall with some specific interpreters of Python and how it can affect multithreaded operations.

The story of GIL

What if someone told you that, even though you have created a multithreaded program, only a single thread can execute at a time? This situation used to be true when systems consisted of a single core that could execute only one thread at a time, and the illusion of multiple running threads was created by the CPU switching between threads frequently.

But this situation is also true in one of the implementations of Python. The original implementation of Python, also known as CPython consists of a global mutex also known as a GIL, which allows only one thread to execute the Python bytecode at a time. This effectively limits the application to executing only one thread at a time.

The GIL was introduced in CPython because of the fact that the CPython interpreter wasn't thread-safe. The GIL proved to be an effective way to workaround the thread-safety issues by trading the properties of running multiple threads concurrently.

The existence of GIL has been a highly debated topic in the Python community and a lot of proposals have been made to eliminate it, but none of the proposals have made it to a production version of Python, for various reasons, which include the performance impact on single-threaded applications, breaking the backward compatibility of features that have grown to be dependent upon the presence of the GIL, and so on.

So, what does the presence of GIL mean for your multithreaded application? Effectively, if your applications exploit multithreading to perform I/O workloads, then you might not be impacted on that much in terms of performance loss due to GIL, since most of the I/O happens outside the GIL, and hence multiple threads can be multiplexed. The impact of GIL will be felt only when the application uses multiple threads to perform CPU-intensive tasks that require heavy manipulation of application-specific data structures. Since all data structure manipulation involves the execution of Python bytecode, the GIL will severely limit the performance of a multithreaded application by not allowing more than one thread to execute concurrently.

So, is there a workaround for the problem that GIL causes? The answer to this is yes, but which solution should be adopted depends completely on the use case of the application. The following options can prove to be of help for avoiding the GIL:

- **Switching the Python implementation:** If your application does not necessarily depend on the underlying Python implementation and a switch to another implementation can be made, then there are some Python implementations that do not come with GIL. Some of the implementations that do not have GIL in place are: Jython and IronPython, which can completely exploit multiprocessor systems to execute multithreaded applications.

- **Utilizing multiprocessing:** Python has a lot of options when it comes to building programs with concurrency in mind. We explored multithreading, which is one of the options for implementing concurrency but is limited by the GIL. Another option for achieving concurrency is by using Python's multiprocessing capabilities, which allow the launching of multiple processes to execute tasks in parallel. Since every process runs in its own instance of Python interpreter, the GIL doesn't become an issue here and allows for the full exploitation of the multiprocessor systems.

With the knowledge of how GIL impacts multithreaded applications, let's now discuss how multiprocessing can help you to overcome the limitations of concurrency.

Concurrency with multiprocessing

The Python language provides some quiet easy ways to achieve concurrency in applications. We saw this with the Python threading library and the same is true for the Python multiprocessing capabilities too.

If you want to build concurrency in your program with the help of multiprocessing, it is quite easy to achieve, all thanks to the Python multiprocessing library and the APIs exposed by the library.

So, what do we mean when we say that we will implement concurrency by using multiprocessing. Let's try to answer this. Usually, when we talk about concurrency, there are two methods that can help us achieve it. One of those methods is running a single application instance and allowing it to use multiple threads. The threads provide a lightweight solution to multithreading and usually live inside the memory space of the application instance only. Most of the time, the executing interpreter or the OS is responsible for scheduling and executing the threads. But there is one other way to achieve concurrency. With this method, instead of using lightweight threads that live inside the application instance itself, we go for multiple processes. Whenever we talk about multiple processes in the context of Python, we essentially mean that every single process executes in its own instance of the Python interpreter. All these processes have their own exclusive memory regions and are usually a bit heavier in comparison to threads, since they need to maintain their own data structures.

The use of multiple processes also allows us to sidestep the GIL in Python, since every process executes in its own instance of the Python interpreter, allowing us to fully exploit the power of a multiprocessor system.

Now, let's take a look at how Python's multiprocessing library helps us to implement concurrency in our applications.

Python multiprocessing module

Python provides an easy way to implement a multiprocess program. This ease of implementation is facilitated by the Python multiprocessing module, which provides important classes, such as the `Process` class to start new processes; the `Queue`, and `Pipe` classes to facilitate communication between multiple processes; and so on.

The following example provides a quick overview of how to use Python's multiprocessing library to create a URL loader that executes as a separate process to load a URL:

```
# url_loader.py
from multiprocessing import Process
import urllib.request

def load_url(url):
    url_handle = urllib.request.urlopen(url)
    url_data = url_handle.read()
    # The data returned by read() call is in the bytearray format. We need
to
    # decode the data before we can print it.
    html_data = url_data.decode('utf-8')
    url_handle.close()
    print(html_data)

if __name__ == '__main__':
    url = 'http://www.w3c.org'
    loader_process = Process(target=load_url, args=(url,))
    print("Spawning a new process to load the url")
    loader_process.start()
    print("Waiting for the spawned process to exit")
    loader_process.join()
    print("Exiting...")
```

In this example, we created a simple program using the Python multiprocessing library, which loads a URL in the background and prints its information to `stdout`. The interesting bit here is understanding how easily we spawned a new process in our program. So, let's take a look. To achieve multiprocessing, we first import the `Process` class from Python's multiprocessing module. The next step is to create a function that takes the URL to load as a parameter and then loads that URL using Python's `urllib` module. Once the URL is loaded, we print the data from the URL to `stdout`.

Next, we define the code that runs when the program starts executing. Here, we have first defined the URL we want to load with the `url` variable. The next bit is where we introduce the multiprocessing in our program by creating an object of the `Process` class. For this object, we provide the target parameter as the function we want to execute. This is similar to the target method we have grown accustomed to while using the Python `threading` library. The next parameter to the `Process` constructor is the `args` parameter, which takes in the arguments that need to be passed to the target function while calling it.

To spawn a new process, we make a call to the `start()` method of the `Process` object. This spawns a new process in which our target function starts executing and doing its magic. The last thing we do is to wait for this spawned process to exit by calling the `join()` method of the `Process` class.

This is as simple as it gets to create a multiprocess application in Python.

Now, we know how to create a multiprocess application in Python, but how do we divide a particular set of tasks between multiple processes. Well, that's quite easy. The following code sample modifies the entrypoint code from our previous example to exploit the power of the `Pool` class from the multiprocessing module to achieve this:

```
from multiprocessing import Pool
if __name__ == '__main__':
    url = ['http://www.w3c.org', 'http://www.microsoft.com',
'[http://www.wikipedia.org', '[http://www.packt.com']
    with Pool(4) as loader_pool:
        loader_pool.map(load_url, url)
```

In this example, we used the `Pool` class from the multiprocessing library to create a pool of four processes that will execute our code. Using the `map` method of the `Pool` class, we then map the input data to the executing function in a separate process to achieve concurrency.

Now, we have multiple processes churning through our tasks. But what if we wanted to make these processes communicate with each other. For example, in the previous problem of URL loading, instead of printing the data on `stdout`, we wanted the process to return that data instead? The answer to this lies in the use of *pipe*, which provides a two-way mechanism for the processes to communicate with each other.

The following example utilizes pipes to make the URL loader send the data loaded from the URL back to the parent process:

```
# url_load_pipe.py
from multiprocessing import Process, Pipe
import urllib.request
```

```
def load_url(url, pipe):
    url_handle = urllib.request.urlopen(url)
    url_data = url_handle.read()
    # The data returned by read() call is in the bytearray format. We need
to
    # decode the data before we can print it.
    html_data = url_data.decode('utf-8')
    url_handle.close()
    pipe.send(html_data)

if __name__ == '__main__':
    url = 'http://www.w3c.org'
    parent_pipe, child_pipe = Pipe()
    loader_process = Process(target=load_url, args=(url, child_pipe))
    print("Spawning a new process to load the url")
    loader_process.start()
    print("Waiting for the spawned process to exit")
    html_data = parent_pipe.recv()
    print(html_data)
    loader_process.join()
    print("Exiting...")
```

In this example, we have used pipes to provide a two-way communication mechanism for
the parent and child processes to talk to each other. When we make a call to
the pipe constructor inside the __main__ section of the code, the constructor returns a pair
of connection objects. Each of these connection objects contains a send() and
a recv() method facilitating communication between the ends. Data sent from
the child_pipe using the send() method can be read by the parent_pipe using
the recv() method of the parent_pipe and vice versa.

If two processes read or write from/to the same end of pipe at the same
time, there is the potential for possible data corruption in the pipe.
Although, if the processes are using two different ends or two different
pipes, this does not become an issue. Only the data that can be pickled can
be sent through the pipes. This is one of the limitations of the Python
multiprocessing module.

Synchronizing processes

As much as synchronizing the actions of the threads was important, the synchronizing of
actions inside the context of multiprocessing is also important. Since multiple processes
may be accessing the same shared resource, their access to shared resource needs to be
serialized. To help achieve this, we have the support of locks here too.

The following example showcases how to use locks in the context of the multiprocessing module to synchronize the operations of multiple processes by fetching the HTML associated with the URLs and writing that HTML to a common local file:

```python
# url_loader_locks.py
from multiprocessing import Process, Lock
import urllib.request

def load_url(url, lock):
    url_handle = urllib.request.urlopen(url)
    url_data = url_handle.read()
    # The data returned by read() call is in the bytearray format. We need to
    # decode the data before we can print it.
    url_handle.close()
    lock.acquire()
    with open("combinedhtml.txt", 'a+') as outfile:
        outfile.write(url_data)
    lock.release()

if __name__ == '__main__':
    urls = ['http://www.w3c.org', 'http://www.google.com',
'http://www.microsoft.com', 'http://www.wikipedia.org']
    lock = Lock()
    process_pool = []
    for url in urls:
        url_loader = Process(target=load_url, args=(url, lock,))
        process_pool.append(url_loader)
    for loader in process_pool:
        loader.start()
    for loader in process_pool:
        loader.join()
    print("Exiting...")
```

In this example, we only added one extra thing. The use of the Lock class from the multiprocessing library. This Lock class is analogous to the Lock class that is found in the threading library and is used to synchronize the actions of multiple processes through the process of acquiring and releasing a lock. When a process accesses a shared resource, it can first acquire a lock before starting its operation. This effectively causes all other processes that may try to access the same shared resource to block until the process that is currently accessing the resource frees up the lock, and hence causing the actions to be synchronized across the processes.

With this, we now have a fair idea about how we can utilize the Python multiprocessing library to achieve the full potential of a multiprocessor system to speed up our application by leveraging the power of concurrency.

Summary

In this chapter, we explored how to achieve concurrency in Python applications and how it can be useful. During this exploration, we uncovered the capabilities of the Python multithreading module and how it can be used to spawn multiple threads to divide workloads on. We then moved on to understand how to synchronize the actions of those threads and learned about various issues that may crop up in a multithreaded application, if not taken care of. The chapter then moved on to explore the limitations that are imposed by the presence of the **global interpreter lock** (**GIL**)in some Python implementations and how it affects multithreaded workloads. To explore possible ways to overcome the restrictions imposed by the GIL, we moved on to understand the use of Python's multiprocessing module and how it can help us to leverage the full potential of a multiprocessor system by achieving parallelism powered by the use of multiple processes instead of multiple threads.

Questions

1. What are the different methods through which Python enables the building of concurrent applications?
2. What happens to an acquired lock if the thread that has acquired it terminates abruptly?
3. How can we terminate executing threads when the application receives a termination signal?
4. How can we share state between multiple processes?
5. Is there a way through which we can create a pool of processes that can then be used to work on the incoming set of tasks in a task queue?

5
Building for Large-Scale Request Handling

In an enterprise environment, as the number of users grow, it is normal for the number of users who try to access the web application at the same time to also grow. This presents us with the interesting problem of how to scale the web application to handle a large number of concurrent requests by the users.

Scaling up a web application to handle a large number of users is a task that can be achieved in multiple ways where one of the simplest ways can be adding more infrastructure and running more instances of the application. However, this technique, though simple, is highly burdensome on the economics of application scalability, since the infrastructure costs associated with running the application at scale can be huge. We certainly need to craft our application in such a way that it is easily able to handle a lot of concurrent requests without really requiring frequent infrastructure scaling.

Building on the foundation laid out in the previous chapter, we will see how we can apply these techniques to build a scalable application that can handle a large number of concurrent requests, while also learning a few other techniques that will help us scale the application in an effortless manner.

Over the course of the chapter, we will be taking a look at the following techniques to scale our web application for large-scale request handling:

- Utilizing reverse proxies in web application deployment
- Using thread pools to scale up request processing
- Understanding the concept of single-threaded concurrent code with Python AsyncIO

Technical requirements

The code listings in this book can be found under `chapter05` directory at `https://github.com/PacktPublishing/Hands-On-Enterprise-Application-Development-with-Python`.

The code samples can be cloned by running the following command:

```
git clone
https://github.com/PacktPublishing/Hands-On-Enterprise-Application-Developm
ent-with-Python
```

For successful execution of the code sample, the python-`virtualenv` package needs to be present.

The problems of accommodating increased concurrency

Over the years, in the time the internet has been around, one of the most common problems that web application architects have commonly faced is how to deal with the increasing concurrency. As more and more users are coming online and utilizing web applications, there is a huge need to scale up infrastructures to manage all these requests.

This stands true even for our enterprise web applications. Even though we can make an estimate of how many users could be concurrently accessing these web applications inside an enterprise, there is no hard and fast rule that will be true for the time to come. As the enterprise grows, the number of clients accessing the application will also increase, putting more stress upon the infrastructure and increasing the need to scale it out. But what options do we have, while trying to scale out the application to accommodate the increasing number of clients? Let's take a look.

The multiple options to scale up

The world of technology provides a lot of options to scale up the application to accommodate the ever increasing user base; some of these options simply ask for increasing the hardware resources whereas the other options require the application to be built around dealing with multiple requests internally itself. Most of the time, the options of scaling fall into two major categories, vertical scaling, and horizontal scaling:

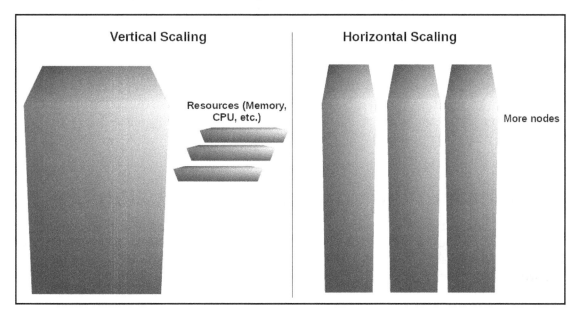

Let's take a look at both of them and figure out their pros and cons:

- **Vertical scaling**: The whole concept of vertical scaling is based upon the fact of adding more resources to the existing hardware to increase the processing power and to accommodate increased concurrency. For example, by adding more processors, we can improve upon the time it takes to process an individual request and, hence, allow for more increased capacity for handling more requests. But vertical scaling also has its own limits; we just can't keep adding more and more resources to the existing hardware and expect that our application will be able to deal with the increasing number of requests. Every hardware has a defined upper limit of how many resources it can accommodate and, once we have reached this limit, it won't be possible to add any further resources to it, hence limiting the scope of how much of a capacity we can increase for the application. This problem brings us to another approach to scalability: horizontal scaling.

- **Horizontal scaling**: The concept of horizontal scaling is based upon adding more nodes to increase the scalability of the application. By adding more nodes where every node shares a part of the responsibility of the application, we can improve upon the capacity of the application to handle a higher number of concurrent requests. Another possible way is that we can run multiple instances of the application on a distributed set of hardware nodes, running behind a load balancer. The load balancer is responsible for distributing the requests across the nodes to provide a higher capacity. The advantage of this approach is that, as the number of users is expected to rise, we can add more nodes so as to help with the increased load. This is one of the approaches the public cloud providers such as AWS have made famous.

Both of these options are available once we have started deploying our application to the production infrastructure. But, is there something which we can do to build the application in such a way that it can maximize the number of concurrent requests it can deal with? Let's explore the answer to this question.

Engineering the application for scalability

At a time when most of the enterprise projects resort to using one framework or another, which usually decides how the application will be served during the production phase, it is still a good idea to take a look beneath the surface and understand how to develop the application while keeping the scalability of the application in perspective.

In this section, we will take a look at the different techniques that can help us build a scalable application, even when we are not using some per-built framework which can do it for us. During the course of this section, we will see how we can use thread/process pooling to handle multiple clients at the same time, and why the pooling of resources is necessary and what prevents us from starting a separate thread or process for dealing with every other incoming request.

But before we dive into the concepts of how we can utilize the thread pooling or process pooling in the application development, let's first take a look at a simple way through which we can hand-off the processing of the incoming requests to a background thread.

The following code implements a simple socket server which first accepts an incoming connection and then hands it off to a background thread for reads and writes, hence freeing the main thread to accept the other incoming connections:

```
# simple_socket_thread.py
#!/usr/bin/python3
import socket
```

```
import threading

# Let's first create a TCP type Server for handling clients
class Server(object):
    """A simple TCP Server."""

    def __init__(self, hostname, port):
        """Server initializer

        Keyword arguments:
        hostname -- The hostname to use for the server
        port -- The port on which the server should bind
        """

        self.server = socket.socket(socket.AF_INET, socket.SOCK_STREAM)
        self.hostname = hostname
        self.port = port
        self.bind_connection()
        self.listen()

    def bind_connection(self):
        """Bind the server to the host."""

        self.server.bind((self.hostname, self.port))

    def listen(self):
        """Start listening for the incoming connections."""

        self.server.listen(10) # Queue a maximum of 10 clients
        # Enter the listening loop
        while True:
            client, client_addr = self.server.accept()
            print("Received a connection from %s" % str(client_addr))
            client_thread = threading.Thread(target=self.handle_client,
args=(client,))
            client_thread.daemon = True
            client_thread.start()

    def handle_client(self, client):
        """Handle incoming client connection.

        Keyword arguments:
        client -- The client connection socket
        """

        print("Accepted a client connection")
        while True:
            buff = client.recv(1024).decode()
```

```
                    if not buff:
                        break
                    print(buff)
                print("Client closed the connection")
                client.close() # We are done now, let's close the connection

    if __name__ == '__main__':
        server = Server('localhost', 7000)
```

In this code, we have implemented a simple `Server` class which initializes a TCP-based server on the machine, ready to accept the incoming connections. Without diverting too much, let's try to focus on the important aspect of this code, where we start the listening loop of the server under the `listen()` method.

Under the `listen()` method, we first call the `listen()` method of the socket and tell it that it can queue up, at most, 10 connections which have not been accepted. Once this limit is reached, any further client connection will be rejected by the server. Now, moving on from here, we start an infinite loop where the first call is made to the `accept()` method of the socket. The call to the `accept()` method blocks until a client attempts to make a connection. On a successful attempt, the `accept()` call returns the client connection socket and the client address. The client connection socket can be used to perform I/O operations with the client.

The fun part happens next: as soon as the client connection is accepted, we launch a daemon thread responsible for handling the communication with the client and hand-off the client connection socket to the thread. This essentially frees up our main thread from dealing with the I/O of the client socket, and hence, our main thread can now accept more clients. This process continues for every other client that connects to our server.

So far so good; we have a nice way through which we can handle the incoming clients and our service can scale up gradually as the number of clients increases. That was an easy solution, wasn't it? Well, apparently during the course of coming up with this solution, we have ignored a major flaw in the process. The flaw lies in the fact that we have not implemented any kind of control related to how many threads can be launched by the application for dealing with the incoming clients. Imagine what will happen if a million clients try to connect to our server? Will we be really running a million threads at the same time? The answer is a big NO.

But why isn't it possible? Let's take a look.

Controlling the concurrency

In the previous example, we came up with a problem of why can't we have a million threads, each dealing with an individual client? That should provide us with a lot of concurrency and scalability. But, there are a number of reasons that really prevent us from running a million threads at the same time. Let's try to take a look at the possible reasons preventing us from scaling our application infinitely:

- **Resource limitations**: Every single client connection that is being handled by the server doesn't come free of cost. With every new connected client, we are expending some of the resources of the machine. These may include file descriptors that map to a socket, some amount of memory that is used to hold the information related to the opened socket, and so on. Every system can have a lot of memory but still it will be finite, and this finite memory is what decides how many sockets we can establish.

- **Costs associated with a new thread**: Every single thread that we launch creates a new space for itself inside the memory. Although a lot of application-related data is shared between the threads, still there are quite a lot of thread-local details which every thread has to maintain. This puts pressure on the system resources and limits how many threads we can have running at the same time.

- **The cost of context switches**: When we are dealing with threads, we need to remember one thing. Not all the threads can be executing in parallel. The number of threads that could be running in parallel depends upon a number of factors that may involve how many cores that the system has, the underlying Python implementation being used, and so on. To provide a fair opportunity for every thread to run, the operating system frequently switches between the threads. Every such switch is called a context switch where the memory structures are unloaded for the thread being switched out and memory structures are being loaded for the thread that will be executing next. This is a highly CPU-intensive operation. Imagine, we have a million threads each contending with each other to execute. This will cause our system to thrash where the CPU spends most of its time handling the context switches of the threads and hence, reducing the system throughput considerably.

These points give us some idea about why we cannot have an infinite concurrency available to our disposal.

But as it turns out, we apparently don't require an infinite concurrency. Rather, with the context to web applications, we should be just fine with a much smaller number of threads. But what makes this possible? Let's try to explore the reasons behind such a claim:

- **Short lived requests**: In most of the web applications, most of the incoming requests are short lived. What that means is, a single request usually deals with the manipulation of a small amount of data that the server can quickly generate and return the results for. This allows for quick freeing up of resources to handle the next request.
- **I/O wait**: Most of the time, as that happens, the requests are bottlenecked by the client side network I/O due to the limited bandwidth of the client. In that case, a few of the threads can be waiting on I/O while the others can quickly process the other requests, significantly reducing the number of threads that needs to be running at the same time.

Now we know we don't necessarily need an infinite number of threads to make our application scale for a large number of requests. This brings us to the concept of resource pooling.

How about if we create a fixed number of threads and a sane connection queue limit for the application and then use this fixed number of threads to cater to the incoming clients. That should provide us with a reasonable trade-off between the resource consumption and how many clients we can handle concurrently.

Using thread pools for handling incoming connections

As we saw in the previous section, we do not need an infinite number of threads to handle the incoming clients. We can manage with a limited number of threads to handle a large number of clients. But, how do we implement this thread pooling in our application. As it turns out, it is quite easy to implement the thread pool functionality with Python 3 and the `concurrent.futures` module.

The following code sample modifies our existing TCP server example to use a thread pool, instead of arbitrarily launching an infinite number of threads to handle the incoming client connections:

```python
# simple_socket_threadpool.py
#!/usr/bin/python3
from concurrent.futures import ThreadPoolExecutor
import socket


# Let's first create a TCP type Server for handling clients
class Server(object):
    """A simple TCP Server."""

    def __init__(self, hostname, port, pool_size):
        """Server initializer

        Keyword arguments:
        hostname -- The hostname to use for the server
        port -- The port on which the server should bind
        pool_size -- The pool size to use for the threading executor
        """

        # Setup thread pool size
        self.executor_pool = ThreadPoolExecutor(max_workers=pool_size)

        # Setup the TCP socket server
        self.server = socket.socket(socket.AF_INET, socket.SOCK_STREAM)
        self.hostname = hostname
        self.port = port
        self.bind_connection()
        self.listen()

    def bind_connection(self):
        """Bind the server to the host."""

        self.server.bind((self.hostname, self.port))

    def listen(self):
        """Start listening for the incoming connections."""

        self.server.listen(10) # Queue a maximum of 10 clients
        # Enter the listening loop
        while True:
            client, client_addr = self.server.accept()
            print("Received a connection from %s" % str(client_addr))
            self.executor_pool.submit(self.handle_client, client)

    def handle_client(self, client):
        """Handle incoming client connection.

        Keyword arguments:
```

```
        client -- The client connection socket
        """

        print("Accepted a client connection")
        while True:
            buff = client.recv(1024).decode()
            if not buff:
                break
            print(buff)
        print("Client closed the connection")
        client.close() # We are done now, let's close the connection

if __name__ == '__main__':
    server = Server('localhost', 7000, 20)
```

In this example, we modified our TCP server code to utilize a thread pool instead of launching an arbitrary number of threads. Let's take a look at how we made it possible.

First, to utilize the thread pool, we need to initialize an instance of the thread pool executor. Under the __init__ method of the `Server` class, we first initialize the thread pool executor by calling its constructor:

```
self.executor_pool = ThreadPoolExecutor(max_workers=pool_size)
```

The `ThreadPoolExecutor` constructor takes a `max_workers` parameter that defines how many concurrent threads are possible inside the `ThreadPool`. But, what will be an optimal value for the `max_workers` parameter?

A general rule of thumb will be to have `max_workers` = *(5 x Total number of CPU cores)*. The reasoning behind this formula is that inside a web application, most of the threads are generally waiting for the I/O to complete, whereas a few threads are busy doing CPU-bound operations.

The next thing after we have created a `ThreadPoolExecutor` is to submit jobs to it so that they can be processed by the threads inside the Executor Pool. This can be achieved through the use of the submit method of the `ThreadPoolExecutor` class. This can be seen under the `listen()` method of the `Server` class:

```
self.executor_pool.submit(self.handle_client, client)
```

The `submit()` method of the `ThreadPoolExecutor` takes in, as the first parameter, the name of the method to execute inside a thread and the parameters that need to be passed to the executing method.

That was quite simple to implement and provides us with lots of benefits, such as:

- Optimal usage of resources provided by the underlying infrastructure
- Ability to handle multiple requests
- Increased scalability and reduced wait times for the clients

> One important thing to take a note of here is, since the
> `ThreadPoolExecutor` utilizes the threads, the CPython implementation
> might not provide the maximum performance due to the presence of GIL,
> which doesn't allow the execution of more than one thread at a time.
> Hence, the performance of the application may vary depending upon the
> underlying Python implementation being used.

Now, the question that arises is, what if we wanted to sidestep the Global Interpreter
Lock? Is there some mechanism while still using the CPython implementation of Python?
We discussed this scenario in the previous chapter and settled with the use of Python's
multiprocessing module in place of the threading library.

Also, as it turns out, using a `ProcessPoolExecutor` is quite a simple feat to achieve. The
underlying implementation inside the concurrent.futures package takes care of most of the
necessities and provides the programmer with a simple-to-use abstraction. To see this in
action, let's modify our previous example to swap in `ProcessPoolExecutor` in place of
the `ThreadPoolExecutor`. To do this, all we need to do is first import the correct
implementation from the concurrent.futures package as described by the following line:

```
from concurrent.futures import ProcessPoolExecutor
```

The next thing we need to do is to modify our __init__ method to create a process pool
instead of a thread pool. The following implementation of the __init__ method shows
how we can achieve this:

```
def __init__(self, hostname, port, pool_size):
        """Server initializer

        Keyword arguments:
        hostname -- The hostname to use for the server
        port -- The port on which the server should bind
        pool_size -- The size of the pool to use for the process based
executor
        """

        # Setup process pool size
        self.executor_pool = ProcessPoolExecutor(max_workers=pool_size)
```

```
# Setup the TCP socket server
self.server = socket.socket(socket.AF_INET, socket.SOCK_STREAM)
self.hostname = hostname
self.port = port
self.bind_connection()
self.listen()
```

Indeed, that was a simple process to carry out and now our application can use the multiprocess model instead of the multithread model.

But, can we keep the pool size the same or does it also need to change?

Every process has its own memory space and internal pointers that it needs to maintain, which makes the process heavier in comparison to the use of threads for achieving concurrency. This provides a reason to reduce the pool size so as to allow for the heavier usage of the underlying system resources. As a general rule, for a `ProcessPoolExecutor`, the `max_workers` can be calculated by the formula `max_workers` = *(2 x Number of CPU Cores + 1)*.

The reasoning behind this formula can be attributed to the fact that, at any given time, we can assume that half of the processes will be busy in performing network I/O while the others might be busy doing CPU-intensive tasks.

So, now we have a fair enough idea about how we can use a resource pool and why it is a better approach in comparison to launching an arbitrary number of threads. But, this approach still requires a lot of context switches and is also highly dependent upon the underlying Python implementation being used. But there should be something better than this, for sure.

With this in mind, let's try to venture into another territory in the kingdom of Python, the territory of asynchronous programming.

Asynchronous programming with AsyncIO

Before we dive into this unknown territory of asynchronous programming, let's first try to recall why we used threads or multiple processes.

One of the main reasons to use threads or multiple processes was to increase the concurrency and, as a result, the ability of the application to handle a higher number of concurrent requests. But this came at a cost of increased resource utilization, and the limited ability to run multiple threads or the launching of heavier processes to accommodate higher concurrency with complex mechanisms of implementing locks between the shared data structures.

Now, in the context of building a scalable web application, we also have a few major differences from a general purpose compute-heavy application. In the functioning of the web application, most of the time, the application is waiting on the I/O so as to receive the complete request or to complete the sending of the response to the client. This was the part where we exploit the use of multiple threads since, at any particular point time, some of the threads can be in a waiting state to complete the I/O and that time can be used in processing other requests by the application.

But we can have something better here. How about if we could use a single thread that executes a task and then, as soon as the task goes into a waiting state (doing some disk I/O or network I/O), the thread swaps out the task for another task. This continues until all the tasks inside the queue have finished executing. This process of asynchronously executing the tasks without really waiting for the results of one task to arrive before calling in the next task is known as asynchronous programming.

A simple example of asynchronous programming might involve a web application which makes a call to three different NEWS feeds, namely `site1`, `site2`, and `site3`. With asynchronous programming, once our program starts executing, it will make a call to `site1` and without waiting for the results to arrive, it will start the execution of a call to `site2`, and so on to `site3`. Since the order in which the results will start arriving can be different anytime, the final output also may differ in the multiple runs of the same program.

This allows us better utilization of the resources while also running the program in a single-threaded mode, where the multiple tasks are multiplexed over a single thread only and are checked periodically for their completion.

Python introduced the support for asynchronous programming by making available the AsyncIO package inside the Python distributions. The way AsyncIO works is through the implementation of an event loop and co-routines.

But, before we dive into the implementation of programs with the Python AsyncIO, let's spend some time understanding the terminology associated with the framework.

AsyncIO terminology

As we recently discussed, the support for asynchronous programming in Python is implemented through the use of an event loop and co-routines. But what exactly are they? Let's take a look:

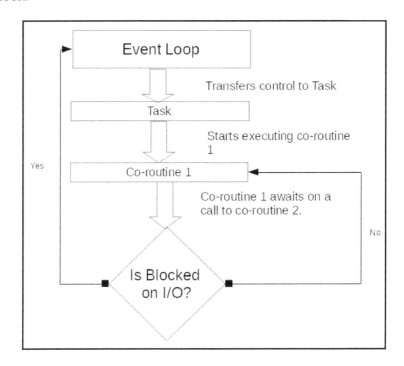

Event loop

An event loop, as its name implies, is a loop. What this loop does is, when a new task is supposed to be executed, the event loop queues this task. Now from here, the control shifts to the event loop. When the event loop runs, it checks whether there is some task in its queue or not. If there is a task present, the control switches to the task.

Now, here is the interesting part in the context of the asynchronous execution of tasks. Suppose there are two tasks, namely Task A and Task B, in the queue of the event loop. When the event loop starts executing, it checks the status of the task queue it has. The event queue finds out that there are tasks in its queue. So, the event queue picks up Task A. Now a context switch happens inside the event loop and Task A starts executing. After a certain point of time, Task A makes a call to an external API and gets blocked on network I/O, waiting for the results to arrive from the API. At this point, the event loop takes back the control and puts the task in a waiting state. Now, the event loop starts checking its task queue again. It finds out that there is another task which is waiting inside the queue to be executed, namely Task B. Now, the event queue picks up Task B, a context switch happens and Task B starts executing. After a certain time, the Task B finishes its execution and the results are generated. Once the results are generated and sent back, the event loop removes the task from the task queue. At this point, the control again comes back to the event queue. Now it finds that Task A which was in blocked state has completed its I/O and is ready for execution again. A context switch happens and control shifts to the execution of Task A. This time, Task A completes its execution and the results are generated and sent back. With this, Task A also gets removed from the event loop queue. The control transfers back to the event loop, which now does not have any other task to execute. The event loop now enters a waiting state, awaiting the arrival of new tasks.

That's how the life of an event queue is spent. It acts as a core part of the process of asynchronous operations and is responsible for the queuing, execution, prioritization, and canceling of tasks.

Co-routines

Co-routines in Python AsyncIO provide a lightweight mechanism of executing multiple simultaneous operations. The co-routines are implemented as a special use case of generators in Python. So, before we dive into understanding what co-routines are, let's spend a little time on understanding the generators.

In general terms, generators are those functions which generate some value. However, that is what every other function does, so how does a generator differ from a regular function. The difference lies in how the life cycle of a general function differs from a generator. When we call a function, it produces some value, returns it, and the scope of the function is destroyed once the call moves out of the function body. When we call the function again, a new scope is generated and executed.

In contrast to this, when we call a generator, the generator can return a value and then goes into a paused state and the control transfers back to the caller. At this time, the scope of the generator is not destroyed and it can pick up the generation of values from where it previously left. This basically provides us with a function through which we can pull or yield some values.

The following code sample shows how to write a simple generator function:

```
def get_number():
    i = 0
    while True:
        yield i
        i = i + 1
num = get_number()
print(next(num))
>>> 0
print(next(num))
>>> 1
```

The interesting part here is that a generator won't continue to provide you with the next result by simply calling the generator again and again. For yielding new results, we need to use the `next()` method on the generator. This allows us to yield new results from the generator.

Now, co-routines implement a special use case of generator in which they can not only yield new results, but can also take in some data. This is made possible with a combination of yield and the `send()` method of the generators.

The following code sample shows the implementation of a simple co-routine:

```
def say_hello():
    msg = yield "Hello"
    yield msg
greeting = say_hello()
next(greeting)
>>> Hello
greeting.send("Joe")
>>> Joe
```

Since co-routines allow for the pausing and resuming of functions, and hence the lazy generation of the results, that makes it a good option for the use case of asynchronous programming, where the tasks are frequently sent into the blocking state and are then resumed from there once their operation completes.

Tasks

A task in Python AsyncIO is a mechanism to wrap the co-routines. Every task has a result associated with it, that may be generated immediately or may be deferred depending upon the kind of task. This result is known as the Future.

In AsyncIO, a task is a subclass of the Future which wraps around a co-routine. When a co-routine has finished generating the values, the task returns and is marked as complete by the event loop and is hence removed from the task queue of the event queue.

Now, we have a fair enough idea of the terminology associated with the use of Python AsyncIO. Let's now dive into some action and write a simple program to understand how the Python AsyncIO really works.

Writing a simple Python AsyncIO program

It's time to buckle up and start taking a dive into the world of asynchronous programming with Python and to understand how the AsyncIO really works.

The following code implements a simple URL fetcher using the Python requests library and AsyncIO:

```python
# async_url_fetch.py
#!/usr/bin/python3
import asyncio
import requests

async def fetch_url(url):
    response = requests.get(url)
    return response.text

async def get_url(url):
    return await fetch_url(url)

def process_results(future):
    print("Got results")
    print(future.result())

loop = asyncio.get_event_loop()
task1 = loop.create_task(get_url('http://www.google.com'))
task2 = loop.create_task(get_url('http://www.microsoft.com'))
task1.add_done_callback(process_results)
task2.add_done_callback(process_results)
loop.run_forever()
```

That was a small and a nice asynchronous program implementing the Python AsyncIO library. Now, let's spend some time understanding what we did here.

Starting from the top, we have imported the Python requests library to make web requests from our Python code and have also imported the Python's AsyncIO library.

Next, we define a co-routine named `fetch_url`. The general syntax of defining a co-routine for AsyncIO requires the use of the `async` keyword:

```
async def fetch_url(url)
```

The next in line is the definition of another co-routine named `get_url`. What we do inside the `get_url` routine is make a call to our other co-routine, `fetch_url`, which does the actual fetch of the URL.

Since `fetch_url` is a blocking co-routine, we proceed the call to `fetch_url` with the `await` keyword. This signifies that this method can be suspended until the results are obtained:

```
return await fetch_url(url)
```

Next in the program is the definition of the `process_results` method. We use this method as a callback to process the results from the `get_url` method once they arrive. This method takes a single parameter, a `future` object, which will contain the results of the function call to the `get_url`.

Inside the method, the results of the future can be accessed through the use of the `results()` method of the `future` object:

```
print(future.results())
```

With this, we have all the basic machinery set up for the execution of the AsyncIO event loop. Now, it's time to implement a real event loop and submit a few tasks to it.

We start this by first fetching an AsyncIO event loop by making a call to the `get_event_loop()` method. The `get_event_loop()` method returns the optimal event loop implementation of AsyncIO for the platform on which the code is running.

 AsyncIO implements multiple event loops which a programmer can use. Usually a simple call to `get_event_loop()` will return the best event loop implementation for the system the interpreter is running on.

Once we have the loop created, we now submit a few tasks to the event loop through the use of the `create_task()` method. This adds the tasks to the queue of the event loop to execute. Now, since these tasks are asynchronous and we don't have a clue about which task will produce the results first, we need to provide a callback to handle the results of the task. To achieve this, we add a callback to the tasks with the help of the tasks `add_done_callback()` method:

```
task1.add_done_callback(process_results)
```

Once everything here is set, we start the event loop into a `run_forever` mode so that the event loop keeps on running and dealing with the new tasks.

With this, we have completed the implementation of a simple AsyncIO program. But hey, we are trying to build a enterprise scale application. What if I wanted to build an enterprise web application with AsyncIO?

So, now let's take a look at how we can use AsyncIO to implement a simple asynchronous socket server.

Implementing a simple socket server with AsyncIO

The AsyncIO library provided by the Python implementation provides a lot of powerful functionality. One of these many functionalities is the ability to interface and manage socket communication. This provides the programmer with the ability to implement asynchronous socket handling and, hence, allows for a higher number of clients to connect to the server.

The following code sample builds a simple socket handler with the callback-based mechanism to handle the communication with the clients:

```
# async_socket_server.py
#!/usr/bin/python3
import asyncio

class MessageProtocol(asyncio.Protocol):
    """An asyncio protocol implementation to handle the incoming
messages."""

    def connection_made(self, transport):
        print("Got a new connection")
        self.transport = transport

    def data_received(self, data):
```

```
        print("Data received")
        self.transport.write("Message received".encode('utf-8'))

loop = asyncio.get_event_loop()
server_handler = loop.create_server(MessageProtocol, 'localhost', 7000)
server = loop.run_until_complete(server_handler)
try:
    loop.run_forever()
except KeyboardInterrupt:
    server.close()
    loop.close()
```

So, we have just implemented a socket server using AsyncIO; there's a lot of new code here. Let's take some time to understand what lies behind the scenes of these magic lines.

So, to start with the implementation, we have first defined a protocol class named `MessageProtocol`. This class inherits from the `asyncio.Protocol` class that provides a base implementation of a streaming protocol, such as TCP:

```
class MessageProtocol(asyncio.Protocol)
```

In the context of the AsyncIO library, a protocol defines how the data from the underlying socket can be dealt with. In other words, the protocol defines the abstraction for the application.

Inside the protocol, we have basically overridden the implementation of two methods, namely, `connection_made` and `data_received`. Let's take a further look at these two methods and try to understand what they do:

- `connection_made`: The method comes from the `BaseProtocol` class, which is the base class for all the protocol classes inside AsyncIO and is responsible for handling the event related to the new clients connecting to the server. The implementation allows for doing extra steps based upon when a new client has joined the server. When such a `connection_event` takes place, the method receives as a parameter, the transport object which signifies the connection type (Streaming, Datagram, Unix Pipe) to the underlying socket. Using this transport object, we can interact with the client by performing read and write operations.

- `data_received`: The method comes from the `Protocol` class of the AsyncIO library and handles the events that occur when the client has sent some data. On a data receive event, the method receives as a parameter, a bytes object which contains the data that has been sent by the client. The underlying transport determines whether the data will be buffered or unbuffered, and hence the method implementation should not make any presumptions and should provide a generic behavior for dealing with the data.

Now, once we have defined our `MessageProtocol`, the next thing to do is to start an asynchronous server to deal with the client connections.

To achieve the same, we start by getting an AsyncIO event loop by making a call to the `get_event_loop()` method.

Once we have attained the event loop, we next make a call to the `create_server()` coroutine of the event loop:

```
loop.create_server(MessageProtocol, 'localhost', 7000)
```

The co-routine is responsible for starting a TCP server on the host. To the `create_server()` co-routine, we provide three basic parameters, a protocol class which will handle the client connections, the host on which the server should run, and the port on which the server should bind.

Since the server is an AsyncIO co-routine, the result of the execution of the server is a future object. We use this property to start our event loop and ask it to run until the server exits by calling the event loop's `run_until_complete` method and passing it the `future` object we received by the call to create_server:

```
server = loop.run_until_complete(server_handler)
```

Once this is done, we are all set to go and our server event loop has started running. The only thing that remains here is the starting of our main event loop, inside which the server will run.

To start our main event loop, we make a call to the `run_forever()` method of the loop and make it exit only when a `KeyboardInterrupt` has occurred.

With this, we get a fair enough idea that the AsyncIO is a powerful library and provides a lot of opportunities over the existing solutions based upon using multiple threads or multiple processes. But when should we go ahead with the use of AsyncIO and what are the advantages we have by going with the option? Let's look into that:

- **Better resource management**: Since AsyncIO uses a single thread to manage the execution of the program, it has better resource usage compared to solutions such as launching multiple threads or multiple processes because the system does not really need to maintain that much data for the individual threads or processes. Also, since there is a single thread, there is no need to do CPU-intensive context switches, which are required to transfer the control from one thread to another, or one process to another.
- **Faster execution**: Since the AsyncIO usually involves the use of light co-routines to execute the tasks and a single event loop, the execution of tasks is generally faster due to the reduced context switching.
- **Better suited for I/O intensive tasks**: The approach of AsyncIO is to switch tasks when a particular co-routine is in blocked state waiting for I/O to complete. For the tasks that involve a considerable amount of I/O, the use of AsyncIO helps to achieve a lot of scalability, because at a given time, quite a lot of tasks could be in blocked state while the others can be consuming the CPU.

Now we know about the different ways through which we can improve the ability of our enterprise applications to scale out to a larger audience. For socket-based applications, this is a good approach, specifically in this century, where more and more business workloads are now moving to the web involving a lot of complex socket communication between the client machines and the application servers.

The techniques we discussed till now will work well to scale out our enterprise web applications and help them achieve a lot of concurrency, but still there is a lot of scope for improvement. So now let's move on to understanding how we can boost the ability of enterprise web applications to handle a lot of clients.

Boosting the application concurrency

Most of the time when we are building some web application through a framework, the frameworks usually provide a small and easy to run web server. Although these servers are good for use in the development environment to quickly realize the changes and debug through the issues inside the application during the development stage, these servers are not capable of handling the production workloads.

Even in the case when the whole application has been developed from scratch, it is generally a good idea to proxy the communication to the web application through use of a reverse proxy. But the question arises is, why do we need to do so? Why shouldn't we just run the web application directly and let it handle the incoming requests. Let's quickly go through all the responsibilities the web application serves:

- **Handling of incoming requests**: When a new request arrives at the web application, the web application might need to decide what to do with that request. If the web application has workers that can process the request, the application will accept the request, hand it over to a worker, and return the response for the request, once the worker finishes processing. If there is no worker, then the web application has to queue this request for later processing. In the worst case, when the queue backlog has exceeded the threshold of the maximum number of queued clients, then the web application has to reject the request.
- **Serving static resources**: If the web application needs to generate dynamic HTML pages, it may also double up as a server to send across the static resources such as CSS, Javascript, images, and so on, hence increasing the load.
- **Handling encryption**: Most of the web applications now come up with the encryption turned on. In this case, our web application will also require us to manage the parsing of the encrypted data and provide a secure connection.

Those are quite some responsibilities to be handled by a simple web application server. What we rather need is a mechanism through which we can offload quite a lot of these responsibilities from the web application server and let it handle only the essential work that it is supposed to do and where it really shines.

Running behind a reverse proxy

So, our first line of action to improve the ability of our web application to handle a lot of clients, is to first take a few responsibilities off its shoulders. A simple option that comes to mind in order to achieve this, is to first start running the web application behind a **Reverse Proxy**:

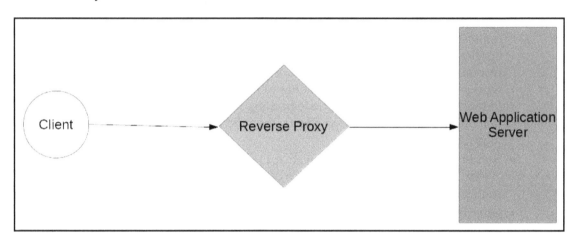

So, what essentially does a **Reverse Proxy** do? The way the reverse proxy works is, when a **Client** request arrives at the **Web Application Server**, the **Reverse Proxy** intercepts the request. Based on the rules defined to match the request to the appropriate backend application, the **Reverse Proxy** then forwards this request to the backend application, which processes the request and sends the response back to the **Reverse Proxy**. Once this response is received, the **Reverse Proxy** relays this response back the **Client**. Now, there are a number of advantages associated with the use of a **Reverse Proxy**. Let's take a look at these advantages provided by the use of a **Reverse Proxy**.

Improved security

One of the first advantages that comes to the mind when considering the use of a reverse proxy is the improved security. This happens because now we can run our web application behind the firewall so that it cannot be accessed directly. The reverse proxy intercepts the request and forwards it to the application without letting the user know what is going on behind the scenes with the request that they made.

This restricted access to the web application helps in reducing the attack surface that can be utilized by a malicious user to break into the web application, and access or modify the critical records.

Improved connection handling

A reverse proxy server can also be used to improve the connection handling capability of the web application. Nowadays, to speed up the fetching of the remote content, the web browsers open multiple connections to a web server to increase the parallel download of the resources. The reverse proxy can queue up and serve the connection requests as the web application is processing the pending requests, hence improving the connection acceptance and reducing the load on the application to manage the connection states.

Resource caching

When the web application generates a response to a particular client request, there is a chance that the same kind of request may arrive again, or the same resource may be requested again. For every similar request, using the web application to generate the response again and again may turn out to be a not so elegant solution.

The reverse proxies can at times help understand the request and response patterns and implement caching for them. When caching is enabled, when the similar request arrives again or the same resource is requested again, the reverse proxy, instead of forwarding the request to the web application can send back the cached response directly, hence offloading a lot of overhead from the web application. This results in the improved performance of the web application and a shorter response time for the clients.

Serving static resources

Most of the web applications have two kind of resources that they serve. One is the dynamic responses generated in accordance to the external input and static content that remains the same, such as CSS files, Javascript files, images, and so on.

It provides a lot of performance gain as well as improved scalability if we can offload either one of these responsibilities from the web application.

The best possibility that we have here is to offload the serving of static resources to the clients. A reverse proxy can also double up as a server which can serve the static resources to the clients without forwarding these requests to the web application server, which dramatically reduces the number of requests waiting to be processed by the web application, hence resulting in improved capability to handle the dynamic requests by the application.

With the use of a reverse proxy in front of the application we are trying to develop, we can now better handle the large number of incoming concurrent clients while also taking off some of the load which the application server might had to deal with to serve the static resources for every request or for other operations which may include termination of SSL, balancing of the load, etc.

Summary

Through the course of this chapter, we got to learn about the different ways through which we can build our web application to handle a large number of concurrent requests. We started off by understanding and learning about the different scaling techniques, such as vertical scaling and horizontal scaling, and learned about the different pros and cons of each technique. We then further dived into the topics to help us improve the ability of the web application itself to process a higher number of requests. This led us to a journey into the use of resource pools and why it is a good idea to use resource pooling instead of arbitrarily allocating the resources for every new request that arrives at the web application. Further on in the journey, we got to know about the asynchronous way of dealing with the incoming requests and why the asynchronous mechanism is better suited for higher scalability in the case of web applications which are more I/O bound. We ended our discussion on scaling the applications for large numbers of clients by looking into the use of reverse proxies and what advantages a reverse proxy provides to help us scale our web application up.

Now with the understanding of how we can make our application handle a large number of concurrent requests, the next chapter will take us through the process of building a demo application taking advantage of the different concepts we have learned so far in the book so far.

Questions

1. How can we use multiple instances of the same application to serve the incoming requests?
2. How do we implement process pools and distribute the client requests over them?
3. Can we implement an application which utilizes both process pooling and thread pooling? What are the issues we may face while implementing the same?
4. How do we implement a basic web server with AsyncIO?

Example – Building BugZot

6

Over the last few chapters, we have discussed numerous techniques that deal with building an enterprise-scale application. But what good is that knowledge if we don't have any idea where to utilize it?

During the course of this chapter, we will walk through the process of building an enterprise-grade web application, which will be used to track bugs reported by various stakeholders of products that are marketed by the Omega Corporation. The system that we will, from now on, call **BugZot**, aims to provide such functionality.

The application will use various concepts to build the system in a manner that allows it to be scaled easily as the number of users interacting with the system grows. We will see how to utilize the various techniques of optimized data access and storage, highly scalable deployments, and caching, to build an application that performs well, even in high load scenarios.

Over the course of this chapter, we will learn about:

- Utilizing existing web frameworks for building an enterprise-grade web application
- Implementing optimizations to database access to speed up the application
- Implementing caching techniques to reduce load on the application backend
- Utilizing multithreading techniques to increase application concurrency
- Deploying application in a scalable manner for production

Technical requirements

The code listings in this book can be found under `chapter06` directory at `https://github.com/PacktPublishing/Hands-On-Enterprise-Application-Development-with-Python`.

The code samples can be cloned by running the following command:

```
git clone
https://github.com/PacktPublishing/Hands-On-Enterprise-Application-Developm
ent-with-Python
```

The chapter aims to build a scalable bug tracking web application. To achieve this, we use quite a lot of pre-existing libraries and tools that are openly available and well tested to suit various use cases over time. The following set of tools will be required to build and run the demo application:

- PostgreSQL 9.6 or above
- Python 3.6 or above
- Flask—Microframework for web development in Python

Any other dependencies that may be required for the application to run properly are already specified in the `requirements.txt` and can be installed by simply executing the following:

```
pip install -r requirements.txt
```

Defining the requirements

The first part of building any enterprise-grade application is to define what the application aims to do. Up to now, we know that our application is going to track bugs for the various products that are marketed by the Omega Corporation. But what things are required from our application that will prove to be useful for bug tracking? Let's take a look and try to define the requirements for the application that we are going to build.

- **Support for multiple products**: One of the fundamental requirements for our bug tracking system is to support the tracking of bugs for multiple products that the organization builds. This is also a required feature considering the future growth of the organization.

- **Support for multiple components per product**: Although we can file the bugs at the product level itself, it will be too clumsy, specifically considering that most of the organizations have a separate team working on orthogonal features of a product. To make the tracking of bugs easier based on which component they have been filed, the bug tracking system should support the filing of bugs on a component to component basis.

- **Support for attachments**: Many a time, the users filing a bug, or the ones involved in any way in the bug life cycle, might want to attach images showing the effect of the bug, or may want to attach patches to the bug so they can be tested before being incorporating into the product. This will require the bug tracking system to provide support for attaching files to the bug reports.

- **Support for comments**: Once the bug has been filed, a user who is responsible for solving that bug might require some other information about the bug, or may require some collaboration. This makes it compulsory for the bug tracking system to have support for comments. Also, not every comment can be made public. For example, if there is some patch that the developers might have attached to the bug report to be tested by the original submitter of the bug, but which has not yet been incorporated into the main product, the developers might want to keep the patch private, so that it can be seen only by people with privileged access. This makes the inclusion of functionality for private comments also a necessity.

- **Support for multiple user roles**: Not everyone in the organization has the same level of access to the bug tracking system. For example, only people at the director level should be able to add new components to a product, and only employees should be able to see private comments on a bug. This calls for the inclusion of role-based access as a requirement for the system.

These are some of the requirements that are specific to our bug tracking system. However, as a consequences of these, there are a few more requirements that obviously need to be included in the system. Some of these requirements are:

- **Requirement for a user authentication system**: The system should provide a mechanism for authenticating the users based on some simple mechanism. For example, a user should be able to sign into the system by providing their username and password, or email id and password combination.

- **Web interface for filing a new bug**: The application should provide a simple to use web interface that can be used by the users to file new bugs.

- **Support for bug life cycle**: Once a bug has been filed into the system, its life cycle starts in the NEW state. From there it may move on to the ASSIGNED state, when someone from the organization picks up the bug for validation and reproduction. From there, the bug can move into various states. This is known as a bug life cycle inside our tracking system. Our bug tracking system should provide the support for this life cycle, and how to handle it when the bug moves from one state to another.

So, with this, we finally have our requirements in place. These requirements play an important role when we move onto designing and defining how our bug tracking web application will be built. So, with the requirements in place, it's time for us to move onto defining how our code base will look.

Entering the development phase

With our project structure defined and in place, it's time for us to get up and start developing our application. The development phase involves various steps, which include setting up the development environment, developing models, creating views that map to the models, and setting up the server.

Setting up the development environment

The first step before we begin our development is to set up our development environment. This involves getting the required packages in place, and setting up the environment.

Setting up the database

Our web application relies heavily on the database for managing the individual records related to the users and the bugs that have been filed. For the demo application, we will set back with the PostgreSQL as the choice for our database. To install it on an RPM-based distribution, such as Fedora, the following command needs to be executed:

```
dnf install postgresql postgresql-server postgresql-devel
```

To install `postgresql` on any other distribution of Linux or any other operating system like Windows or Mac OS, the required commands for the distribution/OS will need to be executed.

Once we have the database installed, the next step is to initialize the database so that it can be used to store our application data. For setting up PostgreSQL, the following steps need to be executed:

sudo postgresql-setup –initdb –unit postgresql

This command helps to initialize the postgresql database server and start the server process. If no configuration has been changed, the server will default to listen to traffic on port 5432.

Once our server has been initialized, the next thing we need to do is to set up our database and the user that will be used by our BugZot application.

Now, let's switch our user to postgres and create the user and database. Once we have switched the user, the following commands need to be executed to create the required user and database:

```
psql
postgres=# CREATE ROLE bugzot_admin WITH LOGIN PASSWORD 'bugzotuser';
postgres=# CREATE DATABASE bugzot;
postgres=# GRANT ALL PRIVILEGES ON DATABASE bugzot TO bugzot_admin;
```

With this, we have our database up and running along with the required user and database that our application needs to connect to. From here on, we can work on our application directly without much of a manual interaction with the database.

Note: Although in the demo application we have granted all the privileges to a single user for the database, this is not a recommended practice for a production use case if security is of top-most concern. For a production use case, we will recommend that different users be created with varying permissions to the database, based on the extent of access required by a particular user.

Setting up the virtual environment

Now with the database in place, let's set up the virtual environment, which we will use for the purpose of application development. To set up the virtual environment, let's run the following commands:

virtualenv –python=python3

This command will set up a virtual environment in our current directory. The next thing after the virtual environment is set up is to install the required framework for the application development and other packages.

However, before we move on to installing the required packages, let's just first activate our virtual environment by executing the following command:

```
source bin/activate
```

As a design decision, we will base our application on the Python Flask micro framework for web application development. The framework is an open source framework, which has been around for quite some years and enjoys the support of various plugins that can be easily installed along with the framework. The framework also is a very light framework, which comes with bare minimum set of modules pre-packaged, hence allowing for a smaller footprint. To install `flask`, execute the following command:

```
pip install flask
```

Once we have Flask installed, let's move onto setting up a few other required packages that we are going to use in the development of our web application by executing the following command:

```
pip install flask-sqlalchemy requests pytest flask-session
```

With this, we are now done with the setup of our virtual environment. Now, let's move onto setting up how our code base will look.

Structuring our project

Now, we are at a stage where we need to decide how our project structure will look. The project structure has a lot of importance, since it decides how the different components in our code will interact with each other and what point will mark the entry point of our application.

A well-structured project will not only help in providing a better navigation for the project, but will also help in providing increased coherency between different parts of the code.

So, let's take a look at how our code structure will look and understand the significance of what a particular directory or file stands for:

```
$ tree --dirsfirst
├── bugzot
│   ├── helpers
│   │   └── __init__.py
│   ├── models
```

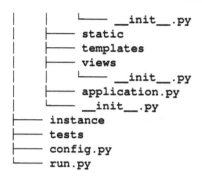

```
|       |       └──── __init__.py
|       ├──── static
|       ├──── templates
|       ├──── views
|       |       └──── __init__.py
|       ├──── application.py
|       └──── __init__.py
├──── instance
├──── tests
├──── config.py
└──── run.py
```

Now, we have an idea about how our code structure looks. Let's spend some time to understand the various parts of this structure and why are they even present.

Our project starts with the BugZot directory as entry point, which encapsulates our complete bug tracking project. Now, let's take a look at the directories and files that comprise the BugZot project directory:

- **Helpers**: The directory acts as a module for the project and provides classes and methods that act as a helper inside the project. For example, methods such as those which provide password salt generation, password hashing, and so on, can be grouped under the helpers directory.
- **Models**: The models directory contains the database models for a component to component basis. For example, the models for storing information related to the users, bugs, comments, and so on, are grouped under the models directory.
- **Views**: The views directory contains the code that is responsible for rendering a response to the user on a component to component basis. For example, the code responsible for rendering the home page of the BugZot application, a new bug file page, and so on, are the views that go under the views directory.
- **Templates**: The templates directory consists of the templates that are rendered by the views. For example, the template that is responsible for rendering the home page of the application, the template which is responsible for rendering the new bug page, and so on, are the ones that go under the templates directory.
- **Static**: There are a few files inside the application that don't change over the time. Their content, once defined, is served again and again without any kind of on-the-fly change by the server or the backend. For example, files such as CSS style sheets or JavaScript files are some examples that are defined once, and are served again and again. The static directory encapsulates these files.
- application.py: The file defines the point where we mark the initialization logic for the application and the application global objects that are shared across the application.

These are a few directories and files that are encapsulated under the BugZot project directory. But beyond these, we also have a few files and directories that lie at the same level as our bugzot project directory. Let's take a look at these directories and files:

- **Instance**: The instance directory contains the files and configuration that are local to a particular deployment of the application. This helps in keeping a global configuration of the application separate from the deployment-specific configuration, as well as allowing for keeping security sensitive content present under permission controlled directories.
- **Tests**: No matter what kind of application is involved, tests form an integral part of the application development process and allows for testing the individual parts of the code in the form of unit tests and the interaction between the different components of the code, through the use of integration tests. These tests come under the tests directory.
- `config.py`: The file defines the global configuration for the application that is required for the application to work and provides expected outputs. Any of the configuration that needs to deviate from the global configuration can be overridden in the instance-specific configuration files under the instance directory.
- `run.py`: The file defines the run point of the application and is responsible for encapsulating the code that is responsible for starting the application server.

With this, we now have a fair enough idea about how our project will be structured and what the role is of the individual directories and files that are present inside the project structure. Now, let's jump into the real fun and start developing the project.

Initializing the Flask project

So, we are finally entering the fun phase of our project where we will be building this project from scratch. So, let's not wait too long before we can see some action. The first thing we will do is to set up a basic project with Flask and get it running. To do this, let's fire up our code editor and set up our initial code base.

Let's open up the file `bugzot/application.py` and initialize our application code base:

```
'''
File: application.py
Description: The file contains the application initialization
             logic that is used to serve the application.
'''
from flask import Flask, session
from flask_bcrypt import Bcrypt
```

```
from flask_session import Session
from flask_sqlalchemy import SQLAlchemy

# Initialize our Flask application
app = Flask(__name__, instance_relative_config=True)

# Let's read the configuration
app.config.from_object('config')
app.config.from_pyfile('config.py')

# Let's setup the database
db = SQLAlchemy(app)

# Initializing the security configuration
bcrypt = Bcrypt(app)

# We will require sessions to store user activity across the application
Session(app)
```

Here we have completed the very basic setup of our application. Let's spend some time trying to understand what we did here.

At the very start of the file, we first imported the required packages over which we will be building our project. We imported the `Flask` application class from the package `flask`. Similarly, we import the code hashing library `bcrypt`, the `Flask` session class, and the SQLAlchemy support package for Flask, which provides SQLAlchemy integration with Flask.

Once we have imported all the required packages, the next thing is to initialize our Flask application. To do this, we create an instance of `Flask` class and store it in an object named `app`.

```
app = Flask(__name__, instance_relative_config=True)
```

While creating this instance, we pass the class constructor two parameters. The first parameter is used to signify the name of the application to Flask. `__name__` provides, which we pass as the application name to the constructor. The second parameter, `instance_relative_config` allows us to override the application configuration from an instance folder.

With this, we have our Flask application instance setup done. Next thing inline is to load up the configuration for the application, which will be used to configure how the different components inside our application behave, and how our application will be served to the user. To do this, we need to read from our configuration file. The following two lines achieve this:

```
app.config.from_object('config')
app.config.from_pyfile('config.py')
```

The first line loads up our `config.py` file under the project root, treats it as an object, and loads up its configuration. The second line is responsible for reading the `config.py` file under the instance directory and loading any configuration that may be present there.

Once these configurations are loaded, they are available under the `app.config` object. Most of the Flask plugins are configured to read the configuration from the `app.config`, hence reducing the clutter that may happen if every plugin had a different mechanism for dealing with the configuration.

With our configuration loaded up inside our application, we can now move on to initialize the remaining modules that we may require. In particular, we require a few more modules to establish our application functionality. These modules include the SQLAlchemy engine, which we will use to build and interact with our database models, a sessions module, which will be required to manage user sessions across the application, and a `bcrypt` module, which will be required to provide encryption support across the application. The following lines of code provide this functionality:

```
db = SQLAlchemy(app)
bcrypt = Bcrypt(app)
Session(app)
```

As we can see from these lines of code, to configure these modules, all we needed to do was pass the Flask application object as a parameter to the respective class constructors and their configuration will be picked up from there itself.

Now, we have our application initialization code in place, the next thing we need to do is to export the required components from our BugZot module so the application can be called from the project root.

To achieve this, all we need to do is to get these modules included in the module entry point. So, let's fire up the code editor and open `bugzot/__init__.py` where we need to get these objects.

```
'''
File: __init__.py
Description: Bugzot application entrypoint file.
'''
from .application import app, bcrypt, db
```

And we are done. We have all the required objects exported in our BugZot module. Now, the question is how to launch our application. So, to launch our application and make it serve the incoming requests, we need to complete a few more steps. So, let's open up the run.py file inside our project root and add the following lines to it:

```
'''
File: run.py
Description: Bugzot application execution point.
'''
from bugzot import app

if __name__ == '__main__':
    app.run(host='0.0.0.0', port=8000)
```

And we are done. Wasn't that simple? All we did here was to import the flask app object we created inside our BugZot module and call the run method of the app object passing it the value for the hostname on which the application will be serving the users, and the port on which the application server should bind to listen to the requests.

We are now all set to start our application server and make it listen to the incoming requests. However, before we do that, we need to just complete one more step, which is to create the configuration for the application. So, let's get going and create the configuration.

Creating the configuration

Before we can start our application, we need to configure our modules that we are going to use in our application. So, let's first go ahead and create the global configuration of our application by opening up config.py in our code editor and adding the following content to it:

```
'''
File: config.py
Description: Global configuration for Bugzot project
'''
DEBUG = False
SECRET_KEY = 'your_application_secret_key'
BCRYPT_LOG_ROUNDS = 5 # Increase this value as required for your
application
```

```
SQLALCHEMY_DATABASE_URI = "sqlite:///bugzot.db"
SQLALCHEMY_ECHO = False
SESSION_TYPE = 'filesystem'
STATIC_PATH = 'bugzot/static'
TEMPLATES_PATH = 'bugzot/templates'
```

With this, we have drafted our global application configuration. Let's try to understand what each line means here.

First, we have set DEBUG = False, which tells Flask not to run in debug mode and hence not to print any back-traces of the application when an error occurs. This allows us to hide sensitive application information when running in production mode.

The next key, SECRET_KEY, provides a way to set a secret key, which will be used by the application to sign the application cookies.

Next key inline BCRYPT_LOG_ROUNDS configures the flask-bcrypt module to run *n* number of rounds for every input provided to generate a hash value.

The following two settings, namely, SQLALCHEMY_DATABASE_URI and SQLALCHEMY_ECHO, configure the flask-sqlalchemy module by setting up how sqlalchemy should connect to the database and whether sqlalchemy should, or should not, print the SQL for the operations it is doing.

With sqlalchemy configured, we next move on to configure our flask sessions by setting SESSION_TYPE to filesystem. This tells the flask session modules to use filesystem-based sessions to manage user activity.

Lastly, in the configuration, we set up two more keys, STATIC_PATH and TEMPLATES_PATH, which tell flask where to look for static files and template files respectively.

We are now done with setting up the global configuration of our application. We next move on to setting up the instance-specific configuration, where we define our unique application related keys. To do this, create a new file named config.py under the instance directory and add the following content to it:

```
'''
File: config.py
Description: Instance specific configuration for BugZot
'''
BCRYPT_LOG_ROUNDS=16
DEBUG=True
SECRET_KEY='hdu8463$$Jh#*@jdjsu937822i__#@*hsiud829aiuwnxhsi'
SQLALCHEMY_DATABASE_URI='postgresql://bugzot_admin:bugzotuser@localhost/bug
```

```
zot'
SQLALCHEMY_ECHO=True
```

Here, we have enabled the debug mode of Flask because we are currently developing our application and any stack-trace can help us better understand the reason behind the errors. We have also defined a URI for `sqlalchemy` to use the `postgresql` based database, which we created earlier in our application, and have also enabled the printing of SQL statements by `sqlalchemy` module for the purpose of development.

With this we are all set to run our application. So, let's give it a try by issuing the following command inside our project root:

python run.py

On a successful execution, we should be getting the following message printed on our terminal:

```
/home/sbadhwar/book_example/Hands-On-Enterprise-Application-Development-
with-Python/chapter6/bugzot/lib/python3.6/site-
packages/flask_sqlalchemy/__init__.py:794: FSADeprecationWarning:
SQLALCHEMY_TRACK_MODIFICATIONS adds significant overhead and will be
disabled by default in the future. Set it to True or False to suppress this
warning.
  'SQLALCHEMY_TRACK_MODIFICATIONS adds significant overhead and '
 * Serving Flask app "bugzot.application" (lazy loading)
 * Environment: production
   WARNING: Do not use the development server in a production environment.
   Use a production WSGI server instead.
 * Debug mode: on
 * Running on http://0.0.0.0:8000/ (Press CTRL+C to quit)
 * Restarting with stat
/home/sbadhwar/book_example/Hands-On-Enterprise-Application-Development-
with-Python/chapter6/bugzot/lib/python3.6/site-
packages/flask_sqlalchemy/__init__.py:794: FSADeprecationWarning:
SQLALCHEMY_TRACK_MODIFICATIONS adds significant overhead and will be
disabled by default in the future. Set it to True or False to suppress this
warning.
  'SQLALCHEMY_TRACK_MODIFICATIONS adds significant overhead and '
 * Debugger is active!
 * Debugger PIN: 174-906-953
```

With this, we are now up and running with our application. But, we still can't do anything. If we go ahead and try to open the URL in our browser, we won't see anything, and will instead be greeted with an error. This happens because we still haven't defined any route inside our application that can be served up by Flask and which the user can see.

So, as a first step, let's define the first route of our application.

To do this, open up `bugzot/application.py` and add the following set of lines to the end of the file:

```
@app.route('/ping', methods=['GET'])
def ping():
    '''Output a pong response as a greeting.'''

    return "Pong", 200
```

What we did here was to create a new route that can be accessed at the `/ping` endpoint of our application. This route is only accessible in the form of `GET` requests and prints a simple response to the browser, along with sending `HTTP 200 – SUCCESS` as a status code to the browser.

With this done, we are now fully prepared to enter the development of database models that we will use to manage the data of our application. So, let's hop onto the model development wagon.

Developing database models

The database model forms an integral part of any real life application. This is because any serious application in enterprises will for sure be dealing with some kind of data that needs to be persisted across the time.

The same is the case for our BugZot. BugZot is used to track the bugs and their life cycle that are encountered in the products of Omega Corporation. Also, the application will have to keep a record of users that are registered on it. To achieve this, we will require multiple models, each serving its own purpose.

For the development of this application, we will group all the related models under their own separate directories, so that we can maintain the clarity about which models serves what purpose. Also, this allows us to keep the code base clean from clutter, which may make it hard for the developers to understand what each file does as the code base grows in the future.

So, let's first get started with the development of the models that are required to manage the user accounts-related information.

To get started with the development of the user account-related models, we first go on and create a directory named `users` inside our models directory:

```
mkdir bugzot/models/users
```

Then initialize it as a submodule inside the models module.

Once we are done with this, we are good to go with the creation of our user model whose definition is shown in the following code:

```
'''
File: users.py
Description: The file contains the definition for the user data model
             that will be used to store the information related to the
             user accounts.
'''
from bugzot.application import db
from .roles import Role


class User(db.Model):
    """User data model for storing user account information.

    The model is responsible for storing the account information on a
    per user basis and providing access to it for authentication
    purposes.
    """

    id = db.Column(db.Integer, primary_key=True, autoincrement=True)
    username = db.Column(db.String(50), unique=True, index=True,
nullable=False)
    password = db.Column(db.String(512), nullable=False)
    email = db.Column(db.String(255), unique=True, nullable=False,
index=True)
    user_role = db.Column(db.Integer, db.ForeignKey(Role.id))
    role = db.relationship("Role", lazy=False)
    joining_date = db.Column(db.DateTime, nullable=False)
    last_login = db.Column(db.DateTime, nullable=False)
    account_status= db.Column(db.Boolean, nullable=False, default=False)

    def __repr__(self):
        """User model representation."""
        return "<User {}>".format(self.username)
```

With this, we just created our user model that can be used to store the information related to our users. Most of the columns just provide the definitions for the data that we expect to store inside the database. However, there are a couple of interesting bits here, so let's go through them:

```
index=True
```

We can see this attribute is mentioned in the username and the email column definition. We set the index attribute to True in the two columns because these two columns can be used frequently to access the data related to a particular user, and hence can benefit from the added optimization that comes with indexing.

The next interesting piece of information here is the relationship mapping to the roles model.

```
role = db.relationship("Role", lazy=False)
```

Since every user inside our database has a role associated to it, we can just add a one to one relationship mapping from our user model to the role model. Also, if we take a look carefully, we have set `lazy=False`. There is a small reason why we want to avoid lazy loading here. The roles model is usually small, and there is only a one-to-one mapping from the users model to the role model. By avoiding lazy loading, we are shedding off some time that would have been spent in waiting, had our database access layer lazily loaded the data from the roles model. Now, the question arises, where is the role model?

The definition of the role model can be found under the `bugzot/models/users/roles.py` file, but we explicitly are not providing that definition here inside the book, to keep the chapter concise.

Also, we need a mechanism for verifying the email address of the users. We can do this by sending the users a small email containing an activation link, which they need to click. To do this, we also have to generate and store an activation key for every new user. For this, we leverage a new model named `ActivationKey` model whose definition can be found under the `bugzot/models/users/activation_key.py` file.

Once all of this is done, we are now ready to export these models out of our users model submodule. To do this, let's fire up the module entrypoint file inside our code editor and export the models by adding the following lines to the `bugzot/models/users/__init__.py` file:

```
from .activation_key import ActivationKey
from .roles import Role
from .users import User
```

With this, we are done with the definition of our data models related to storing the information about the users.

The next thing inside our application is to define data models related to the categorization of the products for which the bugs can be filed. So, let's jump into the creation of the models related to the product categorization.

For creating the models related to the products, we first create a new submodule directory under the `bugzot/models` module and initialize it. Next, we provide the definition for the product model under `bugzot/models/products/products.py` as shown in the following code:

```
'''
File: products.py
Description: The file contains the definition for the products
             that are supported for bug filing inside the bug tracker
'''
from bugzot.application import db
from .categories import Category


class Product(db.Model):
    """Product defintion model.

    The model is used to store the information related to the products
    for which the users can file a bug.
    """

    id = db.Column(db.Integer, primary_key=True, autoincrement=True)
    product_name = db.Column(db.String(100), nullable=False, unique=True,
index=True)
    category_id = db.Column(db.Integer, db.ForeignKey(Category.id))
    category = db.relationship("Category", lazy=True)

    def __repr__(self):
        """Product model representation."""
        return "<Product {}>".format(self.product_name)
```

With this a we have completed the definition of the product model that will be used to keep a track of the products, against which the bugs can be filed in our application.

There are a few more model definitions inside our products submodule as follows:

- **Category**: The category model is responsible for storing the information about the product categories to which a particular product belongs
- **Component**: The component model is responsible for storing the information related to the product components against which a bug can be filed
- **Version**: The version model is responsible for storing the information related to the product versions against which a bug can be categorised

Once all these models are defined, they can be exported out from the product's submodule so that they can be utilized inside the application.

In a similar manner, we define the models related to the tracking of the bugs inside the system. We will skip over mentioning the definition of these models inside this chapter to keep the chapter length reasonable, but, for the curious mind, the definitions of these models can be easily tracked inside the `bugzot/models/bugs` directory in the code repository for this chapter.

Migrating the database models

With our database models created and ready for use, the next thing is to migrate these database models to the database server that we are using to run the application. The process to do this is quite straightforward.

To migrate the models to the database server, we first expose them into the application root. For example, to migrate the database models related to the users and products, all we need to do is to add the following line to the `bugzot/__init__.py` file:

```
from bugzot.models import ActivationKey, Category, Component, Product,
Role, User, Version
```

Once this is done, all we need to do is to call the `create_all()` method of the SQLAlchemy database object we created. This can be done by adding the following line to the end of the `bugzot/__init__.py` file:

```
db.create_all()
```

Once this is done, our `bugzot/__init__.py` it looks something like the following:

```
'''
File: __init__.py
Description: Bugzot application entrypoint file.
'''
from .application import app, bcrypt, db
from bugzot.models import ActivationKey, Category, Component, Product,
Role, User, Version

db.create_all()
```

With this done, the next time we start our application, the database models will be migrated to the database and be made available for use.

Building the views

Once the models are generated and are ready for use, the next thing we require is to have a mechanism through which we can interact with these models in order to access or modify them. One of the ways through which we can achieve this functionality is through the use of views.

With Flask, building the views is quite an easy task. The Flask web framework provides multiple methods for building views. Indeed, the /ping endpoint could also be termed as one of the views only which was built using a procedural style.

Over the course of the example, we will now try to follow object oriented methodology while defining any of the resources in the application. So, let's move on and start developing some of our views.

Developing the index view

Whenever a user visits our application, most likely it will be the case that the user will be landing on the home page of the application. So, the first thing we build is the index view. This will also be one of the places where we can understand how to build simple views in Flask.

So, as the first step, let's create a new module inside the views directory of our project workspace for the index module by executing the following commands:

```
mkdir bugzot/views/index
touch bugzot/views/index/__init__.py
```

With this, we are now ready to code our first view, the code for which follows:

```
'''
File: index.py
Description: The file provides the definition for the index view
             which is used to render the homepage of Bugzot.
'''
from bugzot.application import app
from flask.views import MethodView
from flask import render_template, session


class IndexView(MethodView):
    """Index view provides the method of rendering the homepage.

    The view is responsible for rendering of the index page of the bugzot
    when a HTTP GET request is made to the server.
```

```
    """

    def get(self):
        """HTTP GET request handler."""

        username = session.get('username', None)

        if not username:
            return render_template("index/index.html", logged_in=False)
        else:
            return render_template("index/index.html", logged_in=True,
    username=username)
```

That was quite a simple view to build. So, let's see what we did here to get this view up and functional.

So, starting from the imports, we need to focus on the last two import statements:

```
from flask.views import MethodView
from flask import render_template, session
```

In the first import statement we imported the `MethodView` class from the flask views. This class gives us the ability to build views based on the HTTP method names. This can be achieved by defining a method that has a name similar to the HTTP method we want the method to handle. For example, to handle `HTTP GET` requests in a `MethodView` type view, we will define a new method named `get()` inside our view.

The next import inline provides us one more important method, `render_template`. The method provides us with the functionality to render a defined template.

Now, moving on to our view definition, we create a new view known as `IndexView`, which derives from the `MethodView` class we imported earlier. Inside the view, we provide the definition for the method `get()`, providing our view with the capability to handle the `HTTP GET` type requests.

Now, let's take a look at what we do inside our `get()` method definition.

Inside the method, we first check if we have the username key set inside our session. This key will be set only when the user has successfully signed into the application, and will help us to identify the user who is using the application.

```
username = session.get('username', None)
```

In case the user is not signed in, we return a `None` object to denote a new session.

Now, the next thing we do, based on our identification of the user state, is to render the template with the appropriate variables being passed to it as a parameter. This is where our `render_template` method comes into the picture.

```
return render_template("index/index.html", logged_in=False)
```

As we can see from this call to the `render_template` method, the first parameter it takes is the path to the template that should be rendered.

> The `render_template()` method can render Jinja2 templates. This allows us to generate dynamic views based on the set of parameters and conditions that can be passed to the `render_template()` method. For the index view, the templates can be found under the `bugzot/templates/index` directory of the project workspace.

Once we have provided the name of the template that needs to be rendered, the next parameter to the method defines the variables that we want to pass to the template. These variables can be used in different ways across the template. For example, based on the value of the `logged_in` variable, we can decide whether we want to render the login form or display the username of the logged-in user.

Getting the index view to render

Now, we have the index view ready. But, before this view can be served to the user, we need to provide Flask with a mapping about the endpoint on which this view will be rendered. To achieve this, let's fire up our code editor and open `bugzot/__init__.py` and add the following lines to the file:

```
from bugzot.views import IndexView
app.add_url_rule('/', view_func=IndexView.as_view('index_view'))
```

Here, our focus is on the second line, which is responsible for mapping our view with a URL endpoint. The `add_url_rule()` of our flask application is the one that is responsible for providing these mappings. The method takes as its first parameter the URL path on which the view should be rendered. The `view_func` parameter provided to the method takes in the view that needs to be rendered on the provided URL endpoint.

Once this is done, we are now ready to serve our index page. All we need to do now is to run the following command:

python run.py

Then visit `http://localhost:8000/` on your browser.

Building the user registration view

Now, with the index view deployed and ready for use, let's move on to building a more complicated view where we allow the users to register on BugZot.

The following code implements a view known as `UserRegisterView`, which will allow the users to register to BugZot.

```python
'''
File: user_registration.py
Description: The file contains the definition for the user registration
             view allowing new users to register to the BugZot.
'''
from bugzot.application import app, brcypt, db
from bugzot.models import User, Role
from flask.views import MethodView
from datetime import datetime
from flask import render_template, session


class UserRegistrationView(MethodView):
    """User registration view to allow new user registration.

    The user registration view allows for the registering of the new users
    to the bugzot bug tracking system. The view allows the application
    to render the user registration page along with the handling of the
    submitted data.
    """

    __keys = ['username', 'password', 'confirm_password', 'email']

    def get(self):
        """HTTP GET handler."""

        username = session.get('username', None)

        # Check if there is an active user session
        if username is None:
            return render_template('user/registration.html')

        return render_template('index/index.html', logged_in=True,
username=username)

    def post(self):
        """HTTP POST handler."""

        form_data = {}
```

```
        # Iterate over the form to validate the existence of all the
        # required keys and store their data
        for form_key in self.__keys:
            if not request.form.has_key(form_key):
                return "All fields are required"
            else:
                form_data[form_key] = request.form.get(form_key)

        # Validate if the passwords match
        if not self.__validate_passwords(form_data['password'],
form_data['confirm_password']):
            return "Passwords do not match"

        # Generate a new model
        user = self.__generate_model(form_data)

        # Save the model to the database
        db.session.add(user)
        db.session.commit()

        return render_template("user/registration_success.html")


    def __generate_model(self, form_data):
        """Generate the user data model.

        Returns:
            db.Model
        """

        username = form_data['username']
        email = form_data['email']
        password =
bcrypt.generate_password_hash(form_data['password']).decode('utf-8')

        # Determine the user role and id
        role = Role.query.filter(role_name='user').first()
        joining_date = datetime.now()
        last_login = datetime.now()

        user = User(username=username, email=email, password=password,
role=role, joining_date=joining_date, last_login=last_login)
        return user


    def __validate_passwords(self, password, confirm_password):
        """Validate if the passwords match or not.
```

```
        Returns:
            Boolean
        """
        if password != confirm_password:
            return False
        return True
```

With this, we finish the implementation of the user registration view. So, let's take a look at a few things that we did differently here.

The first and the foremost thing inside `UserRegistrationView` is the fact that the view contains the definitions for two different methods, namely, `get()` and `post()`.

This is done for a purpose. To handle the user registration, we have two options at our disposal:

1. Create separate views for rendering the user registration form and processing the registration data.
2. Handle the form rendering and data processing in the same view based upon the type of requested.

For the registration view, we sided up with the second option to avoid the unnecessary complexity of adding two different endpoints just to handle the user registration. Also, this keeps the logically related functionalities under the same view.

For us, the `get()` method is responsible for rendering the user registration form when the user navigates to the registration page in their browser. When the user has filled up the data and clicks **submit**, the form sends the data to the same URL endpoint, but this time, as a `POST` request, which is handled by the `post()` method of the view.

Our `get()` user method is a simple method that checks if there is an existing user session going on the machine, and, if one is found, we redirect back to the index page, not allowing the user to re-register. If no active user session is found, the registration page is rendered.

Now, coming to our `post()` method, things become a little bit interesting (as a matter of fact, all the form data processing is being handled here). So, let's take a look at what this method is doing.

The first thing that happens here is, we check if the form data we got contains all the required keys or not. This is done by validating the request.form, which is a type of dictionary containing the required keys, or not. In Flask, this is done by calling the `has_key()` method of the request.form, which takes in the name of the key to be checked and returns true if it is found, and false otherwise.

If the keys are found, we store the keys in a local dictionary for later processing.

Once this is done, the next thing is to validate if the passwords match or not, which is done so that the user does not accidentally input an incorrect password that they might not remember in the future, causing them the added pain of going through the password reset process.

If the passwords are validated correctly, we then move on to the generation of the data model. Most of the data model generation is pretty straightforward, except the setting of the role field in the user model. Since the role field maps to the roles model in our application, we need to provide it with the correct value; otherwise, the database will report a constraint violation when we try to save the data model to the database.

By default, when a new user signs up, we assign that user the category of the user. To retrieve the user role, we can simply search by the name of the role and take the first object as our correct output. We assume here that the database returns only a single object for the query, as can be figured out from the following statement:

```
role = Role.query.filter(role_name='user').first()
```

With this, we get our role field figured out for storing into our user model.

Once our model definition is built, all we need to do is to add it to our database session and commit it. This is done through the following statements:

```
db.session.add(user)
db.session.commit()
```

Once we have successfully committed the model to the database, we can now render a success page telling the user the next steps for activating their account.

Similarly, we can now work on the development of the other models and views for the application.

 For the complete code base and assisting documentation for the application, please head towards the online repository for the book, where you can learn more about the other design choices we have taken to build the application and how they work.

Deploying for concurrent access

Until now, we were in the development stage and we could easily use the development server that comes packaged with Flask to quickly test our changes. But this development server is not a good choice if you are planning to run the application in production, and we need something more dedicated for that. This is because, in a production environment, we will be more concerned about the concurrency of the application, as well as its security aspects, like enabling SSL and providing more restricted access to some of the endpoints.

So, we need to figure out some choices here based on the fact that we need our application to handle a lot of concurrent accesses, while constantly maintaining a good response time for the users.

With this in mind, we end up with the following set of choices, which, by their nature are also fairly common in many production environments:

- **Application server**: Gunicorn
- **Reverse Proxy**: Nginx

Here, Gunicorn will be the application that will be responsible for handling the requests that are to be served by our Flask application, while Nginx takes care of request queuing and handling the distribution of the static assets.

So, first, let's set up Gunicorn and how we are going to serve the application through it.

Setting up Gunicorn

The first step that is involved in the setup of Gunicorn is its installation, which is quite an easy task. All we need to do is run the following command:

```
pip install gunicorn
```

Once this is done, we have Gunicorn available to be run. Gunicorn runs the application through **WSGI**, which stands for Web Server Gateway Interface. For Gunicorn to run our application, we need to create an additional file in our project workspace, known as `wsgi.py`, with the following contents:

```
'''
File: wsgi.py
Description: WSGI interface file to run the application through WSGI
interface
'''
from bugzot import app
```

```
if __name__ == '__main__':
    app.run()
```

Once we have defined the interface file, all we need to do is to run the following command to make Gunicorn serve our application:

```
gunicorn –bind 0.0.0.0:8000 wsgi:app
```

Wasn't this simple?

Now, the next thing is to set up Nginx as our reverse proxy to proxy the requests to the application server.

Setting up Nginx as reverse proxy

To use Nginx as our reverse proxy solution, we first need to get it installed on our system. For Fedora-based distributions, this can be easily installed by using the dnf or yum based package manager by running the following command:

```
$ sudo dnf install nginx
```

For other distributions, their package managers can be used to install the Nginx package.

Once the Nginx package is installed, we now need to do its configuration to allow it to communicate with our application server.

To configure Nginx to proxy the communication to our application server, create a file named bugzot.conf under the /etc/nginx/conf.d directory, with the following contents:

```
server {
    listen 80;
    server_name <your_domain> www.<your_domain>;

    location / {
        include proxy_params;
        proxy_pass http://unix:<path_to_project_folder>/bugzot.sock;
    }
}
```

Now with the Nginx configured, we need to establish a relationship between our Gunicorn application server and Ngnix. So, let's do it.

Establishing communication between Nginx and Gunicorn

One thing to note inside the Nginx configuration that we just completed was the `proxy_pass` line:

```
proxy_pass http://unix:<path_to_project_folder>/bugzot.sock
```

The line tells Nginx to look for a socket file through which Nginx can communicate to the application server. We can tell Gunicorn to create this proxy file for us. This can be done by executing the following command:

```
gunicorn –bind unix:bugzot.sock –m 007 wsgi:app
```

After executing this command, our Gunicorn web server will create a Unix socket and bind to it. Now, all that is remaining is to start our Nginx web server, which can be easily achieved by executing the following command:

```
systemctl start nginx.service
```

Once this is done, we can visit `http://localhost:80` to access our web application.

With this, our web application is now ready to be served in production and is able to take up a large number of concurrent requests.

Summary

In this chapter, we gained hands-on experience of how we can develop and host an enterprise-scale web application. To achieve this, we first started by making some technology decisions about which web frameworks and databases we were going to use. We then progressed to defining our project structure and how it will look on disk. The main aim was to achieve high modularity and less coupling between code. Once the project structure was defined, we then initialized a simple Flask application and implemented a route to check whether our server worked fine or not. We later progressed on to defining our models and views. Once these were defined, we altered our application to enable new routes that provide access to our views. Once our application development cycle was over, we then moved on to understanding how an application can be deployed using Gunicorn and Nginx to handle a large number of requests.

Now as we move on to the next chapter, we will take a look at how we can work on to develop an optimized frontend for the applications we are developing and how can a frontend affect the experience of the user while interacting with our application.

Questions

- What are some of the other pre-built view classes provided by Flask?
- Can we remove the foreign key constraint to role table from our user table without removing the relationship?
- What are the other options apart from Gunicorn for serving the application?
- How can we increase the number of Gunicorn workers?

Building Optimized Frontends

7

We have come quite far in this book while trying to understand how to build applications for enterprises in Python. The chapters we've covered so far consisted of how to build a scalable and responsive backend for our enterprise application that can cater for a large number of concurrent users, so that our enterprise application is a success with its users. However, there is one topic we have been missing and which usually gets very little attention when building enterprise level applications: the application frontend.

When a user interacts with our application, they are hardly concerned with what is going on in the backend. The experience of the user is directly connected with how the frontend of the application responds to their inputs. This makes the application frontend not only one of the most important aspects of the application, but also makes it one of the major deciding factors for the success of the application among its users.

Throughout this chapter, we will take a look at how we can build application frontends that not only provide an easy to use experience, but also a fast response to their inputs.

While going through this chapter, we will learn about the following topics:

- The need for optimizing the application frontends
- Optimizing the resources your frontend depends upon
- Leveraging the client-side caching to streamline the page loading
- Utilizing web storage for persisting user data

Technical requirements

The code listings in this book can be found under bugzot application directory built in `chapter06` at `https://github.com/PacktPublishing/Hands-On-Enterprise-Application-Development-with-Python`.

The code samples can be cloned by running the following command:

```
git clone
https://github.com/PacktPublishing/Hands-On-Enterprise-Application-Developm
ent-with-Python
```

The execution of the code does not require any particular set of special tools or frameworks and is a pretty straightforward process. The `README.md` file points to how to run the code samples for this chapter.

The need for optimizing frontends

The UI of the application is one of its most important user facing components. It decides how the user is going to perceive the application. A smooth and fluid frontend goes a long way in defining the user experience with the application.

This requirement for a smooth user experience brings in the need for optimizing the application frontend, in that it provides an easy to use interface, fast response times, and fluidity in the operations. If we go ahead and look toward the web 2.0 companies such as Google, Facebook, LinkedIn, and so on, they spend a huge amount of resources just on optimizing their frontends to shave off a few milliseconds of the rendering time. That is how important an optimized frontend is.

Components of an optimized frontend

We are discussing optimizing the frontends. But what does an optimized frontend consist of? How can we decide whether a frontend is optimized or not? Let's take a look.

An optimized frontend has several components, where it is not compulsory that every component needs to be reflected from the frontend. These components are as follows:

- **Quick rendering times**: One of the first focuses of frontend optimization is to reduce the rendering time of the page. Although there is no predefined set of rendering times that can be considered good or bad, you can think that a good rendering time will be the one where the user does not have to wait too long for the page to load on a decent internet connection.
  Also, a decent rendering time is not only dependent upon the speed of the internet connection of the user—it also depends upon the complexity of the frontend code. For example, a page consisting of deep nesting of the HTML components will take a longer time to render than a page that has shallow nesting of the HTML components.

- **Reduced data transfer**: One of the major components of optimizing a frontend is the reduction in the amount of data that needs to be transferred between the server and the client while an operation is performed. As a matter of fact, when the amount of data that needs to be transferred reduces, the responsiveness of the frontend increases, resulting in a positive experience for the users of the application.

- **Easy to navigate**: An optimized frontend will provide the user with the power to reach any part of the application in no more than a few clicks. A frontend that has a very deeply nested navigation, where a user has to hop through several pages before they can achieve what they want to do, acts as a really negative experience for the user, and hence an optimized frontend tries to deal with these problems of content navigation.

These are only a small set of components that define an optimized frontend, and there are several more, as we will see in the upcoming sections. But before we go ahead and start optimizing a frontend, we need to understand what the possible causes of problems in a frontend are. So, let's take a look.

What causes frontend issues

Frontend issues are a category of issues that are easily perceived by the users because they affect the way the user interacts with an application. For the sake of clarity here, when we say frontend of an enterprise web application, we are not only talking about its UI, we are also talking about the code and the templates that are there to render the required UI. Now, let's move on to understand what possible causes of frontend-specific issues are:

- **Excessive amount of objects**: In most of the dynamically populated templates that are responsible for rendering the frontend, the first problem comes with the rendering of an excessive amount of objects. When a lot of objects are passed to a template that needs to be rendered, the page response times tend to increase, causing an imminent slowdown in the process.

- **Excessive includes**: One of the major things that is focused on in software engineering is how to increase the modularity of the code base. The increase in modularity benefits in the increased reusability of the components. However, everything done in excess can be a signal of a major problem that might occur. When the frontend templates are modularized to an extent that goes beyond what is required, the rendering performance of the templates decreases. The reason for this is that for every include that is there, a new file needs to be loaded from the disk, which is an exceptionally slow operation.
One of the counter points here could be that once the template is loaded with all it includes resolved, the rendering engine can cache the template and serve the later requests from the cache. However, most of the caching engines have a limit on how much level of included depth they can cache, beyond which the performance hit will be imminent.

- **Unnecessary set of resources**: Some of the frontends could have an unnecessarily large amount of resources being loaded that are not used anywhere on a particular page. This includes JavaScript files that contain functions that are executed only on a small set of pages. Every extra file that is being loaded not only adds to increased consumption of the bandwidth but also affects the loading performance of the frontend.

- **Forcing the code to be loaded serially**: Most modern browsers are now optimized to load a lot of resources in parallel to efficiently utilize the network bandwidth and to reduce the page loading times. However, at times, some of the tricks that we use to reduce the amount of code may force the page to get loaded sequentially instead of being loaded in parallel. One of the most common examples that may cause the page resources to be loaded in sequence is the use of CSS imports. Although CSS imports provide the flexibility of loading third-party CSS files directly inside another style sheet, it also reduces the ability of the browser to load the contents of the CSS file in parallel, hence increasing the time it takes to render a page.

This set of causes forms a non-exhaustive list of issues that can cause a slowdown in the page rendering time and hence provide an unpleasant experience to the user.

Now, let's take a look at how we can optimize our frontends to be responsive in nature and provide the best possible user experience.

Optimizing the frontend

Until now, we learned about the various issues that may hamper the performance of the frontend. Now, it's time to take a look at how we can reduce the performance impact on the frontends and make them fast and responsive in an enterprise grade environment.

Optimizing resources

The first and foremost optimization that we are going to take a look at is the optimization of resources that a particular page loads when it is requested. For this, consider the following code snippet from the user data display page in the admin panel, which is responsible for displaying a table of users in the database:

```
<table>
{% for user in users %}
  <tr>
    <td class="user-data-column">{{ user.username }}</td>
    <td class="user-data-column">{{ user.email }}</td>
    <td class="user-data-column">{{ user.status }}</td>
  </tr>
{% endfor %}
</table>
```

So far, so good. As we can see, the code snippet just loops over a user's object and renders the table based on how many records are stored in the user's table. This is essentially good for most of the purposes where the user records are only in a small number (for example, 100 or so). But this code will start to become problematic as the number of users in the application grows. Imagine trying to load 1 million records from the application database and making them display on the UI. There are certain issues with this:

- **Slow database queries**: Trying to load up 1 million records from the database at the same time is going to be very slow and can take quite a significant time, hence blocking the view from rendering for a long time.
- **Decoding the objects in the frontend:** In the frontend, to render the page, the templating engine has to decode the data from all the objects so that it is able to display the data on the page. This kind of operation is not only CPU intensive, but also slow.
- **Large page size:** Imagine transferring over a page consisting of millions of records over the network from the server to client. This process is time-consuming and also makes the page unfavorable to load over slow connections.

So, what can we do here? The answer to this is pretty simple: let's optimize the amount of resources that are going to be loaded. To achieve this, we are going to utilize a concept known as pagination.

To implement pagination, we need to make a few changes to the view that is responsible for rendering the frontend template, as well as the frontend template. The following code describes how the view will look if it had to support pagination:

```
From bugzot.application import app, db
from bugzot.models import User
from flask.views import MethodView
from flask import render_template, session, request

class UserListView(MethodView):
    """User list view for displaying user data in admin panel.
       The user list view is responsible for rendering the table of users
that are registered
       in the application.
    """

    def get(self):
        """HTTP GET handler."""
        page = request.args.get('next_page', 1) # get the page number to be
displayed
        users = User.query.paginate(page, 20, False)
        total_records = users.total
        user_records = users.items
        return render_template('admin/user_list.html', users=user_records,
next_page=page+1)
```

We are now done with the modifications to the view—it now supports pagination. Implementing this pagination was quite an easy task with the facilities already provided by SQLAlchemy to paginate the results from the database table using the `paginate()` method. This `paginate()` method asks for three parameters, namely the page number, which should start from one, the number of records on each page, and `error_out`, which is responsible for setting the error reporting for the method. A `False` here disables the errors from being displayed on `stdout`.

With the view developed to support the pagination, the next thing is to define the template so that it can take advantage of the pagination. The following code shows the modified template code that takes advantage of the pagination:

```
<table>
{% for user in users %}
  <tr>
    <td class="user-data-column">{{ user.username }}</td>
```

```
    <td class="user-data-column">{{ user.email }}</td>
    <td class="user-data-column">{{ user.status }}</td>
  </tr>
{% endfor %}
</table>
<a href="{{ url_for('admin_user_list', next_page) }}">Next Page</a>
```

And with this, we have our view code ready. This view code is quite simple as we have just extended the previous template by adding a `href`, which loads the data for the next page.

With our resources being sent to the page now optimized, the next thing we need to focus on is how we can make our frontend load more and more resources faster.

Fetching CSS in parallel by avoiding CSS imports

CSS is one of the major parts of any frontend that helps in providing the styling information to the browser for how it should style the page it has received from the server. Usually, a frontend may have a number of CSS files associated with it. One of the possible optimizations that we can achieve here is by making these CSS files get fetched in parallel.

So, let's imagine we have the following set of CSS files, namely `main.css`, `reset.css`, `responsive.css`, and `grid.css`, which our frontend needs to load. The way we allow the browser to load all these files in parallel is by linking them into the frontend using the HTML link tag instead of CSS imports, which causes the CSS files to be loaded synchronously.

Here, the following code snippet is preferred:

```
<link rel="stylesheet" href="css/main.css" />
<link rel="stylesheet" href="css/reset.css" />
<link rel="stylesheet" href="css/responsive.css" />
<link rel="stylesheet" href="css/grid.css" />
```

This is preferred over the use of the following code snippet:

```
# main.css
@import url("css/reset.css")
@import url("css/responsive.css")
@import url("css/grid.css")
```

Most current browsers have the optimization to not block the rendering of a page until the link resource has been fetched. This allows the user to have a quick page load, and the styles are then later applied to the page as the style sheets are made available to the browser. Also, all of these resources mentioned through the link tag are loaded in parallel by the browser by sending multiple requests to the server, hence allowing for a faster page load.

Bundling JavaScript

In the current time and hopefully the future as well, we will constantly see increasing bandwidths for the networks, be it broadband networks or mobile networks that allow for faster downloading of resources in parallel. But for every resource that needs to be fetched from a remote server, there is still some network latency involved due to the fact that every separate resource demands a separate request to be made to the server. This latency can bite when there are a lot of resources that need to be loaded and when the user is on a high latency network.

Usually, most modern web applications heavily utilize JavaScript for a wide set of purposes, which may include input validation, dynamically generating content, and so on. All of this functionality is split into multiple files, which may include some libraries, customized code, and so on. Although having all of these split into different files can help in parallel loading, sometimes the JavaScript files contain code for generating dynamic content on the web page, which may block the rendering of the web page until all the necessary files required for successfully rendering the page are not loaded.

One of the possible ways through which we can reduce the amount of time a browser takes to load up these script resources is to bundle them all together into a single file. This allows all the scripts to be combined into a single large file that the browser can fetch in a single request. Although this may cause the user a bit of a slow experience when they first visit a website, once the resource has been fetched and cached, the subsequent loads of the web page will be significantly faster for the user.

Today, a lot of third-party libraries are available that allow us to bundle this JavaScript. Let's take an example of a simple tool called Browserify, which allows us to bundle our JavaScript files. For example, if we had multiple JavaScript files, such as `jquery.js`, `image-loader.js`, `slideshow.js`, and `input-validator.js`, and we want to bundle these files together with Browserify, all we have to do is run the following command:

```
browserify jquery.js image-loader.js slideshow.js input-validator.js >
bundle.js
```

This command will create a bundle of these JavaScript files into a common file known as `bundle.js`, which can now be included in our web application through the use of a simple script tag like the following:

```
<script type="text/javascript" src="js/bundle.js"></script>
```

With the JavaScript bundled to load up in one request, we may start seeing some improvements in terms of how quickly a page is fetched and displayed to the user in the browser with the subsequent page loads. Now, let's take a look at one other interesting topic that may be of a good use to really make a difference in how quickly our web application loads up for repeated visits to the website.

 The technique we discussed for bundling of JavaScript can also be a good optimization for the inclusion of CSS files.

Utilizing client-side caching

Caching has long been used to speed up the loading of resources that are frequently used. For example, most of the modern operating systems utilize caching for providing faster access to the most frequently used applications. The web browsers also utilize caching to provide quicker access to resources when the user visits the same website again. This is done so as to avoid fetching the same files from the remote server again and again if they haven't changed and hence reducing the amount of data transfer that may be required, while also improving the rendering time for the page.

Now, in the world of enterprise applications, something like client-side caching can prove to be really useful. This happens because of the following reasons:

- Enterprise applications, once designed, usually do not see abrupt changes to their code base. This keeps most of the resources required to render a web page the same over a long period of time, which makes them a good candidate for caching.
- Enterprise web applications usually have a defined workflow, which basically means that a user trying to work on something will follow a particular page navigation order. This is useful in the cases where a certain set of pages are visited often and hence can have a higher chance of benefitting from the caches.

- Most of the enterprise applications often see repeated visitors, hence requiring the same resources to be fetched again and again from the server. Caching these resources on the client side can be of real high benefit to speed up the response time of the application, as well as in decreasing the network usage.

With these points in mind, we now know that client-side caching, in the case of enterprise applications, could be of real help. But now the question is, how do we get the client-side caching in place for the content?

With our web application, implementing client-side caching is an easy task.

Setting application-wide cache control

Since our application is based upon Flask, we can leverage several simple mechanisms for setting up the cache control for our application. For example, adding the following code to the end of our `bugzot/application.py` file enables site-wide cache control, as follows:

```
@app.after_request
def cache_control(response):
    """Implement side wide cache control."""
    response.cache_control.max_age = 300
    response.cache_control.public = True
    return response
```

In this example, we utilize the Flask's inbuilt `after_request` decorator hook to set up the HTTP response header once the request has arrived to the Flask application. The decorated function needs a single parameter that takes in an object of the response class and returns a modified response object.

For our use case, inside the code for the method for the `after_request` hook, we set the `cache_control.max_age` header, which specifies the upper boundary for the time for which the content will be served from the cache before it is fetched from the server again, and the `cache_control.public` header, which defines if the cached response can be shared with multiple requests or not.

Now, there could be times when we want to set up the cache control differently for a particular kind of request. For example, we may not want `cache_control.public` to be set for the user profile page so as to avoid displaying the same profile data to the different users. Our application allows us to achieve these kinds of scenarios pretty quickly. Let's take a look.

Setting request level cache control

In Flask, we can modify the response headers before we send the response back to the client. This can be done fairly easily. The following example shows a simple view implementing response-specific header control:

```
from bugzot.application import app, db
from bugzot.models import User
from flask.views import MethodView
from flask import render_template, session, request, make_response

class UserListView(MethodView):
  """User list view for displaying user data in admin panel.

  The user list view is responsible for rendering the table of users that
are registered
  in the application.
  """

  def get(self):
    """HTTP GET handler."""
    page = request.args.get('next_page', 1) # get the page number to be
displayed
    users = User.query.paginate(page, 20, False)
    total_records = users.total
    user_records = users.items
    resp = make_response(render_template('admin/user_list.html',
users=user_records, next_page=page+1))
    resp.cache_control.public = False
    return resp
```

In this example, we first use the `make_response()` method of Flask to build a response with the `render_template` call. The next thing we do here is set the cache-control to use the private cache for holding the response data using the `resp.cache_control.public` property. Once we have the headers set, all we have to return is the modified response back to the client.

Wasn't this quite simple to use while providing a lot of benefits? With this kind of approach, we can set the cache for static files to be maintained for a longer duration, hence providing speedup in terms of page loading while also reducing data usage.

Now, let's take a look at a slightly more sophisticated way of utilizing the client storage to store some frequently accessed data, so that we can avoid making web requests when a user requests the same data again and again.

Utilizing web storage

Any web application developer who has worked on any application that involves even a little user management will for sure have heard about web cookies, which in essence provide a mechanism for storing some of the information on the client side.

Utilizing cookies provides an easy way through which we can maintain small amounts of user data on the client side and can read it multiple times until the cookies expire. But as easy as it is to deal with cookies, there are certain limitations that restrict the cookies being used for anything useful, other than maintaining a small amount of application state on the client side. Some of these limitations are as follows:

- Cookies are transferred with every request, hence adding to the data that is transferred with every request
- Cookies allow for storing a little amount of data that is restricted to a maximum of 4 KB

Now, the question that comes is, what can we do if we want to store more data or we want to avoid fetching the same set of stored data again and again with every request?

For dealing with such scenarios, the latest version of HTML, HTML 5, provides various functionalities that allow for dealing with client-side web storage. This web storage provides a number of benefits over the cookies-based mechanism, such as the following:

- Since the web storage is available directly on the client side, the information doesn't need to be sent by the server again and again to the client with every request
- The web storage API provides a maximum of 10 MB of storage, which is multiple times grater than what can be stored with the cookies
- Web storage provides the flexibility of storing the data either in local storage, for example, the data will be accessible even after the user closes and opens a browser again, or on a per session basis, where the data stored in the web storage will be cleared off as soon as the session is invalidated, either when the user session is destroyed by your application handler responsible for handling the user log out, or the browser is closed

This makes web storage an attractive place to put in the data and avoid loading it again and again.

For our enterprise applications, this can provide a lot of flexibility by storing the results of the intermediate steps in the user browser only, and then submitting them back to the server only when all the required input fields have been filled up.

One other use case that may be more specific to Bugzot is that, we can store the bug report that a user is filing into the web storage and send it to the server when the bug report is completed. In this case, the user gets the flexibility to come back to working on their bug reports as and when they wish, without worrying about starting from scratch again.

Now that we know about the benefits that web storage provides, let's take a look at how we can leverage the use of web storage.

Working with local web storage

The use of local web storage is easy with HTML 5, since it provides a number of APIs to interact with the web storage. So, without wasting much time, let's take a look at a simple example of how we can use local web storage. For this, we will create a simple JavaScript file known as `localstore.js` with the following contents:

```
// check if the localStorage is supported by the browser or not
if(localStorage) {
  // Put some contents inside the local storage
localStorage.setItem("username", "joe_henry");
  localStorage.setItem("uid", "28372");
  // Retrieve some contents from the local storage
  var user_email = localStorage.getItem("user_email");
} else {
  alert("The browser does not support local web storage");
}
```

This was a very simple example of how to use the local webstorage API provided by HTML 5 in a compatible browser. Let's spend some time understanding what we did in the script:

At the start of the script, we first checked if the browser supports the HTML 5 local storage API or not; in case it does not support the local storage API, we just display an alert showing the unavailability of the feature. If the browser supports the API, we move on to using some simple `localStorage` APIs to store and retrieve some content from the local web storage. The `setItem(key, value)` method allows for storing a new key value pair inside the storage, or using the `getItem(key)` method, which allows us to retrieve the content of the key from the web storage.

Now, we have a little bit of an idea about the local storage API and how we can use it to store some data that we can access any time without worrying about the state of the session. But what if we wanted to store some data up until the point where the user's browser session was valid? For this, the HTML 5 web storage API provides a session storage mechanism, which provides similar methods as local storage but stores the data only until a user session is valid. Let's take a look at how we can use the session store to store data.

Working with session storage

As simple as it is to use the local storage, session storage also doesn't add any kind of complexity. For example, let's take a look at how easy it is to port our example of localStorage to sessionStorage:

```
// check if the sessionStorage is supported by the browser or not
if(sessionStorage) {
  // Put some contents inside the local storage
sessionStorage.setItem("username", "joe_henry");
  sessionStorage.setItem("uid", "28372");
  // Retrieve some contents from the session storage
  var user_email = sessionStorage.getItem("user_email");
} else {
  alert("The browser does not support session web storage");
}
```

From this example, it is evident that moving away from local storage to session storage is very easy, with both the storage options providing a similar storage API, the only difference being how long the data in the storage is kept.

With the knowledge of how we can optimize frontends to provide completely scalable and responsive enterprise web applications, now it's time for us to visit some aspects of the enterprise application development that ensure what we are building is secure and works as per expectations, and doesn't delivers random surprises.

Summary

Throughout the course of this chapter, we learned about why it is important to have an optimized frontend for our enterprise applications, and how a frontend may affect the use of our application inside the enterprise. We then moved on to understand what kind of issues usually plague the performance of web frontends, and what possible solutions we can take to improve the application frontend. This involves reducing the amount of resources that are loaded by the frontend, allowing the CSS to load in parallel, bundling JavaScript, and so on. We then moved on to understand how caching can prove to be useful considering the use case of an enterprise web application. Once we understood the concept of caching, we then moved into the territory of web storage, which allows us to store a large amount of data in the client browser, allowing easy access to the data without making a request to the server again and again.

Now, we are ready to take a look at how to mature the process of our application development, and to make sure that we deliver an application with the least number of defects as possible. The next chapter of this book takes us through the process of making sure that the application we are building contains the least number of defects through the use of different testing techniques.

Questions

1. How can the use of CDN provide a boost to frontend performance?
2. Can we do something to make the browser utilize existing connections to the server for loading resources?
3. How can we remove a particular key from web storage or clear the contents of web storage?

8
Writing Testable Code

With this chapter, we have entered part two of our book, which covers the development of enterprise-grade applications using Python. While part one of this book focused on how to build an enterprise-grade application with scalability and performance in mind, part two of this book focuses on the internal development aspects of the application, such as how we can make sure our application is secure, how well it is performing, and how to ship an application with the higher quality checks in place so as to minimize the occurrence of unexpected behaviors during the production phase.

In this chapter, we would like to bring your focus to a very important aspect of the enterprise application development or, for that sake, an important aspect for the development of any kind of application. This important aspect is the testability of the code.

Writing code that can be easily tested can prove to be really useful. This involves the ability to identify bugs early in the application development phase, providing software with high quality standards, allowing for more and more automated testing of the code, and hence resulting in an application development process that is mature enough to release a stable application for the enterprise use cases.

Over the course of this chapter, we will learn about the following:

- The need for elaborate testing of the application code
- Different types of testing during the development life cycle
- Building a code base that can be tested easily
- Utilizing frameworks for improving our testing process
- Utilizing **Continuous Integration/Continuous Delivery (CI/CD)** pipelines for automating application testing

Technical requirements

The code listings in this book can be found under `chapter08` directory at `https://github.com/PacktPublishing/Hands-On-Enterprise-Application-Development-with-Python`.

The code samples related to the unit testing and functional testing for the bugzot application developed in `chapter 6`, *Example – Building BugZot*, can be found under the `chapter06` directory.

The code samples can be cloned by running the following command:

```
git clone
https://github.com/PacktPublishing/Hands-On-Enterprise-Application-Developm
ent-with-Python
```

This includes the instructions regarding how to run the code. In addition to that, this chapter requires the installation of a Python library, which allows us to simplify the writing of our test code. The library and all the related dependencies can be installed by running the following command:

```
pip install -r requirements.txt
```

The importance of testing

As developers, we usually aim at working on challenging problems, trying to navigate through the complex connections, and coming up with a solution. But how many times do we care to look at all the possible ways through which our code can fail to provide the expected outcome? As much as it is hard to try to break something that we as developers have written ourselves, it forms one of the most important aspects of the development cycle.

This is the time when testing becomes an important aspect of the development life cycle. The aim of application testing can be summed up by answering the following questions:

- Are the individual components in the code performing as per the expectations?
- Does the flow of the code from one component to another as is desired?
- Was the final outcome of the application the same that we thought of?
- Are there some deviations in the standard behavior?
- Did the application handle all the expected scenarios and provided a fail-safe over for the unexpected ones?

With the preceding questions answered, we are now able to define how well our application has been built and how robust the application is in case some unexpected input is given to the application. This results in various benefits, such as the following:

- **Early detection of bugs**: With the testing being a part of the development cycle itself and the individual components of the code base being subject to separate tests, we can ensure that a large number of bugs can be detected early in the development phase itself.
- **Increased reliability**: With the testing in place to detect the bugs early, we can see how much our application is reliable in generating accurate results for the expected set of inputs without causing trouble to the user.
- **Robustness in check**: No matter what we do, there will be cases when a user may input an incorrect set of inputs, and how our application responds to that is important. One of the aims of testing is to ensure that our application is able to handle the incorrect set of inputs without generating a crash or causing a major loss to the data.
- **Reduced maintenance costs**: When an application has undergone a thorough testing phase during its development and post-development phases, most of the critical bugs are already identified and fixed before the application is deployed in the production environment. This indirectly results in the reduction of maintenance costs due to the smaller number of hours required from the engineers trying to fire fight the issues that may arise due to failure in testing the behavior of the application when an unexpected input is provided.

For an enterprise-grade application, a thorough testing that starts early from the development phase itself will result in the users of the application having a pleasant time using the application. Thus they will be able to achieve more productive output instead of spending time dealing with how to handle a particular use case because the application doesn't handle it properly.

Now, we know why testing of the application is an important aspect. But is there just one kind of testing? What kind of application testing should a developer be doing before handing off the application to the quality engineering teams? Let's take a look.

The different kinds of testing

When the focus is on shipping a quality application, whether it be for general customers or for an enterprise, there are multiple kinds of testing that need to be performed. These testing techniques may start at different points in the development life cycle of the application, and hence are categorized accordingly.

In this section, instead of focusing on some testing methodologies that can be grouped as black-box testing and white-box testing, we will rather focus our effort on understanding the terminology associated with the developers. So, let's take a look.

Unit testing

When we start to build our application, we have the application divided into a number of submodules. These submodules contain a number of classes or methods that interact together to achieve a certain output.

For the correct output to be generated, all the individual classes and methods need to work correctly, otherwise the results will differ.

Now, when our target is to check the correctness of the individual components of a code base, we usually write tests that target these individual components independently from the other components of the application. This kind of testing, where an individual component is tested independently of the other components, is known as **unit testing**.

To state this briefly, the following are some features of unit tests:

- **Starts early in the development cycle:** Unit testing usually starts early from the development phase itself, and the unit tests are written so as to cover the individual components inside a code base.
- **Isolation of components:** Each component is tested in complete isolation from the other components. In case there are some components that may depend upon other components, stubs or fakes can be used to simulate the interaction.
- **Increased automation:** Since the unit tests usually cover individual components and are mostly a piece of code trying to mock some method or class, these tests may be easily automated, and can be run again and again over the code quite quickly without manual intervention.

Unit testing allows a developer to detect issues early in their code base and hence enable the developer to quickly fix pieces of code that might be providing an incorrect behavior that can later affect the functionality of the application. But the ability of the unit tests to find all the issues is quite limited. Since unit tests are used to check a component in isolation, they are not able to evaluate all the execution paths that a code may take, hence limiting their scope of finding all the bugs.

To overcome the shortcomings of unit tests, there are additional testing techniques that are used. Let's take a look at one of the techniques that is often used to test the behavior of the application when the different components of the application interact with each other.

Integration testing

An application is not merely complete once all of its individual components have been written. To produce any meaningful output, these individual components need to interact with each other in different possible ways based upon the type of input that has been provided. To have a complete check of the application code base, the components that make up the application not only need to be tested in isolation, but also when they are interacting with each other.

Integration testing starts once the application is out of the unit testing phase. Inside integration testing, individual components are made to interact with each other through the use of interfaces, and this interaction is then tested to see if the results being produced are according to the expectations or not.

During the integration testing phase, not only the interaction between the components of the application is tested, but also the interaction between the components and any other external service, such as third-party APIs and databases.

In brief, here are some of the features of integration testing:

- **Focus on testing the interfaces:** Since the different components of an application interact with each other through the use of interfaces exposed by the components, the role of integration testing is to validate that these interfaces are working as expected
- **Usually starts after unit testing:** Once the components have passed the unit tests, they are then integrated together to connect with each other and integration testing is then performed
- **Code flow testing:** In contrast to unit testing, where the individual components are tested in isolation and any dependency on any other component is usually mocked, the integration tests usually focus on the flow of data from one component to another, and hence also check the outcome of the code flow

As we can see, integration testing forms an important part of the application testing process, where the aim is to validate if the different components of an application are able to interact with each other properly or not.

Once integration testing is complete, the next phase in the testing process is to move to system testing, followed by the final stage of acceptance testing. The following image shows the flow of testing from the Unit testing stage to the acceptance testing stage and the different kinds of testing that may happen during the development of the application.

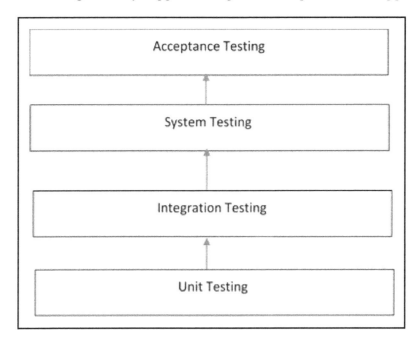

To keep the length of this book in check, we will skip over the explanation of these two testing techniques and instead focus the rest of this chapter on implementing some hands-on unit testing.

For the rest of this chapter, we will keep our focus on the unit testing practices and how we can implement them in our demo application.

Building an application with testing in mind

So, we now know that testing is important and we've also got to know about the different kinds of testing. But are there any important things that we need to do while building our application so that we are able to test it properly?

The answer to this question is a bit complicated. Although we can easily write the code in any particular manner we desire, and subject the code to testing through a number of procedures, for example, unit testing, it is still better to follow a general set of guidelines so that the code can be tested easily and efficiently. So, let's go ahead and take a look at the guidelines:

- **Every component should have one responsibility:** For testing to be efficient and to cover all the possible code paths, every component should play a single responsibility. For example, take a look at the following code:

```
def encrypt_password(password):
    """Encrypt the provided password.

    Keyword arguments:
    Password - The password to be encrypted

    Returns:
      Tuple
    """

    salt = secrets.token_bytes(8)
    passwd_hash = hashlib.pbkdf2_hmac('sha256', password.encode('utf 8'),
salt, 10000).hex()
    return (passwd_hash, salt)
```

In this code, we can see that the method is responsible for playing two different responsibilities of first generating a random salt that is used to pad the password with, and then generate a new password hash for the supplied password. This kind of method can be tested using unit tests, which is hard because of the multiple roles it is playing. Changing even a single statement in the method can result in multiple unit tests having to be modified.

- **Avoid non-determinism:** Going with the previous example, our method generates a random salt in every iteration, which is independent of the inputs we have provided to the method. This results in non-deterministic behavior, which might be hard to test because the output of the method might be different, even for the same kind of inputs. To have successful unit tests in place, avoiding non-determinism is important.

- **Avoid global state:** While writing a particular component, do not make it depend on a global state. When a global state is used to coordinate between the different components, it creates a mess during the testing because this state needs to be maintained for all the unit tests to execute successfully. This kind of problem usually defeats the purpose of unit testing, which aims to test the components in isolation from each other without any kind of coordination between them.

- **Avoid inserting too much logic in constructors:** When programming in an object-oriented language, constructors are called when the objects of a particular class need to be instantiated. The constructors are responsible for setting up the object instance and initializing it with any required data. While testing the method of a class, every test will instantiate a new object of the class. If your constructors are responsible for doing anything other than setting up the state of the newly constructed object, all these settings will need to be tracked in all the test cases, making the tests much more complicated.

So, we need to take a look at some of the tips that we can follow to make our code testable. So, let's go back to our previous example and see what can we do to make the method testable, for example:

```
def encrypt_password(password, salt):
    """Encrypt the provided password.

    Keyword arguments:
    password: The password to be encrypted
    salt: The salt to be used for padding the password

    Returns:
      String
    """
    passwd_hash = hashlib.pbkdf2_hmac('sha256', password.encode('utf-8'),
salt, 10000).hex()
    return passwd_hash
```

In this example, we modified our `encrypt_password()` method a little bit. Our modification involved removing the logic for salt generation out of the method and replacing it with ingesting a salt through parameters. With this, we removed two problems from our method. The first of these problems was the same method having more than one responsibility—the generation of a salt and generating a hash of the password. The second problem was of non-determinism, where the salt generated could be different in every iteration of the test.

These were a few rules that if followed can not only make the process of testing easy, but also much more useful, because we are easily able to test the different edge cases of a particular component with quite some ease. During the development of some large scale applications, some of the teams even follow the principles of **test-driven development (TDD)**.

Test-driven development

Test-driven development is a software development process where the process of software development involves the writing of tests for the individual requirements first, and then building or improving methods that will pass those tests. This kind of process usually benefits in terms of producing an application with a smaller number of defects than it would have if the tests would have been written once the components were developed.

During test-driven development, the following steps are followed:

1. **Add a test:** Once the requirements are specified, the developers start by writing a new test for a new component of improvement in the previous component. This test sets the expected outcome from the particular component.
2. **Run the tests to see if the new test fails:** When the new test has been added, the tests are run against the code to see if the new test fails for the expected reasons. This assures us that the test works as expected and does not pass in unfavorable conditions.
3. **Write/modify the component:** Once the tests have been run and an expected result can be seen, we move on to either writing the new component or modifying the existing component so that the newly added test case passes.
4. **Run tests:** Once the required modification has been made for the test to pass, the test suite is made to run again to see if the previously failing test now passes or not. This assures that the modifications are working as expected.
5. **Refactor:** As we progress in the development life cycle of the application following the TDD process, there will be times when there will be tests that will be duplicated or components that might be playing the same responsibility. To remove these issues, constant refactoring is required so as to reduce the duplication.

Now, we have quite an understanding about how much the testing plays an important role in the development of any successful application, and also about how to write code that can be tested easily. Now, it's time for us to get our hands dirty and start writing some tests for the application that we built in `chapter 6`, *Example – Building BugZot*.

Writing unit tests

So, it's time to start writing our unit tests. The Python library provides us with a lot of options to write tests and that too, quiet easily. We are usually spoilt for choice. The library in itself provides a unit testing module which can be used to write unit tests, and then there is no shortage of the frameworks that we can use to make our life easier while writing unit tests.

So, let's first take a look at writing some simple unit tests with the Python `unittest` module, and then we will move on to writing unit tests for our application using one of the renowned Python testing frameworks.

Writing unit tests with Python unittest

Python 3 provides a really nice and quite a featured library that allows us to write unit tests for our applications. This library, known as `unittest`, is used for writing unit tests that may range from the complexity of very simple tests to very complex tests involving a proper setup before a unit test is made to run.

Some of the features that we see supported in the Python `unittest` library are as follows:

- **Object-oriented:** The library facilitates the writing of unit tests in an object-oriented manner. What this means is that, the objects are written in an object-oriented form through the use of classes and methods. This in no sense means that only object-oriented code can be tested with the library. The library does support testing object-oriented and non-object-oriented code alike.
- **Ability for test fixtures:** Some of the tests may require the environment to be set up in a certain way before the test is run and then cleaned up properly once the test completes execution. This is known as test fixture and is fully supported by the Python `unittest` library.
- **Ability to write test suites:** The library provides the functionality for writing fully featured test suites that are composed of multiple test cases. The results of a test suite are aggregated and displayed at once.
- **Built-in test runner:** A test runner is used to orchestrate the tests and compile the results of the executed tests to generate a report. The library provides a built-in test runner to achieve this functionality.

Now, let's take a look at following code, which we will use to write our unit tests on:

```python
import hashlib
import secrets

def strip_password(password):
    """Strip the trailing and leading whitespace.
    Returns:
        String
    """
    return password.strip()
def generate_salt(num_bytes=8):
    """Generate a new salt

    Keyword arguments:
    num_bytes -- Number of bytes of random salt to generate

    Returns:
        Bytes
    """

    return secrets.token_bytes(num_bytes)

def encrypt_password(password, salt):
    """Encrypt a provided password and return a hash.

    Keyword arguments:
    password -- The plaintext password to be encrypted
    salt -- The salt to be used for padding

    Returns:
        String
    """

    passwd_hash = hashlib.pbkdf2_hmac('sha256', password.encode('utf-8'),
salt, 10000).hex()
    return passwd_hash
```

In this code, we have defined some functions that aim to help us with the generation of the password hash that can than be safely stored inside the database.

Now, our aim is to utilize the Python `unittest` library to write some unit tests for the preceding code.

The following code aims to implement a small set of unit tests for the passwords helper module:

```
from helpers import strip_password, encrypt_password
import unittest

class TestPasswordHelpers(unittest.TestCase):
    """Unit tests for Password helpers."""

    def test_strip_password(self):
        """Test the strip password function."""

        self.assertEqual(strip_password(' saurabh '), 'saurabh')

    def test_encrypt_password(self):
        """Test the encrypt password function."""

        salt = b'\xf6\xb6(\xa1\xe8\x99r\xe5\xf6\xa5Q\xa9\xd5\xc1\xad\x08'
        encrypted_password =
'2ba31a39ccd2fb7225d6b1ee564a6380713aa94625e275e59900ebb5e7b844f9'

        self.assertEqual(encrypt_password('saurabh', salt),
encrypted_password)

if __name__ == '__main__':
    unittest.main()
```

We created a simple file for running our unit tests. Now, let's take a look at what this file does.

Firstly, we import the functions that we want to test from their required module. For this example, we have these functions defined inside a file named `helpers.py` from which we are going to import them. The next import gets us the Python unittest library.

Once we have the required things imported, the next step is to start writing the unit tests. To do this, we start with defining a class named `TestPasswordHelpers` that inherits from the `unittest.TestCase` class. The class is used to define a set of test cases that we may want to execute, as follows:

```
class TestPasswordHelpers(unittest.TestCase):
```

Inside the class definition, we then move on to defining individual test cases for the methods that we want to test. The methods that define a test case must start with the word `test` so as to signify that this particular method is a test and needs to be executed by the test runner. For example, the method that is responsible for testing our `strip_password` method is named as `test_strip_password()`:

```
def test_strip_password(self):
```

Inside the method definition, we are using assertions to validate if the output of a particular method is what we expected or not. For example, the `assertEqual` method is used to assert whether the parameter 1 matches with the parameter 2 or not:

```
self.assertEqual(strip_password(' saurabh '), 'saurabh')
```

Once these tests have been defined, the next thing to do is define an entry point for our test file when it is run through the Terminal. This is done by calling the `unittest.main()` method from the entry point. Once the call is made, the test cases mentioned in the file are run and an output is displayed, as follows:

```
python helpers_test.py
..
------------------------------------------------------------------
Ran 2 tests in 0.020s

OK
```

This is as easy as it can get when you want to write unit tests with Python. Now, it's time for us to move on to something that is more important. Let's write some unit tests for our demo application.

Writing unit tests with pytest

As we discussed, writing unit tests in Python can be done with a number of options at our disposal. For example, in the previous section, we utilized Python's `unittest` library to write our unit tests. In this section, we will move on to writing unit tests with `pytest`, which is a framework for writing unit tests for applications.

But what benefits does `pytest` provide that mean we should move toward it? Why can't we just stick with the `unittest` library that comes bundled with Python?

Although the `unittest` library provides us with a lot of flexibility coupled with the ease of use, there are still a number of improvements that `pytest` brings to the table, so let's take a look at what these improvements are:

- **Modified assertions:** In the example for writing test cases with `unittest`, we saw the use of assert statements and how they are used to validate the outcome of a particular test. With `pytest`, these assert statements have been modified to provide more descriptive errors that are causing the test to fail.
- **Fixtures:** The `unittest` library provides us with the functionality of setting up a test environment before executing a test and cleaning the environment once the test has been executed. `pytest` provides something similar but better through fixtures. These fixtures can be used to set up the environment, and can also be reused in different tests. One of the great advantages of using fixtures is the fact that the use of fixtures can be scoped. A fixture can be made available to a function, a class, or a complete module.
- **Write tests as you desire:** With the `unittest` library, the tests need to be encapsulated into a class for them to run. This kind of forces the use of the object-oriented style for writing unit tests. With `pytest`, this is not the case and the developer is free to write the test cases in procedural or object-oriented style as they desire.

Now, we have an idea about the advantages that are provided by `pytest` over the use of the `unittest` library. Now, let's take a look at how can we write a simple test for our BugZot application.

Let's set up pytest

The `pytest` framework is a standalone framework that comes as a separate library outside of standardized Python distribution. Before we can start writing tests using the `pytest`, we need to install `pytest`. Getting `pytest` installed is not a big task, and can be done easily by running the following command:

```
pip install pytest
```

Now, before we start writing tests for our application, let's first create a new directory named *tests* under our application directory and at the same level as where our `run.py` resides, to store these test cases by running the following command:

```
mkdir -p bugzot/tests
```

Now, it's time to write our first test with `pytest`.

Writing our first test with pytest

In our demo application, we defined a number of models that will be used to store the data in the database. As our first test, let's target writing a test case for our models.

The following code snippet shows a simple test case for our User model:

```
'''
File: test_user_model.py
Description: Tests the User database model
'''
import sys
import pytest

# Setup the import path for our application
sys.path.append('.') # Add the current rootdir as the module path
# import our bugzot model we want to test
from bugzot.models import User

@pytest.fixture(scope='module')
def create_user():
  user = User(username='joe', email='joe@gmail.com', password='Hello123')
  return user
def test_user_creation(create_user):
  assert create_user.email == 'joe@gmail.com'
  assert create_user.username == 'joe'
```

With this, we are done writing our most basic unit test for the user model. Now, let's take some time to understand what we did here.

First, we import the required libraries that we will use to build our tests. The next thing is to get our project into the system path from where the imports can be resolved. This is required because we never installed our project, nor did we set up the PYTHON_PATH to look for our project. To do this, we simply append the path of the rootdir of our project to the sys.path, as follows:

```
sys.path.append('.')
```

Once our project is in the path, we can now easily import the required model from the project, as follows:

```
from bugzot.models import User
```

Now, it's time for us to start writing a very simple test.

This test will cover the creation of a new user class object, and then we will validate if its attributes were set properly or not.

We will break this test down into two parts, where one part is responsible for creating a new `User` class object that can be reused easily, and another part where we actually write the validation logic of the test.

So, let's focus on the first part. Here, we will use one of the features that is provided by the `pytest` library known as the fixtures. Fixtures help us write logic that can be used to set up the environment before a test starts, and gets cleaned up once the test finishes. Since fixtures are built as a separate method, we can reuse these fixtures any number of times we want in any of the tests. For our test, we will build a fixture for the creation of the `User` class object. This is done by using the `@pytest.fixture` decorator. In our case, we have built a fixture named as `create_user()`, as follows:

```
@pytest.fixture(scope='module')
def create_user():
```

Once the fixture is built, we can now move on to our second part of the test. Here, we will build a simple method that is used to validate the newly created `User` class object. One important thing to note in this method, `test_user_creation()`, is how we have passed our fixture, `create_user`, as a parameter to the method. This makes sure that our fixture is run before the method logic is made to execute. The newly created object is available in the name of the fixture, as can be seen in the following statement:

```
assert create_user.email == 'joe@gmail.com'
```

Now, once this test finishes execution, any of the changes made to the test environment by the fixture will be cleaned up and then the results will be displayed.

Now, to run these tests, we can execute the following command:

```
pytest tests/
```

Any of the tests stored under the tests directory will now be executed by `pytest` and their results will be reported.

Now, we have an idea about how we can write a simple unit test for our application. The next thing for us is to write a functional test for our application so that we can validate the APIs we have created. So, let's enter the journey of writing our first functional test for the APIs we are building.

Writing functional tests with pytest

The `pytest` framework, along with its unique fixtures and the power of `flask`, allows us to write functional tests easily for our application. This allows us to test the API endpoints we have built with quite some ease.

Let's take a look at one of the sample tests for our index API endpoint, and then we will deep dive into how we wrote the test.

The following piece of code shows a sample test case written using `pytest` to test the index API endpoint:

```
'''
File: test_index_route.py
Description: Test the index API endpoint
'''
import os
import pytest
import sys
import tempfile

sys.path.append('.')
import bugzot

@pytest.fixture(scope='module')
def test_client():
  db, bugzot.app.config['DATABASE'] = tempfile.mkstemp()
  bugzot.app.config['TESTING'] = True
  test_client = bugzot.app.test_client()

  with bugzot.app.app_context():
    bugzot.db.create_all()

  yield test_client

  os.close(db)
  os.unlink(bugzot.app.config['DATABASE'])

def test_index_route(test_client):
  resp = test_client.get('/')
  assert resp.status_code == 200
```

This was a very simple functional test that we wrote for testing our index API route to see if it was working properly or not. Now, let's take a look at what we did here to get this functional test working:

The first few lines of code are more or less general, where we import some of the libraries that we will be requiring to build our tests.

The interesting work starts from the `test_client()` fixture we have built. The fixture is used to get us a flask-based test client that we can use to test our application endpoints to see if they are working correctly or not.

Since our application is a database-oriented application that will require a database to function correctly, the first thing we need to do is set up a database configuration for our application. For the purpose of testing, we can settle with an SQLite3 database that can be created quite easily in most of the operating systems. The following call provides us with the database we will be using for our testing purposes:

```
db, bugzot.app.config['DATABASE'] = tempfile.mkstemp()
```

The call returns a file descriptor to the database and a URI that we will store in the application config.

Once the database has been created, the next thing is to tell our application that it is running in a testing environment so that the error handling inside the application is disabled to improve the output of the tests. This is done easily by setting the `TESTING` flag inside the application configuration to `True`.

Flask provides us with a simple test client that we can use to run our application tests. This client can be obtained by making a call to the application `test_client()` method, as follows:

```
test_client = bugzot.app.test_client()
```

Once the test client is obtained, we need to set up the application context, which is done through calling the `app_context()` method of the Flask application.

With the application context established, we create our database by calling the `db.create_all()` method.

Once our application context is set up and a database has been created, the next thing we do is start the testing. This is achieved by yielding the test client:

```
yield test_client
```

Once this is done, the tests now execute and control transfers to the `test_index_route()` method where we simply try to load the index route by calling the `get` method of the `test_client`, as follows:

```
resp = test_client.get('/')
```

Once this is done, we check whether the API provided a valid response or not by checking the HTTP status code of the response and validating that it was a `200`, SUCCESS or not, as follows:

```
assert resp.status_code == 200
```

Once the test finishes executing, the control transfers back to the fixture and we perform our cleanup by closing the database file descriptor and removing the database file, as follows:

```
os.close(db)
os.unlink(bugzot.app.config['DATABASE'])
```

Quite simple, wasn't it? That's how we can write a simple functional test with `pytest` and `Flask`. We can even write tests that handle the user authentication and database modifications this way, but we will leave this as an exercise for you as the reader.

Summary

In this chapter, we took a look at how testing forms an important aspect of the application development project and why it is necessary. Here, we took a look at the different types of testing that are usually employed during the development life cycle and what the uses of different techniques are. We then moved on to taking a look at how we can craft our code in a way that makes testing an easy and effective process. Moving on, we started digging deeper into the Python language to see what facilities it provides for writing up tests. Here, we discovered how to use the Python `unittest` library to write unit tests, and how to run them. Moving on, we took a look at how we can utilize testing frameworks like `pytest` to write test cases for our demo application, Bugzot, and how to run these test cases. Once familiar with the art of writing test cases, we tried to understand why we need to automate the running of test cases and how we can achieve that.

With the knowledge of testing the code base, now we can take a look at one more important aspect of making our application enterprise ready. We achieve this by running our application through the performance benchmarks and by providing functionality to trace the performance bottlenecks easily inside the code base.

In the next chapter, we will take a look at how we can measure the performance of our application through the use of different tools, and how we can make sure that our code performs according to the expectations by running it through a certain set of benchmarks.

Questions

1. What are the differences between unit tests and functional tests?
2. How can we write unit test suites using Python `unittest`?
3. What is the role of fixtures in `pytest`?
4. What are scopes in `pytest` while writing fixtures?

Profiling Applications for Performance

9

Over the course of this book, we have seen how much the performance and scalability of an application matters inside an enterprise environment; with this in mind, we dedicated a significant portion of the book to understanding how to build an application that is not only performant but is also scalable.

So far, we have just seen some best practices for what we can do to build a performant and scalable application, but not how to figure out whether a particular piece of code in our application is slow and what might be causing it.

For any enterprise-grade application, improving its performance and scalability is an ongoing process, as the user base of the application keeps growing and the application's functionality continues to get more and more sophisticated. All of this effort requires an understanding of what is going on inside the application and on which parts of the application we need to focus for possible optimizations that can give us significant results.

In this chapter, we'll look into loopholes of how we can point out which portion of our application is turning out to be a performance bottleneck, and how we can build our application in such a way that we are able to track down the potential bottlenecks quite easily.

Over the course of this chapter, we will get to learn about the following:

- The behind the scenes of performance bottlenecks and their causes
- Profiling bottlenecks inside the code base
- Building an application with performance profiling built into its core

Technical requirements

The code listings in this book can be found under `chapter09` directory at `https://github.com/PacktPublishing/Hands-On-Enterprise-Application-Development-with-Python`.

The code samples related to the profiling and benchmarking of bugzot sample application can be found under the `chapter06` directory itself under the tests module of the code base.

The code samples can be cloned by running the following command:

```
git clone
https://github.com/PacktPublishing/Hands-On-Enterprise-Application-Developm
ent-with-Python
```

This chapter also has some dependencies on third-party Python libraries, which can be easily installed by running the following command on your development system:

```
pip install memory_profiler
```

Behind the scenes of performance bottlenecks

Before an application enters the development phase, there is a thorough discussion on what the application is supposed to do, how it will do it, and what kind of third-party components the application will need to interact with. Once all of this is finalized, the application enters the development phase, where the developers are responsible for building the application in such a way that the tasks to be performed by the application can be achieved in the most efficient manner possible. This efficiency is usually measured in terms of how much time an application takes to complete a provided task and how many resources it uses while working on that task.

When the application is deployed into production, the real test of the application begins. Most of the time, if the work being done by the application is the same as was defined during the requirements-gathering and design phases, the application usually performs well and provides an adequate scalability. But as developers, we know this is seldom the case.

Most of the time, workloads in production differ significantly from what was conceptualized during the design phase. Usually the data that the application is dealing with grows over time as the application is used in production and can become orders of magnitude larger than what was initially conceived during the application development phase. Another factor that may impact the performance are the side-effects exerted by the production environment on the application such as poor execution performance of certain workloads.

The result is that some of the workloads are efficient while the performance of others suffers. This deviation can range from very small and insignificant which may easily get unnoticed to considerably significant that may disrupt the regular workflow of the organization.

Once these kinds of issues are identified, developers work to optimize them over time and improve the efficiency of completing a provided workload. This is perfectly normal in any enterprise or consumer environment, because some of the issues can only be identified when the application is subject to varied workloads in production, which differ significantly from the ones that were tested during the internal testing phases.

To fix these performance bottlenecks in workloads, you should have an idea of why and where a particular bottleneck is happening, and then a developer can work to fix the bottleneck or to improve it so that its impact is reduced. So, let's take a look at some of the possible factors that might cause performance issues, and then we'll move to trying to understand how we can figure out the places where these performance issues are happening and how can we possibly fix them.

Looking at the causes of performance bottlenecks

Usually, performance bottlenecks can be caused by a number of factors, which may include shortage of physical resources in the environment where the application is deployed or choosing a bad algorithm to process a particular workload when a better algorithm was available. Let's take a look at some of the possible issues that may lead to performance bottlenecks in a deployed application:

- **Not having enough hardware resources:** Initially, most of the bottlenecks in performance and scalability are due to poor planning of the hardware resources required to run an application. This may happen due to incorrect estimations or a sudden unplanned surge in the user base of the application. When this happens, the existing hardware resources get stressed and the system slows down.

- **Incorrect design choices:** In `Chapter 2`, *Design Patterns – Making a Choice*, we looked at how important design choices are to any enterprise-grade application. Constantly allocating new objects for something that could have been done through the allocation of a single shared object is going to impact the application's performance by not only stressing the available resources but also by causing unnecessary delays due to repeated allocations of objects.
- **Inefficient algorithms:** The places where a large amount of data is being processed or the systems that perform a large amount of calculations to generate a result may often see degraded performance due to choosing inefficient algorithms. A careful study of the availability of alternative algorithms or in-place algorithmic optimizations may help boost the performance of the application.
- **Memory leaks:** In large applications, there could be places where memory leaks may happen in an unexpected manner. Although this is difficult in garbage-collected languages such as Python, it's still a possibility. There could be times when objects, although no longer in use, still aren't garbage collected because of the way they have been mapped inside the application. Over a longer period of runtime, this will cause the available memory to decrease and eventually will bring the application to a halt.

These were a few reasons why performance bottlenecks in a system happen. Fortunately for us as software developers, we have a number of tools that can help us pinpoint bottlenecks, as well as find things such as memory leaks or even just profile the memory usage of individual portions.

With this knowledge about why some performance bottlenecks happen, it's time for us to move onto learning how to look for these performance bottlenecks in an application and then trying to understand some of the ways we can reduce their impact.

Probing an application for performance issues

Performance is a critical component of any enterprise-grade application, and you cannot afford to have an application that slows down often and impacts the business process of the whole organization. Unfortunately, performance issues are also one of the most complex issues to understand and debug. This complexity arises because there's no standard way to access the performance of a particular piece of code inside the application, and because once the application has been developed, the complete flow of code needs to be understood so as to pinpoint the possible areas that might cause a specific performance issue.

As developers, we can reduce these hardships by building our application in such a way that the application reports its own performance metrics. Along with this, we can write benchmark tests that run alongside unit tests to help us flag the components that may become a possible bottleneck once the application is deployed in production. So, let's take a look at how we can achieve these goals within our application development cycles.

Writing performance benchmarks

Let's start with a discussion about how we, as software developers, can build the application in a way that helps us flag the performance bottlenecks early in the development cycle and how we can make our life easy in terms of debugging these bottlenecks.

The first and most important thing we can do during our application development cycle is to write benchmark tests for the individual components of our application.

Benchmark tests are simple tests that aim to evaluate the performance of a particular piece of code by executing it for multiple iterations and averaging the time required to execute the code over those iterations. Do you remember hearing the name of a library known as Pytest, which we used to write unit tests in Chapter 8, *Writing Testable Code*?

We're going to utilize the same library to help us write our performance benchmark tests. But, before we can make Pytest usable for writing benchmark tests, we need to make it understand the benchmarking concept, which is very easy with Python, specifically because of the availability of a huge Python ecosystem. To make Pytest understand the concept of benchmarking, we are going to import a new library known as pytest-benchmark, which adds benchmarking fixtures to Pytest and allows us to write benchmarking tests for our application. To do this, we need to run the following command:

```
pip install pytest-benchmark
```

Once we have the library installed, we are ready to write our performance-benchmarking tests for our application.

Writing our first benchmark

With the required library installed, it's time for us to write our first performance benchmark. For this, we will use a simple example and then move forward to understand how we can write a benchmark test for our application:

```
'''
File: sample_benchmark_test.py
Description: A simple benchmark test
'''
import pytest
import time
def sample_method():
  time.sleep(0.0001)
  return 0

def test_sample_benchmark(benchmark):
  result = benchmark(sample_method)
  assert result == 0

if __name__ == '__main__':
  pytest.main()
```

We have written our first benchmark test. A very simple one indeed, but there are quite a few things which we need to understand to see what we are doing here:

First, as we started writing the benchmark test, we imported `pytest`. When we did this, there was one more thing that happened behind the scenes without us knowing: the import of the `pytest-benchmark` library, which `pytest` included automatically.

With the inclusion of `pytest-benchmark`, we got hold of an important fixture, named `benchmark`, which allows us to run benchmark tests.

The benchmark fixture is a callable fixture that takes in the name of the method that needs to be benchmarked and, once executed, runs the benchmark on the method.

For our sample benchmark test, we create a simple method, known as `sample_method()`, which does nothing except go into sleep for a fraction of a second and then return.

Next, we define a new test method, known as `test_sample_benchmark()`, to which we pass the benchmark fixture as a parameter. Now, inside the method, we pass the `sample_method()` method to the benchmark fixture:

```
result = benchmark(sample_method)
```

Once we run this test, it will run a benchmark over the method and will provide us with the results of the call through which we can also validate the output of the tested method.

Now, let's run this test to see what kind of results it produces for us. To do this, we execute the following command:

```
python3 simple_benchmark_test.py
```

Once the test runs, we see the following output:

```
=============================================== test session starts
=================================================
platform linux -- Python 3.6.7, pytest-4.0.1, py-1.7.0, pluggy-0.8.0
benchmark: 3.1.1 (defaults: timer=time.perf_counter disable_gc=False
min_rounds=5 min_time=0.000005 max_time=1.0 calibration_precision=10
warmup=False warmup_iterations=100000)
rootdir: /home/sbadhwar, inifile:
plugins: benchmark-3.1.1
collected 1 item

simple_benchmark_test.py . [100%]


----------------------------------------------------- benchmark: 1 tests -
-----------------------------------------------------
Name (time in us) Min Max Mean StdDev Median IQR Outliers OPS (Kops/s)
Rounds Iterations
-----------------------------------------------------------------------------
-----------------------------------------------------
test_sample_benchmark 199.0000 1,081.0000 791.5421 97.5851 821.0000 24.7500
207;368 1.2634 1271 1
-----------------------------------------------------------------------------
-----------------------------------------------------

Legend:
  Outliers: 1 Standard Deviation from Mean; 1.5 IQR (InterQuartile Range)
from 1st Quartile and 3rd Quartile.
  OPS: Operations Per Second, computed as 1 / Mean
=============================================== 1 passed in 2.19 seconds
=================================================
```

Now, if we take a look at the output produced, we can see that the results show us the name of the method that was benchmarked, followed by the different mathematical calculations related to its runtime and the operations the method was able to perform in a given second, as well as for how many iterations of the method call these results have been gathered.

Now, what if we wanted to benchmark the method for more than one iteration? This is a simple feat to achieve. All we have to do is to mention another parameter to our benchmark call and specify the number of iterations:

```
result = benchmark.pedantic(sample_method, iterations=1000)
```

Here, the `benchmark.pedantic` method helps us to set up the benchmark to customize it for various parameters, which may include the number of iterations and the number of rounds the benchmark should run to provide the results.

Writing an API benchmark

With this, we know how to write a simple benchmark. So, how about writing something similar for our API? Let's take a look at how we can modify one of our API tests that we used to validate the functioning of our index API endpoint and see how we can run a benchmark on that.

The following code modifies our existing index API test case to include a benchmark test for the API:

```
'''
File: test_index_benchmark.py
Description: Benchmark the index API endpoint
'''
import os
import pytest
import sys
import tempfile

sys.path.append('.')
import bugzot

@pytest.fixture(scope='module')
def test_client():
    db, bugzot.app.config['DATABASE'] = tempfile.mkstemp()
    bugzot.app.config['TESTING'] = True
    test_client = bugzot.app.test_client()

    with bugzot.app.app_context():
        bugzot.db.create_all()

    yield test_client

    os.close(db)
    os.unlink(bugzot.app.config['DATABASE'])
```

```
def test_index_benchmark(test_client, benchmark):
  resp = benchmark(test_client.get, "/")
  assert resp.status_code == 200
```

In the preceding code, all we did to make the API endpoint benchmark was add a new method, known as `test_index_benchmark()`, which takes in two fixtures as a parameter. One of the fixtures is responsible for setting up our application instance, and the second fixture—the benchmark fixture—is used to run the benchmark on the client API endpoint and generate the results.

Also, one important thing to note here is how we were able to mix the unit test code with the benchmark code so that we do not need to write two different methods for each class of the test; all of this is made possible by Pytest, which allows us to run the benchmark on the method as well as allow us to validate if the method being tested provides a correct result or not through the use of a single testing method.

Now we know how to write benchmark tests inside the application. But what if we had to debug something that was slow but for which the benchmark operation doesn't flags any concern. What can we do here? Fortunately for us, Python provides a lot of options that allow us to test for any kind of performance anomalies that may happen inside the code. So, let's spend some time looking over them.

Doing component-level performance analysis

With Python, a lot of facilities come built-in and others can be easily implemented with third-party libraries. So, let's take a look at what python has in store for us for running component-level performance analysis.

Measuring slow operations with timeit

Python provides a very nice module, known as `timeit`, that we can use to run some simple time-analysis tasks on small snippets of code or to understand how much time a particular method call is taking.

Let's take a look at a simple script that shows us how we can use `timeit` to understand how much time a particular method is taking, and then we will understand a bit more about how we can use the functionality provided by `timeit` to run time-profiling for the applications that we intend to build.

The following code snippet shows a simple use of `timeit` for running timing analysis on a method call:

```
import timeit

def calc_sum():
    sum = 0
    for i in range(0, 100):
        sum = sum + i
    return sum
if __name__ == '__main__':
    setup = "from __main__ import calc_sum"
    print(timeit.timeit("calc_sum()", setup=setup))
```

On running this file, we get an output that looks like this:

```
7.255408144999819
```

As we can see from the preceding example, we can use `timeit` to do a simple time analysis for the execution of a given method.

Now, this is handy, but we cannot go on writing multiple setup statements when we have to time more than a couple of methods. What should we do here? There should be a simple way to achieve this.

So, how about we create a simple decorator that we can use to time our methods that may need time profiling.

Let's create this simple decorator method. The following example shows us how to write a decorator method that we can use later to do time comparisons on our methods:

```
import time
def time_profile(func):
    """Decorator for timing the execution of a method."""
    def timer_func(*args, **kwargs):
        start = time.time()
        value = func(*args, **kwargs)
        end = time.time()
        total_time = end - start
        output_msg = "The method {func} took {total_time} to execute"
        print(output_msg.format(func=func, total_time=total_time))
        return value
    return timer_func
```

This was a decorator that we created. Inside the decorator, we take in the function that we want to profile as a parameter, along with any of the arguments that were passed to it. Now, we initialize the start time for the function, followed by a call to the function and then we store the end time of the call once the execution of the function returns. Based on this, we calculate the total time it took for the function to execute.

But how can we use this decorator to profile our methods? The following example shows a sample of that:

```
@time_profile
def calc_sum():
    sum = 0
    for i in range(100):
        sum = sum+i
    return sum
```

This was very simple and far easier to do than importing individual methods again and again for the timing profile.

So, our `timeit` method is a very simple method to use and can provide us with some basic information about how much time it took for a particular method to execute. We can even profile individual statements with these methods. But what if we wanted a more detailed explanation of how much time individual statements are taking inside a particular method or to understand what exactly is causing a given method to slow down? For things such as these, our simple timing solution isn't an ideal option. We need something more sophisticated.

As a matter of fact, Python provides us with some built-in profilers that we can use to perform in-depth performance profiling of an application. Let's take a look at how we can do this.

Profiling with cProfile

The Python library provides us with an application profiler which can help ease the life of the developers by allowing to easily profile not only the whole application, but also the individual components of the application.

Profile is a built-in code profiler that comes bundled as a module with some of the python distributions. The module is able to collect the information about the individual method calls that have been made, along with the profiling of any of the calls made to third-party functions.

Once these details are collected, the module provides us with a host of statistics that can help us get a better picture of what's going on inside the component. Before we dive into what details are collected and represented, let's see how we can use cProfile in our application.

The following code snippet shows us a sample of how to use cProfile in our code:

```
import cProfile
import hashlib
def encrypt_password(password, salt):
    """Encrypt the provided password.

    Keyword arguments:
    password - The password to be encrypted
    salt - The salt to be used for padding the password

    Returns:
        String
    """
    profiler = cProfile.Profile()
    profiler.enable()
    passwd_hash = hashlib.pbkdf2_hmac('sha256', password.encode('utf-8'),
salt, 10000).hex()
    profiler.disable()
    profiler.print_stats()
        return passwd_hash
```

In the preceding code, we enabled the profiling using cProfile. Getting cProfile to work for us is a straightforward process. We first import the module as usual through the use of import statements. Once the module has been imported, we need to create a new cProfile Profile instance. This is done by calling the `Profile()` constructor of the cProfile module:

```
profiler = cProfile.Profile()
```

Once the profiler instance is created, we start the profiler by calling the `enable()` method on the profiler. After this, whatever operations we do will be profiled by our profiler. Once we are done executing, we call the `disable()` method on the profiler to stop the collection of the metrics.

Now, to get the collected statistics, we make a call to the `print_stats()` method of the profiler instance that was created.

Let's take a look at what statistics were generated based on when we ran the preceding piece of code:

```
        3 function calls in 0.015 seconds

   Ordered by: standard name

   ncalls tottime percall cumtime percall filename:lineno(function)
        1 0.015 0.015 0.015 0.015 {built-in method _hashlib.pbkdf2_hmac}
        1 0.000 0.000 0.000 0.000 {method 'disable' of '_lsprof.Profiler'
objects}
        1 0.000 0.000 0.000 0.000 {method 'encode' of 'str' objects}
```

As we can see from the preceding output, we got some detailed statistics about what our method did. These statistics consist of a number of details, such as the function that was called, how many calls were made to the function (`ncalls`), the total time spent in a function (`tottime`), and how much time an individual call took (`percall`).

These are some really important statistics from a production-grade-application point of view because these statistics not only provide the information about a particular slow operation, but also about how many times that operation was called so that it can be determined why something is performing slower than expected.

Now, we know of a built-in profiler that can help us profile the calls with much more timing detail than we were doing previously, and this can help us in understanding the slowdowns. What if the performance issue was not a slowdown but an anomaly related to the increased memory usage of the application while doing a certain job? Our cProfile profiler doesn't provides us with those details, and we need to know about them to properly address the issue.

For this, we get out of our comfort zone of utilizing the Python standard library, and move into the third-party libraries that are available to us through the use of the python package manager.

Profiling for memory usage with memory_profiler

Memory profiling forms a very important aspect of the performance analysis of an application. When building an application, there are places where we may implement an incorrect mechanism of dealing with the dynamically allocated objects and hence may land up in a situation where these objects which are no longer in use are still having a reference pointing to them preventing their garbage collection by the Garbage Collector.

This results in the growth of the application-memory usage over time, causing the application to come to a halt once the system runs out of memory that can be allocated to the application for performing its regular activities.

Now, to address these kinds of issues, we don't require a profiler that will help us analyze the call stack of the application and provide us details about how much time an individual call took. Instead, what we need here is a profiler that can tell us about the memory trends of an application, such as how much memory individual methods might be consuming and how that memory grows as the application continues to run.

This is the place where memory_profiler comes in, which is a third-party module that we can easily include in our application to allow memory profiling. But, before we dive into how to use memory_profiler, we need to get the module into our development environment first. The following line of code fetches the required module into our development environment:

```
pip install memory_profiler
```

Once the memory profiler has been fetched into the developer environment, we are now ready to get up and running with it. Let's take a look at a sample program and see how we can use memory_profiler to understand the memory usage patterns of our application.

The following code snippet shows us an example of how we can use memory_profiler:

```
from memory_profiler import profile

@profile
def calc_sum():
    sum = 0
    for i in range(100):
        sum = sum + i
    print(str(sum))

if __name__ == '__main__':
    calc_sum()
```

Now, with the code in place, let's try to understand what we did here.

At the start, we imported a decorator known as profile, which is provided by the memory_profiler library. This decorator is used to notify memory_profiler of which methods needs to be profiled for the memory usage.

To enable memory profiling for a method, all we need to do is decorate that method with the decorator. For example, in our sample application code, we decorated the calc_sum() method with the decorator.

Now, let's run our sample code and see what we get as an output by running the following command:

python3 memory_profile_example.py

Once the command is executed, we get the following output:

```
4950
Filename: memory_profile.py

Line # Mem usage Increment Line Contents
====================================================
     3 11.6 MiB 11.6 MiB @profile
     4 def calc_sum():
     5 11.6 MiB 0.0 MiB sum = 0
     6 11.6 MiB 0.0 MiB for i in range(100):
     7 11.6 MiB 0.0 MiB sum = sum + i
     8 11.6 MiB 0.0 MiB print(str(sum))
```

As we can see from the preceding output, we got some detailed statistics about the memory allocation for the method. The output provided us information about how much memory was being used and how much memory increment each of the steps caused to the application.

Now, let's take one more example to see how the memory allocation changes when one method calls another method. The following code showcases this:

```
from memory_profiler import profile

@profile
def calc_sum():
    sum = 0
    for i in range(100):
        sum = sum + i
    say_hello()
    print(str(sum))

def say_hello():
    lst = []
    for i in range(10000):
        lst.append(i)

if __name__ == '__main__':
    calc_sum()
```

On executing the preceding code, we get to see the following output:

```
Line # Mem usage Increment Line Contents
==================================================
    3 11.6 MiB 11.6 MiB @profile
    4 def calc_sum():
    5 11.6 MiB 0.0 MiB sum = 0
    6 11.6 MiB 0.0 MiB for i in range(100):
    7 11.6 MiB 0.0 MiB sum = sum + i
    8 11.7 MiB 0.1 MiB say_hello()
    9 11.7 MiB 0.0 MiB print(str(sum))
```

As we can see, when a call to the `say_hello()` method was made, the call caused an increment of 0.1 MB of memory usage. This is quite a handy library in case we suspect that there's some memory leak that may be happening somewhere in the code.

Collecting live performance data

So far, we have seen how we can use the different profiling tools to profile the performance of the application when needed so as to assist us in figuring out which portion of the code is causing performance bottlenecks. But how will we know whether an operation is taking long than it should?

One of the answers to this could be the slow response times being reported by users, but that could have quite a lot of factors behind it, which may involve a slowdown at the user end only.

There are a few other mechanisms that we can use to monitor the performance issues in our application in real time. So, let's take a look at one of these methods, which allows us to gather information about the time taken for individual requests.

Logging performance metrics

Inside an application, there could be several steps. Each of these steps can be profiled for their performance through the use of different tools. One of the most basic tools is logging. In this, we collect the execution time of the different methods and keep the entry for it inside the log file.

The following snippet of code shows a small example of how this can be achieved inside the demo application that we built in `Chapter 6`, *Example – Building BugZot*:

```
@app.before_request
def before_request_handler():
    g.start_time = time.time()

@app.teardown_request
def teardown_request_handler(exception=None):
    execution_time = time.time() - g.start_time
    app.logger.info("Request URL: {} took {} seconds".format(request.url,
str(execution_time)))
```

This was a simple code and logs the execution time of every API endpoint called in a request. What we do here is very minimalistic. We first create a `before_request` handler, which initializes a property, `start_time`, in the flask global namespace. Once this is done, the request is sent to processing. Once the request has been processed, it goes to the `teardown` handler that we have defined.

Once the request reaches this `teardown` handler, we calculate the total time it took to process the request and log it inside the application logs.

This kind of approach allows us to query or process our log files to understand how much time every request is taking and which API endpoints are taking the longest amount of time.

Avoiding performance bottlenecks

Over the last few sections, we took a look at the different ways we can profile our application for different kinds of performance bottlenecks that may involve slowdowns to memory leaks. But once we're aware of these issues and why they're happening, what other options do we have to prevent them from occurring again?

Fortunately, we have a couple of helpful guidelines that may help prevent performance bottlenecks or can limit the possible impact of these bottlenecks. So, let's take a look at some of these guidelines:

- **Choosing the correct design patterns:** Design patterns are an important choice in the application. For example, a logging object doesn't need to be reinitialized in every submodule of the application and can easily be reused as a global object or a shared object. Making a logging class a singleton can help us in this.

- **Cleaning up the objects as soon as they go out of scope:** As a developer, we need to take care of cleaning up the objects as soon as they go out of scope. One of the most basic mistakes that happens during development is keeping the objects in a list or dictionary to track them and later forgetting to clean them up. This causes the memory usage to grow.
- **Using native libraries:** Python allows the use of native extensions. These are the extensions that have been compiled internally and are optimized for the machine they are running on. This provides a huge boost in the performance of an application in comparison to using the methods that need to be converted into bytecode every time they are supposed to be used.
- **Monitoring the Garbage Collector:** In some of the applications that are allocating a large chunk of objects, one of the bottlenecks that may happen is due to the runs of the garbage collector. In these applications, the garbage collector needs to be monitored and optimized where required, so that we can avoid the slowdowns it may cause.

Summary

In this chapter, we took a look at how the performance of an application is an important aspect of the software's development and what kind of issues usually cause performance bottlenecks to appear in the application. Moving forward, we took a look at the different ways in which we can profile an application for performance issues. This involved, first the writing of benchmark tests for individual components as well as the individual APIs and then moving to more specific, component-level analysis, where we took a look at different ways of profiling the components. These profiling techniques included the use of simple timing profiles of methods using the Python `timeit` module, then we moved on to using more sophisticated techniques with Python cProfile and covered memory profiling. Another topic we took a look at during our journey is the use of logging techniques to help us evaluate slow requests whenever we want. Finally, we took a look at some of the general principles that can help us to prevent performance bottlenecks inside an application.

In the next chapter, we will take a look at how important it is to secure our application. If not done, it'll not only pave the way to serious data theft, but also a lot of liabilities and can erode the trust of your users.

Questions

1. What factors can cause a performance bottleneck when the application is deployed?
2. What are the different ways in which we can run a time profile on a method?
3. What may cause a memory leak in Python, which is a garbage-collected language?
4. How can we profile an API response and figure out what could be the cause of its slowing down?
5. Can choosing an incorrect design pattern result in a performance bottleneck?

Securing Your Application

10

With all the chatter about the performance and scalability of an application, and the best practices to ensure an application is stable in the enterprise environment, we have covered a lot. We got to learn about how important the user experience is to make an application successful inside an enterprise. But do you think we are missing something here?

Imagine that we had all the components for building a successful enterprise application and that we were able to make it scale, while also providing a decent response time to the user with the fewest deviations from the expected behavior. However, it's easy for anyone to just access the records from our application. What if there are loopholes that allow a user to gather sensitive data from the application without even performing a login? Yes, that's the missing link: the application security. Inside an enterprise, the security of an application is a really big factor. An application that is not secure may leak sensitive and confidential data to unintended parties and can also wreak legal havoc on the organization.

Application security is a big topic and even a 500-page book might not be enough to cover the topic in depth. But over the course of this chapter, we will go through a quick primer of how to handle application security and make our users feel secure while using our application.

As a reader, by the end of this chapter, you will have learned about the following:

- The importance of enterprise application security
- Different types of attack vectors that are used to breach application security
- Common mistakes in application development giving rise to breaches
- Making your application secure

Technical requirements

For this chapter, we expect the user to have an understanding of the basics of configuring a web server and basic knowledge of network communication.

Enterprise application security

Application security is such a big topic, where you might be talking about how to protect confidential data from leaking out, to making the application resilient enough to deal with defacement attacks.

When it comes to the enterprises, the topic becomes even more serious. This happens because most enterprises are dealing with a huge amount of personal data, which may include information that can be used to identify individual users or information related to their financial details, such as credit card numbers, CVV codes, or payment records.

Most enterprises spend a huge amount of their capital on improving the security of their business because they cannot afford to have a weak link in their chain that may result in a breach of the confidential information that they store. The repercussions that a breach may bring to an organization start with fines imposed on the organization that failed to maintain the security of the confidential data and extend to a loss of trust that may bring an organization to bankruptcy.

Security is no joke and there is no one-solution-fits-all approach. Rather, to make things more complicated, the attacks that have been used to breach an organization's security barriers have become more and more sophisticated and harder to build protection against. If we take a look at the history of cybersecurity breaches, we can find examples that show how hard a cybersecurity issue can hit. For example, in recent years, we saw a number of breaches involving major organizations where one of the organizations saw a breach of more than 3,000,000,000 user accounts; in another attack, a gaming network saw a security breach and remained down for approximately a month, costing the organization a huge amount of financial losses.

There is one thing that the field of cybersecurity demonstrates clearly: it is an ever-evolving field where new types of attacks are discovered every day and new mitigations are being researched to overcome them in a timely manner.

Now, let's take a look at understanding why enterprise application security is an important topic and one that should not be compromised.

The importance of enterprise security

Most enterprises, no matter their size, deal with a decent amount of user data. This data may involve something about the users that might be available publicly, or it may involve data that is confidential. Once this data enters the storage of the organization, it becomes the responsibility of the organization to protect the confidentiality of the data so that it cannot be accessed by any unauthorized party without permission.

To achieve this, most enterprises amp up their cybersecurity and build multiple barriers to prevent unauthorized access to their user-data systems. So, let's take a look at some of the reasons why enterprise security is so important:

- **Confidentiality of data:** A lot of organizations may possess data that can be deemed confidential in nature. This may involve the storage of data that relates to its users or to the business practices of the organization, such as information about their business plan or upcoming products, that should not be disclosed to any unauthorized person.
- **Maintaining user trust:** When a user onboards a particular application, they also put their trust in the organization that is going to deal with their information. They expect that the data they have provided will be kept confidential and no one who is not authorized to access that data will gain access to it. Once a cybersecurity breach happens, users quickly lose trust in the organization and are wary of sharing data with them.
- **The growth of devices connected to the internet:** For organizations that are dealing with the development of products that stay connected to the internet to provide users with a desired functionality, the concept of cybersecurity becomes even more important. This is because these devices can be used to spy on their users or to collect highly sensitive information about the users that can be used to target them individually. The security of the devices and the ways they are communicating with the outside world become highly important in these scenarios so as to avoid any kind of information leak.
- **Compliance with the law:** Most countries have their own set of laws that defines the collection and security of its citizens' data, and any organization that is operating in a country must adhere to these laws. Most of these laws impose heavy fines over the organizations involved in an incident of cybersecurity breach.

So, now we have an idea about why it is important for organizations to maintain the security of their systems. But doing this is not an easy task, and most organizations face a wide variety of challenges in dealing with the security of their systems. But why does this happen? What's really a challenge here? Let's take a look.

Challenges in system security

The information technology field is growing at a rapid pace, with new technologies popping up every day. The mode of communication between two parties is also evolving, providing more efficient long-distance communication. But this evolution comes up with its own set of challenges with respect to the security of systems. Let's take a look at the challenges that make system security difficult for organizations:

- **The increasing amount of data:** With most organizations building their systems to leverage AI and ML to provide more personalized experience to their users, they are also gathering a huge amount of information about their users so as to improve recommendations. This huge amount of data storage makes the security of that data more difficult to maintain, because now more and more confidential information is being retained, making the system a lucrative shot for the attackers.
- **Distribution of data over public service providers:** A lot of enterprises are now cutting down on their storage infrastructure and are becoming more and more reliant on third-party public storage providers, which provide the same amount of storage at much lower costs, along with reduced maintenance costs. This also puts the enterprise security at risk because now the data is governed by the security policies of the third-party service provider, and the owner of the data has very little control over the security policy of the data through which it is protected. A single breach on the part of the storage service provider can expose the data of multiple users of different organizations.
- **The increasing number of devices connected to the internet:** With more and more devices joining the internet, the attack surface also increases. If even a single device has a weak segment inside it, be it in terms of the encryption standard or because of not implementing proper access controls, the security of the whole system can be breached easily.

- **Sophisticated attacks:** The attacks have became more and more sophisticated, where the attackers are now using day-zero vulnerabilities in systems and even utilizing vulnerabilities that have not yet been discovered by the organization. These attacks compromise a large amount of data and pose as a huge security risk to the whole system. To complicate matters even more, since the vulnerabilities are new, they don't have an immediate solution, resulting in a delayed response, or at times even a delayed identification that an attack occurred.

- **Increase in state-sponsored attacks:** With the ever increasing move to the Information Technology powered communication and processes in the whole world, the context of wars is also changing. Where wars were previously fought on the ground, now they are being fought over the network, and this has given rise to state-sponsored attacks. These attacks usually target enterprises to either collect intelligence or to cause major disruptions. The problem with state-sponsored attacks is the fact that these attacks are highly sophisticated in nature and utilize a huge amount of resources, which makes them difficult to overcome.

With this, we now know what are the different factors that make it hard for the enterprises to improve the security of their systems. This is why cybersecurity is always playing a catch-up game, where the enterprises are improving their security against the ever changing attack vectors being used by the attackers to attack the IT systems.

Now, with this knowledge, it's time for us to understand what really affects application security. Only with this knowledge of the different attack vectors can we move forward and make our application secure against attacks. So, let's embark on this journey.

Taking a look at the attack vectors

Every attack that breaches the security of the system or takes it down, exploits either one or the other vulnerability of the system the application is running on. These vulnerabilities differ for every kind of application. An application that has been built natively for a system may have different attack vectors than an application that has been developed for the web.

To adequately protect the application against attacks, we need to understand the different attack vectors that are used against the different application types.

For here onwards, we will take a brief look at two of the most common application types and the attack vectors that may be used to target those applications.

Security issues with native applications

Native applications are those applications that have been built specifically for the platform they are running on. These applications take advantage of the libraries and functions that are provided by a given platform to make the best use of the platform features. The security issues that may be experienced by these applications are usually the security issues that affect the underlying platform on which these applications are running, or because of the vulnerabilities that have been left by the application developers. So, let's take a look at some of the issues that affect the security of native applications:

- **Vulnerabilities of the underlying platform:** When an application runs over a platform, its functionality is governed by what the underlying platform exposes. If the underlying platform is vulnerable to security issues, the applications running on top of the platform will also be vulnerable, unless they implement proper measures to mitigate those vulnerabilities at the application level. These kinds of issues may involve issues with the hardware, such as the recent Spectre and Meltdown vulnerabilities that affected the x86 platform.

- **Use of third-party libraries:** Some applications that use third-party libraries, specifically the ones for implementing security inside the application, can indeed leave the application more vulnerable to security breaches if the developer stops maintaining those libraries or if there are some vulnerabilities that are left unfixed. Usually, a better alternative is to use the libraries that are provided by the platform itself, at least for the use case of implementing security in the application and not utilizing undocumented platform APIs, which may have unexplained security implications for the use of the application.

- **Unencrypted storage of data:** In case an application that may involve the storage and retrieval of data stores, the data in an unencrypted format may cause the data to be accessed by untrusted sources and may leave the data vulnerable to misuse. An application should make sure that the data it is storing is in an encrypted form.

- **Unencrypted communication with third parties:** A lot of applications these days depend upon third-party services to achieve a particular functionality. This is true, even inside a corporate network where an application might be making a call to a third-party authentication server inside the network to validate the user's identity. If this communication between the applications is unencrypted, it can lead to attacks, such as a man-in-the-middle attack.

- **Avoiding bound checks:** Those native applications that are implementing their own memory management techniques may become vulnerable in case the developers of the application miss a possible bounds check, which may allow an attacker to access data outside the application boundaries. This may cause a huge breach of the system's security, where data not only from the affected application but also from the other applications is left exposed.

This is a non-exhaustive list of issues that may affect the security of native applications. Some of these issues can be fixed easily, while others require a lot of effort from the application developers as well as the platform provider to mitigate the possible security breaches.

Now, with the knowledge of possible attack vectors that may affect the native apps, it's time for us to move on to understanding the attack vectors that may affect the web applications.

Security issues with web applications

Web applications have been seeing an ever-growing rise in their usage. With the increasing use of the internet, more and more organizations are shifting their day-to-day office work to the web applications that help establish a connect between the different offices located in different geographies. But these advantages come with their own costs in terms of security.

The security of web applications has been a challenging domain due to the sheer amount of ways an attack can take place over a web application. So, let's take a look at the ones plaguing the security of web applications:

- **SQL Injections**: One of the common attacks with web applications that are backed by SQL databases is the use of SQL Injections. In these attacks, an attacker usually crafts a malicious SQL statement that tricks the application into executing some database operation intended by the attacker. Usually, this happens when the application developer does not take enough care to filter the user input that's taken in through a form or an API. The repercussions of this attack can be very severe, which may involve access to the records stored in the database or wiping the database clean.
- **Cross-Site Scripting Attack** (**XSS**): XSS attacks are another variety of attack that plagues web applications. In this case, the attack usually tricks a user into opening a web page that contains some malicious script. This usually happens when an attacker is able to insert malicious content into a dynamic page through the use of an HTTP input. In this case, when the target user opens the page, the malicious code is executed.

- **Cross-Site Request Forgery (CSRF)**: Here, an attacker usually constructs a malicious URL to perform some state-change operation on the web service they are currently authenticated with. These state-change operations may be an email address change, password reset, or transfer of funds from one bank account to another. Usually, this happens when the web application does not require any kind of randomness that can be used to distinguish actual user input from malicious user input.

- **Defacement attacks (such as Denial of Service (DoS) or Distributed Denial of Service (DDoS))**: These days, DoS attacks or DDoS attacks are used to deface a web service. In these attacks, the web servers serving the web application are bombarded with a huge number of requests in a short span of time. This causes the web server to overload with a request backlog and hence the web application stops accepting new requests. How a DoS attack differs from a DDoS attack is in the way these attacks originate. In a DoS attack, a fixed set of machines is usually sending a huge number of requests in a short span of time, whereas in a DDoS attack, a large set of machines distributed over a large geography might be sending a large number of packets to the vulnerable application. Usually, the scale at which a DDoS attack occurs is orders of magnitude larger than a DoS attack.

- **Credential theft**: A lot of web applications depend upon cookies to authenticate users. In this case, a malicious user with access to the cookies of the victims can trick the web application into providing access to secure areas of the application that would not have been possible if the user was not authenticated. This happens when a web application validates the authentication status of the user, but only on the basis of cookies, and does not have any other kind of checks in place.

- **Man-in-the-middle attacks**: In this kind of attack, an attacker is usually sitting in-between the victim and the party with which the victim is communicating. The attacker can do some simple malicious stuff, such as as eavesdropping on the conversation, or could be active, such as actively modifying the conversation between the two parties while the victim thinks that they are communicating directly with the third party. This usually happens when there is no, or very weak, encryption between the victim and the third party.

With this, we have learned about some of the issues that plague the security of web applications. Most of these issues can be avoided by the developers of web applications by simply performing some additional checks or by validating what data their application gets through the use of web forms or HTTP requests.

Now, we know about the different ways in which the security of either a web application or a native application is compromised. Let's spend some time understanding the mistakes that can happen during the development of an application, which may result in security breaches later.

Security anti-patterns

It's time for us to understand what kind of practices usually land the application in the vulnerability zone of security breaches. There could be a number of things that can cause the application to suffer from security issues,as we move through this section we will take a look at some of the mistakes that usually leaves an application vulnerable to security breaches. So, let's go through them one by one.

Not filtering user input

As an application developer, we want our users to trust our application. That is the only way we can make sure that our users will use our application. But how about trusting our users equally and expecting them not to do anything wrong? Specifically, trusting them with the input they will provide us through the use of input mechanisms our application exposes to the user for taking input from them.

The following snippet of code shows a simple example of not filtering the input provided by the user:

```
username = request.args.get('username')
email = request.args.get('email')
password = request.args.get('password')
user_record = User(username=username, email=email, password=password)
#Let's create an object to store in database
# Let's store the object into the database
db.session.add(user_record)
db.session.commit()
```

This code snippet takes the input of some of the details of the users, creates an object out of those details, and then performs a simple SQL insert in the background by running a statement, as shown here:

```
INSERT INTO users(username, email, password) VALUES(username, email, password);
```

With this code, we are now assured that we trust our users. The code is absolutely fine and will store the user details in the database, but only until the point when a user comes in and issues the following as an input to one of the fields:

```
(select password from mysql.user where user='root')
```

As soon as this statement is executed, based on the configuration of the database server, it can result in the exposure of the password of the root user of the database.

Another kind of issue that may arise due to such trust is a cross-site scripting attack. Imagine a user submitting the following as an input to your application:

```
<script>alert('XSS attack');</script>
```

Now, since the application does not filter any of the user input, this HTML snippet will be stored inside the database. When the user visits a page that requests this information from the server, the browser will consider the data as valid HTML and render the HTML, thus executing the code inside the script tags.

Now, this was a harmless input, but a real attacker may craft something more serious to steal data from the user, maybe to do a session hijack of the user.

Storing Sensitive Data Unencrypted

Now, as application developers, we love to have simplicity in the application code base so that we can maintain the application later with ease. While keeping this simplicity in mind, we thought that we already had our application running behind a nice firewall and every access was thoroughly checked, so why not just store the passwords of the user in plaintext in the database? This will help us to match them with ease and will also help us save a number of CPU cycles.

One day while the application was running in production, an attacker was able to compromise the security of the database and somehow was able to fetch the details from the user table. Now, we are in a situation where the login credentials of the user are not only leaked but are also available in cleartext format. Going with general psychology, many people will reuse the same password on a number of services. In this case, we have not only risked the credentials of users on our application but also on a number of other applications that the user might be using.

Such an attempt to have security-sensitive data stored without any strong encryption not only put the application at risk of security issues that may happen at any time, but also its users.

Ignoring bound-checking

Security issues pertaining to missing bound checks is quite a common scenario in software applications. This happens when the developers accidentally forget to implement a bounds check in the data structure they are implementing.

When a program attempts to access the memory region outside the one that was allocated to it, it causes the program to experience a buffer overflow.

For example, consider the following code snippet:

```
arr = [None] * 10

for i in range(0,15):
    arr[i] = i
```

When this program is executed, the program tries to alter the contents of memory that are not actually managed by it. If the underlying platform does not raise any kind of memory protection, this program will be successfully able to overwrite a memory region that was out of its scope, resulting in a buffer overflow attack that can be used to trigger malicious code.

Not keeping the libraries updated

Most of the production applications depend upon third-party libraries to enable some sets of functions. Keeping these libraries outdated can save you upon the few extra kilobytes of update or maintaining your software so that it continues to work with the updated libraries. However, this can also lead your application to have unfixed security vulnerabilities that may be exploited by an attacker later to gain illegal access to your application and the data that is being managed by the application.

Giving full privileges of the database to a single user

A lot of applications will actually give full database privileges to a single user of the application. Sometimes, these privileges are enough to allow your application database user to have the same set of permissions as the root user of the database.

Now, this kind of implementation helps a lot in solving the issue of validating whether a certain user has a particular permission to conduct a database operation and having to switch the users to complete the database operation, but also opens a huge vulnerability with your application.

Imagine if somehow the credentials of one of the database users gets leaked. The attacker will now have complete access to your database, which makes them free to execute any kind of operation on the data stored inside the database. This can not only harm the data stored by your application in the database, but also the data that the other applications may also be storing in the same database environment, in case the user permissions provided the flexibility to have complete control of the database environment.

These were some of the anti-patterns that can help an attacker to exploit your application and risk the data associated with the application. So, what can we do so that our applications remain secure? Well, it turns out that some simple steps can easily improve the application's security. Let's take a look.

Improving your application's security

Keeping your application secure can be achieved if we follow some basic rules of software security and implement them tightly in the application's development and production cycles:

- **Never trust your user input:** As developers of the application, we should make sure that we don't trust any user input. Everything that may come from the user side should be filtered appropriately before it is processed by the application for storage or any other kind of operation that may cause the provided input to be executed.
- **Encrypt sensitive data:** Any kind of sensitive data should have a strong encryption supporting its storage and retrieval. Having some amount of randomness in generating the encrypted version of the data can help a lot in making it difficult for attackers to get anything useful out of the data, even if they somehow got access to it.
- **Properly secure the infrastructure:** The infrastructure that is being used to run the application should be secured properly, with firewalls configured to restrict any kind of unauthorized access to the internal networks or nodes.
- **Implement end-to-end encryption:** Any communication that happens between two services should be end-to-end encrypted to avoid any man-in-the-middle attacks or sniffing of the information.

- **Carefully implement bounds checks:** If your application uses any kind of data structures, make sure that proper bounds-checking is in place so as to avoid vulnerabilities, such as Buffer overflow, which may allow malicious code to get executed.
- **Restrict user permissions:** No application should have a single user with all permissions given to them. The user permissions should be restricted so as to define the boundaries for a user to execute an operation. Following this kind of recommendation can help to restrict the amount of damage a breach may cause in case the credentials for a less privileged user are compromised.
- **Keep the dependencies updated:** The dependencies of an application should be kept updated so as to make sure that the dependencies are free of any known security vulnerability.

Following these kinds of guidelines can help a lot in improving the application security of your application and making sure that the application, as well as the data, is kept safe, which maintains user trust as well as data security.

Summary

As we progressed through this chapter, we got to learn about the different security principles that govern the development and operation of software applications. We talked about needing to maintain high security standards with respect to enterprise applications, and what happens if the application's security is breached. We then learned about the challenges that system security faces nowadays. Then, we moved on to the common attack vectors that are used to compromise an application's security.

Once we had an idea about the attack vectors, we took a look at some common security anti-patterns that compromise the security of your application, as well as the data associated with the application. Once we had the knowledge of these anti-patterns, we went through some of the recommendations that can help us to tackle the problem of application security.

Now, as we move on to the next part of this book, we will take a look at a new way of building enterprise applications, in which an application is not a single, large application built using different, glued-together components, but a set of small services that communicate with each other to handle certain business use cases. Let's take a look at this approach of application development in the next chapter.

Questions

1. What are the different issues that make application security hard?
2. What is an XSS attack?
3. How can we prevent a DoS attack?
4. What are some of the mistakes that compromise the security of the application?

Further reading

If you found application security to be an interesting topic and want to learn more about how to use Python to improve the security of your application, take a look at this awesome video series, "Python for Continuous Delivery and Application Security," authored by Manish Saini and produced by Packt.

11
Taking the Microservices Approach

So far in this book, we have learned about how to develop an enterprise-grade application and how to mature our processes so that the application we deliver meets our standards of quality and provides a robust and resilient experience to its users. In this chapter, we will take a look at a new paradigm for developing applications, where the application is not a single product but rather a combination of multiple products interacting with each other to provide a unified experience.

Over recent years, development scenarios have changed rapidly. Application development has moved from developing large monoliths to developing smaller services, all of which interact with each other to provide the desired result to the user. This change has come to meet the demand for faster shipping of projects in order to increase the ability to add new features and improve the scalability of the application.

Over the course of this chapter, we will take a look at this new paradigm of application development where teams have become smaller and the ability to ship new features inside an application at an ever-reducing cost has become the new standard. This paradigm, known as the microservices development approach, has radically changed the way in which application development cycles work, and has also led to the current trend toward techniques related to DevOps, continuous integration, and deployments.

As you progress through this chapter, you will learn about the following:

- Moving toward the microservices development approach
- API-driven communication between services
- Building robust microservices
- Handling user-server interaction in microservices
- Asynchronous communication between microservices

Technical requirements

The code listings in this book can be found under `chapter11` directory at `https://github.com/PacktPublishing/Hands-On-Enterprise-Application-Development-with-Python`.

The code samples can be cloned by running the following command:

```
git clone
https://github.com/PacktPublishing/Hands-On-Enterprise-Application-Developm
ent-with-Python
```

The steps to set up and run the code have been included inside the `README.md` file inside the directory to give a deeper context about the code samples.

The shift toward microservices

Over the last few years, developers have been trying to experiment with new ways in which they can develop applications. The aim of this is to reduce the time of development life cycles, increasing the ability to ship projects faster into production, increasing the decoupling between the components so that they can be developed independently, and improving the parallelism of the teams working on the development of the application.

With this came the development technique of using microservices, which helped in solving the aforementioned use cases. In this approach, the application is not a single large repository of code where all the components are placed together, and where a single change to any of the components requires the deployment of the whole application again. First, let's look at how the microservices model differs from the monolithic model and then see what advantages there are in following the microservices approach.

Monolithic development model versus microservices

We are all accustomed to building an application where a single code base consists of all the functional components of an application, closely tied together to achieve a certain desired result. These applications follow a rigorous development approach where the functioning and architecture of the application is first thought of during the initial requirement-gathering and design phases, and then the rigorous development of the application starts.

It is only after all the components have been developed and thoroughly tested that an application enters the production stage, where it is deployed on the infrastructure for regular use. This model is shown in the following diagram:

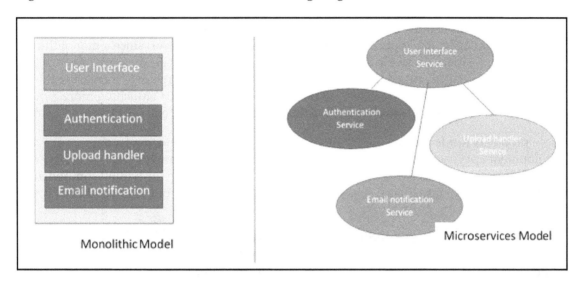

This process is slow, and every step depends upon the successful completion of the previous step. The addition of any new feature to the application once it has been deployed poses a challenge because now the whole development cycle has to be followed again; once the development of the new feature has been completed, the whole application in its entirety needs to be redeployed. This gives rise to a certain number of challenges, as shown in the following list:

- **Slow development:** Since the whole application is a one large code base, a change to one component may affect the functioning of the other components. A huge amount of care needs to be taken so that the existing functionality does not break and new bugs are not introduced.
- **Highly serialized development approach:** When an application is developed as a single monolith, the development approach is highly serialized, where the execution of a step heavily depends on the success of the preceding step. This causes an increased serialization of steps.
- **Higher risks:** When a large code base is modified to add a new feature or to set up a major refactoring, it risks breaking up the previous functionality or introducing new bugs inside the code. This increases the risk of development, and means that there needs to be rigorous testing of the application in its entirety so as to make sure that the functionality still works in the way it was supposed to.

- **Higher downtimes during deployments:** When an upgraded version of the application needs to be deployed, it means that the whole application has to be taken down. The side effect of this is that the user experiences an increased amount of downtime.
- **Difficult to scale the application up:** Usually, when an application grows in popularity, the application needs to be scaled up. However, since a monolithic application is a single application, when the load increases, the options to scale up are fairly limited. Generally speaking, these options relate to increasing the resources that are dedicated to running the application or launching more instances of the complete application running behind a load balancer.

These problems needed to be solved, and the solution came in the form of a new development approach that welcomes faster development-to-production release cycles. This solution was to develop the application in such a way that the individual components can be broken down into logical services, where each service does one thing and does it perfectly.

This development model of building an application by modelling its individual components as separate services came to be known as the microservices development model. Let's take a look at some of the features of the microservices development approach, as shown in the following list:

- **Modelling as a service:** With the microservices approach, the individual functionality of an application is broken down into a set of logical services that are then developed independently of each other. For example, the functionality of allowing a user to authenticate their identity for an application can be segregated into an authentication service.
- **Built for the business:** The microservices architecture enables modelling as a business requirement. This allows each team to work on a complete component on their own. These teams are not only responsible for the development of the component, but are also responsible for the functioning of that component throughout their lifetime into the production environment.
- **Decentralized throughout:** The microservices approach provides a highly decentralized way of deployment and management of these services. In the microservices architecture, every service is responsible for the management of its own data. This is in contrast to the monolithic architecture, where a single database is used to store the information that is managed by the different components of the application.

- **Simple request handling:** Microservices implement a simple RESTful API through which they can take in a request from another entity, process the request, and then provide a suitable response based on the results of the processing of the request. These services do not utilize the highly sophisticated ways of applying business logic to orchestrate the flow of data from one endpoint to another endpoint, and so provide a simple mechanism of routing the requests.
- **Polyglot:** Microservices do not follow the principle of one size fits all. The team responsible for the development of a microservice is usually free to choose the tools and technologies that will power a particular microservice. This may include the choice of language, the operating system, and the hardware on which the service will be made to run.

These are some features that make using microservices a great option. With microservices in the picture, we can now work to solve some of the problems that we face with monolithic applications while also gaining quite a lot of different advantages. So, let's take a look at the advantages that the microservices architecture has to offer.

Advantages of the microservices architecture

The microservices architecture solves a lot of problems for us, mostly because of the changes in the way in which we develop and deploy the microservices. Let's go through some of the advantages that the microservices architecture brings to our development process, as shown in the following list:

- **Small teams:** Since a particular microservice usually focuses on doing one thing and doing it well, the teams responsible for building that microservice can usually be small. A team can own multiple microservices end to end, where they are not only responsible for their development but also their deployment and management, giving rise to a good DevOps culture.
- **Increased independence:** In a microservices architecture, the team responsible for the development of one microservice does not need to have complete knowledge of how another microservice works internally. The teams only need to take care of the API endpoints that have been exposed by the microservice in order to interact with it. This avoids the dependence of teams on each other to carry out their development activities.

- **Increased resilience to failures:** In a microservices architecture, the failure resilience is quite high because of the fact that a malfunction in one microservice won't affect the whole application, and will rather provide a gradual degradation of the service. During this time, a new instance of the failing service might be launched, or the failing service can be easily isolated for debugging so as to reduce the impact.

- **Increased scalability:** The microservices architecture provides a lot of freedom in the scalability of the application. Now, as the load increases, the individual microservices can be scaled up independently instead of scaling the whole application up. This scaling can happen as horizontal scaling, where more instances of a select set of microservices can be launched depending upon the load being experienced by the application, or these services can be individually scaled up using vertical scaling, where more resources are dedicated to a particular service to allow for better handling of the increasing load.

- **Easy integration:** With microservices, the integration between the different services is easy, as no knowledge of the internals of the other microservices is required. All the integration happens while assuming the other microservices to be black boxes.

- **Increased reusability:** Once developed, a microservice can be utilized in different applications. For example, a microservice that's responsible for the handling of user authentication can be reused in multiple applications, which may require user authentication without the replication of the code.

- **Freedom to roll out new features with ease:** With the microservices architecture, new features can be rolled out easily. In most cases, a particular feature is converted into its own microservice, and the service is then deployed in production after proper testing. Once the service is live in production, its features are available for use. This differs from the monolithic approach, where the whole application needs to be redeployed when a new feature or improvement needs to be deployed to production environments.

From this list, we can see a number of benefits that the move toward a microservices architecture provides us with. From the choice of the tools to the ease in rolling out new features, the microservices architecture makes it lucrative for developers to hop into the wagon and quickly start rolling out new microservices.

But all of these advantages do not come for free. As much as there are advantages, there is also the possibility of creating a mess of the infrastructure while working on the microservices architecture, which may not only create increased costs. However, this may also impact the overall productivity of the team, which may end up more focused on firefighting the issues that may arise because of the flawed implementation of the architecture rather than focusing on the improvement and development of the features that may be essential to the users of the application.

This is nothing to worry about. We can follow a few simple pieces of advice that can help a lot during our journey with the microservices architecture. So, let's spend some time understanding these simple tips, which can go a long way in helping us make our microservices journey smooth.

Guidelines for microservice development

The development of microservices is challenging, and getting them right is quite hard. Is there something we can do to make this process easier? It turns out that there are a couple of guidelines that, if followed, can help a lot in getting microservices right. So, let's take a look at these guidelines, as shown in the following list:

- **Design before developing**: When microservices development takes place, they are usually supposed to model a particular domain of responsibility. But this is also the point where the biggest mistakes occur. Usually, the boundaries of a service are not defined. During the later stages, as the domain evolves, the microservice also becomes complex so as to handle the increased context of the domain. This complexity makes the microservice bulky and increases the cost of running and maintaining the microservice.
- **Single responsibility principle** (**SRP**): Following on from the preceding point, the principle of single responsibility comes into the picture. This principle states that a microservice should do only one task and do it well. As the underlying domain increases, new microservices should be rolled out instead of adding newer and newer functionalities to the existing microservice.
- **Maintain the abstractions**: A microservice should provide an increased independence. If a service requires the other services to have knowledge about its internals to allow them proper integration, then there is something wrong with the design. A good microservice design will focus on providing services that act as black boxes for the other services that take in a response in a well-defined format and produce a response in a well-defined format.

- **Keep the message format simple:** The message format through which the microservices communicate with each other should be simple enough to enable the simple processing of data without stressing too much about the decoding of the data.

- **Every service should be self-sustained:** When designing the microservices, it should be kept in mind that every microservice should be able to handle all of the operations related to its functionality independently. This may involve logic to process a particular message or store data.

- **Avoid centralization of data:** To efficiently employ the use of microservices architecture and to have increased failure resiliency, the microservices should not utilize a single data source for handling the data. If all the services use a single data source, then in the event of the data source going down, all the services will fail to operate, thereby ending up with a single point of failure, which is not a desired pattern inside the microservices architecture.

Now, we know about a few simple tips, which, if followed, can help us avoid a lot of hardships that may be experienced when using a microservices architecture. But even when we follow these principles, there are still a few questions that need to be answered, questions such as what will happen if a particular service goes down, how much time it will take for a particular microservice to respond to a request, and so on.

To answer these questions, usually, the teams write agreements that provide guarantees about the uptime of the microservices, how these services will be monitored, their response times, and the requests they can take at any given point in time. These agreements are called **service-level agreements** (**SLAs**), and provide a contract that is followed by the services. So, let's take a look at what these SLAs do and how they can help us in the development of microservices.

Service-level agreements in microservices

During the development of any production-grade application based upon microservices architecture, the services might depend a lot upon the availability of the other services deployed in production. For example, a service providing functionality to the administration panel for the application might require the availability of the user authentication service to allow for administrator logins and privilege management. In case the user management service goes down, there can be severe consequences in the stability of the operations provided by the application.

To guarantee these kinds of requirements, we need to have SLAs that act as contracts between the teams delivering particular microservices. These contracts provide guarantees about the different aspects of the microservices, and cover a lot of different parts. Let's take a look at the kind of things that are covered by the SLAs, as shown in the following list:

- **Uptime guarantees:** If there are two services, say Service *A* and Service *B*, where Service A depends upon the functionality provided by Service B, then Service *A* might require an uptime guarantee from Service B. The SLAs may specify this uptime guarantee in the form of the redundant deployment of Service *B* so as to provide higher uptime and failure resilience. It may also specify the functionality related to alert generation in case the service goes down.
- **API stability:** Most of the microservices communicate through the API endpoints that are exposed through them. If these API endpoints keep changing in every other release of a particular service, then this may cause the developers of other services increased headache because of the fact that they need to keep altering their services so as to accommodate the changing endpoints of one service. SLAs provide the contract between services regarding the lifetime of the API endpoints, how frequently these API endpoints might change, and so on.
- **Rate limiting:** Practically, no microservice can scale infinitely. Most of the time, these services can handle only a certain number of transactions that are dependent upon the availability of the infrastructure resources on which the service is deployed. The SLAs specify the rate-limiting policies of the service. This explains at what point a particular service might start limiting the number of requests it will process from another service.
- **Error rate guarantees:** A service that has a high error rate might be good for nothing because most of the transactions that are being processed by the service end up in an error state. A SLA specifies the error rate guarantee, which, if breached, may flag the service as malfunctioning.

These are just a few parameters that can be covered by a SLA. These SLAs provide a kind of guarantee that the services operating in a given environment adhere to a certain set of standards, and they also lay out the information required to monitor the performance and stability of a given service.

Now that we have all the basic knowledge that is required to understand how microservices work, it's time for us to see some microservices in action.

Building your first microservices application

We are now ready to build our first application using the microservices architecture. During the development of this application, we will get to see how we can utilize the knowledge that we have gained so far to roll out a working application.

Now, regarding our example, to keep this application simple and provide an easy understanding of how the microservices architecture works, we will build a simple to-do-list-creation application: Let's take a look at how this application will look, as stipulated in the following list:

- The application will consist of two microservices—namely the to-do manager service and the user authentication service
- The services will be developed in Python
- For the purpose of this exercise, the services will utilize their own SQLite databases
- The to-do service will depend upon the user service to gather any kind of information related to the user operations, including user authentication, profile fetching, and so on
- The services will communicate through the use of RESTful APIs, each providing a JSON-encoded response

With the basic requirements specified, it's now time for us to start writing our microservices.

The user microservice

The user microservice is responsible for handling anything related to user profile management. The service facilitates the following functionalities:

- Registration of new users
- Management of user profiles
- Authentication of existing users
- Generating unique authentication tokens for the user to log in with
- Providing user authentication functionality to other services

For this service to operate, we need to have the following two database models:

- **User database model:** The user database model is responsible for the management of the user records, such as their username, hashed passwords, and so on.
- **Token database model:** The token database model is responsible for storing information about the tokens that has been generated for a particular user to use to authenticate. For our purposes, every user can only have a single token at any given point in time, and this token will be valid for only 60 minutes from the point of generation, after which the user needs to log in again.

So, let's move on to building the database models for this service.

The following code snippet shows the definition of the database models:

```
'''
File: models.py
Description: The models for the User service.
'''
from user_service.user_service import db
import datetime

class User(db.Model):
    """User database model.

    The User database model is used to store the information related to the
individual users
    allowing for their identification and authentication.
    """

    id = db.Column(db.Integer, primary_key=True)
    username = db.Column(db.String(25), unique=True, nullable=False)
    password= db.Column(db.String(255), nullable=False)
    email = db.Column(db.String(255), nullable=False, unique=True)

    def __repr__(self):
        """Provide a representation of the Model."""
        return "<User {}>".format(self.username)

class Token(db.Model):
    """User Authetication Token Model.

    The authentication token model is used to store the authentication
tokens
    for a given user which can be used to authenticate the user with the
    service.
    """
```

```
        id = db.Column(db.Integer, primary_key=True)
        user_id = db.Column(db.Integer, db.ForeignKey(User.id))
        auth_token = db.Column(db.String(64), nullable=False, unique=True)
        token_timestamp = db.Column(db.DateTime, nullable=False,
    default=datetime.datetime.now())

        def __repr__(self):
            """Provide a representation of the model."""
            return "<Token {}>".format(self.id)
```

With this code snippet, we have defined two important data models for the user service: the user model and the token model. Here, inside the token model, we can see that the model depends upon the user model for storing and relating the authentication tokens to a user account.

Once the models have been developed, it's time for us to work on the API of the user service. The user service provides the following set of APIs to work with:

- /auth/register: This API is responsible for taking in the details for a new user and registering them with the service.
- /auth/login: This API is responsible for taking in the login credentials of the user and authenticating them with the service to validate the user. Once the user is validated, the endpoint generates an authentication token.
- /auth/validate: This API endpoint is responsible for the validation of the authentication token that is given to it. Upon successful validation, the endpoint returns the user ID of the authenticated user.

The following snippet of code shows the implementation of the API endpoints:

```
def check_required_fields(req_fields, input_list):
    """Check if the required fields are present or not in a given list.

    Keyword arguments:
    req_fields -- The list of fields required
    input_list -- The input list to check for

    Returns:
        Boolean
    """

    if all(field in req_fields for field in input_list):
        return True
    return False

@app.route('/auth/register', methods=['POST'])
def user_registration():
```

```
"""Handle the user registration."""

required_fields = ['username', 'email', 'password']
response = {} # Initialize a response dictionary
user_data = request.get_json()
if not check_required_fields(required_fields, user_data.keys()):
    response['message'] = "Required fields are missing"
    return jsonify(response), 400

# Create a user object
username = user_data['username']
password = generate_password_hash(user_data['password'])
email = user_data['email']

user = User(username=username, password=password, email=email)
db.session.add(user)
try:
    db.session.commit()
except Exception:
    response['message'] = 'Unable to register the user'
    return jsonify(response), 400

response['message'] = "User registration successful"
return jsonify(response), 200

@app.route('/auth/login', methods=['POST'])
def user_login():
    """Handle the user login."""

    ...
    # The remaining code can be found inside the code directory of this
chapter
```

With the preceding code, we have completed the deployment of the required API that will facilitate the communication with the user service.

Now, to get this service up and running, run the following command inside the `user_service` directory of the code repository for this chapter:

python3 run.py

Once this command is executed, the user service will start to run on `http://localhost:5000`. To test whether the service is working fine, navigate to `http://localhost:5000/ping` and see whether the web page shows the response **PONG is generated**.

Once this is done, we will be ready to build our to-do manager service, which will help us record our `todo` items in a list.

The to-do manager service

The to-do manager service is the service that will help our users manage their `todo` items. This service provides the functionality for the user to create a new list and add items to the list. For this, the only requirement is that the user should be authenticated.

To work correctly, the service will require the presence of a list database model, which will be used to store the information about the user-created `todo` list and an items model, which will contain the list of items for a particular `todo` list.

The following snippet of code implements these models:

```
'''
File: models.py
Description: The models for the todo service.
'''
from todo_service.todo_service import db
import datetime

class List(db.Model):
    """The list database model.

    The list database model is used to create a new todo list
    based on the input provided by the user.
    """

    id = db.Column(db.Integer, primary_key=True)
    user_id = db.Column(db.Integer, nullable=False)
    list_name = db.Column(db.String(25), nullable=False)
    db.UniqueConstraint('user_id', 'list_name', name='list_name_uiq')

    def __repr__(self):
        """Provide a representation of model."""
        return "<List {}>".format(self.list_name)

class Item(db.Model):
    """The item database model.

    The model is used to store the information about the items
    in a particular list maintained by the user.
    """
```

```
    id = db.Column(db.Integer, primary_key=True)
    list_id = db.Column(db.Integer, db.ForeignKey(List.id))
    item_name = db.Column(db.String(50), nullable=False)
    db.UniqueConstraint('list_id', 'item_name', name='item_list_uiq')

    def __repr__(self):
        """Provide a representation of model."""
        return "<Item {}>".format(self.item_name)
```

Once these models have been developed, the next thing we have to do is implement the APIs.

For the to-do manager service, the following APIs will be in place, providing the interaction endpoints for the service:

- /list/new: This API endpoint takes in the name of the list to be created and creates a new list.
- /list/add_item: This API endpoint takes in the list of the items that need to be added to the list and the name of the list in which the items are supposed to be added. Once validated, the items are added to the list.
- /list/view: This API endpoint takes the name of the list for which the contents need to be displayed and displays the content of the list.

The following snippet of code shows the endpoint implementations for the service:

```
def check_required_fields(req_fields, input_list):
    """Check if the required fields are present or not in a given list.

    Keyword arguments:
    req_fields -- The list of fields required
    input_list -- The input list to check for

    Returns:
        Boolean
    """

    if all(field in req_fields for field in input_list):
        return True
    return False


def validate_user(auth_token):
    """Validates a user and returns it user id.

    Keyword arguments:
    auth_token -- The authentication token to be used
```

```
    Returns:
        Integer
    """

    endpoint = user_service + '/auth/validate'
    resp = requests.post(endpoint, json={"auth_token": auth_token})
    if resp.status_code == 200:
        user = resp.json()
        user_id = user['user_id']
        return user_id
    else:
        return None

@app.route('/list/new', methods=['POST'])
def new_list():
    """Handle the creation of new list."""

    required_fields = ['auth_token', 'list_name']
    response = {}
    list_data = request.get_json()
    if not check_required_fields(required_fields, list_data.keys()):
        response['message'] = 'The required parameters are not provided'
        return jsonify(response), 400

    auth_token = list_data['auth_token']

    # Get the user id for the auth token provided
    user_id = validate_user(auth_token)

    # If the user is not valid, return an error
    if user_id is None:
        response['message'] = "Unable to login user. Please check the auth
token"
        return jsonify(response), 400

    # User token is valid, let's create the list
    list_name = list_data['list_name']
    new_list = List(user_id=user_id, list_name=list_name)
    db.session.add(new_list)
    try:
        db.session.commit()
    except Exception:
        response['message'] = "Unable to create a new todo-list"
        return jsonify(response), 500
    response['message'] = "List created"
    return jsonify(response), 200

@app.route('/list/add_item', methods=['POST'])
```

```
def add_item():
    """Handle the addition of new items to the list."""

    ...
    # The complete code for the service can be found inside the assisting
code repository for the book
```

With the preceding code in place, we are now ready with our to-do manager service, which will help us create and manage our to-do lists through the use of RESTful APIs.

But before we get the to-do manager service to execute, we need to remember one important thing. The service is dependent upon the user service to perform any kind of user authentication and to fetch information about the user profile. For this to happen, our to-do manager needs to know where the user service is running so that it can interact with the user service. For this example, we achieve this by setting up a configuration key for the user service endpoint inside the to-do manager service configuration file. The following snippet shows the contents of the to-do manager service configuration file:

```
DEBUG = False
SECRET_KEY = 'du373r3uie3yf3@U#^$*EU9373^#'
BCRYPT_LOG_ROUNDS = 5
SQLALCHEMY_DATABASE_URI = 'sqlite:///todo_service.db'
SQLALCHEMY_ECHO = False
USER_SERVICE_ENDPOINT = 'http://localhost:5000'
```

To get the to-do manager service running, the following command needs to be executed from inside the `todo_service` directory, inside the repository:

python3 run.py

Once the command executes successfully, the to-do manager service will be available at `http://localhost:5001/`.

Once the service is up and running, we can utilize its API to manage our inventory. For example, if we wanted to create a new to-do list, all we need to do is send an HTTP POST request to the `http://localhost:5001/list/new` API endpoint, passing the following keys as JSON formatted inputs:

- `auth_token`: This is the authentication token the user receives after successfully logging in with the user service using the `http://localhost:5000/auth/login` API endpoint
- `list_name`: This is the name of the new list that is to be created

Once the API endpoint call is made, the to-do manager service first makes an attempt to validate the `auth` token provided in the API call by interacting with the user service. If the `auth` token is validated, the to-do manager service then receives a user ID that is used to identify the user. With this complete, the to-do manager service creates an entry for the new to-do list inside its database against the user ID that has been retrieved.

This was a simple workflow of the to-do manager service.

Now that we understand how we can build a simple microservice, we can now focus on some interesting topics regarding the microservices architecture. Did you notice how we informed our to-do manager service of the presence of the user service? We utilized a configuration key to achieve this. Using the configuration key is by no means a bad option when all you have is two or three services that, no matter what happens, will always run on the same endpoints. However, this approach breaks down badly when the microservices number even moderately more than two or three services, which may run anywhere on the infrastructure.

To add on to these troubles, the problem intensifies even further if new services are being brought into production frequently to add new features to the application. At this point, we will need something better that should not only provide an easy way to identify the new services, but also automatically resolve their endpoints.

Service discovery in microservices

In traditional models of application development, the services pertaining to a particular application are usually deployed in a static manner where their network locations do not change automatically. If this is the case, then maintaining a configuration file that is updated occasionally to reflect the changed network location of the services is absolutely fine.

But in modern microservice-based applications—where the number of services may go up and down based on a number of factors, such as load balancing, upscaling, the launch of new features, and so on—maintaining a configuration file turns out to be a bit hard. In addition, most cloud environments these days do not offer static network deployments for these services, meaning that the network location for the services may keep on changing, adding more trouble to the maintenance of the configuration file.

To tackle these kinds of scenarios, we need to have something that is more dynamic and can adapt to the changing environment. Enter the concept of service discovery. Service discovery allows for the dynamic resolution of the network endpoints of a required service and removes the need for a manually updated configuration file.

The service discovery usually comes in the following two flavors:

- Client-side service discovery
- Server-side service discovery

But before we cover these two approaches, we need to understand one more important component of the service discovery system. Let's take a look at what this important component is and how it facilitates the service discovery process.

Service registry inside microservices

Say there is a magic show that is going to take place inside an auditorium. This show is open to everyone, and anyone can come to the auditorium to attend it. At the gate of the auditorium, there is a registration desk where you need to register before you can enter the auditorium. As soon as the audience members start coming, they first go to the registration desk, provide their information—such as their names, addresses, and so on—and are then given a ticket to enter the auditorium.

The service registry is something like this. It is a special kind of database that keeps a record of which services are running on an infrastructure and where they are located. Whenever a new service comes up, it registers itself with the service registry, identifying itself.

The service registry also acts as a lookup point for these services. For example, if Service *A* wants to communicate with Service *B*, then Service *A* makes a call to the service registry, asking for the network location of Service *B*. If Service *B* was registered with the service registry, then the service registry looks up the network address of Service *B* inside its internal database and sends it back to Service *A*. After this, Service *A* can make calls to Service *B*.

But what happens if Service *B* went down because of some issue? The service registry is responsible for keeping its service database updated through multiple mechanisms. One of the simplest mechanisms to implement is the use of heartbeats. Here, any service that is registered to the service registry sends periodic heartbeats to the service registry to mark itself as alive. If Service *B* goes down, these heartbeats will cease to exist, prompting the service registry to remove the entry for Service *B* from its database.

So, this is how a service registry functions. Now that we know about the service registry, we are ready to explore the patterns of service discovery.

Client-side service discovery

With the client-side service discovery method, the individual services need to be aware of the service registry. For example, in this model, if **Service Instance A** wants to make a request to **Service Instance C**, then the process of making this request will be as shown in the following diagram:

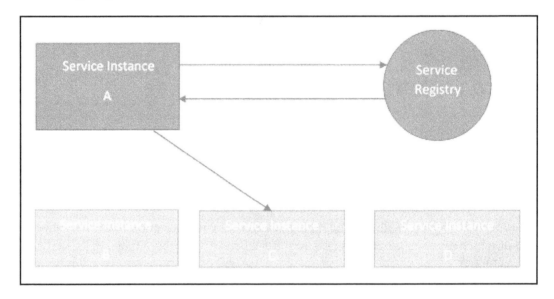

The flow of the request is explained as follows:

- **Service Instance A** queries the service registry for the network address of **Service Instance C**.
- The **Service Registry** checks its database for the network address of **Service Instance C** and returns it to **Service Instance A**. In case **Service Instance C** is a load balanced service with more than one network location, the **Service Registry** is supposed to run an appropriate load balancing algorithm to return the correct network address of **Service Instance C**.
- Once **Service Instance A** receives this network address, it makes the request to **Service Instance C**.

This is a straightforward process of service discovery, but has the drawback that now the service discovery logic needs to be added to all the services in the infrastructure, making the services more complicated.

To tackle these kinds of issues, there is another pattern of service discovery that means that the service discovery logic doesn't have to be replicated inside every other service. Let's take a look at this pattern of service discovery.

Server-side service discovery

With the server-side service discovery pattern, the ability to resolve the network address of the services is not present inside the individual clients—rather, this logic is moved into the load balancer. Inside a server-side service discovery pattern, a request flow looks like the following diagram:

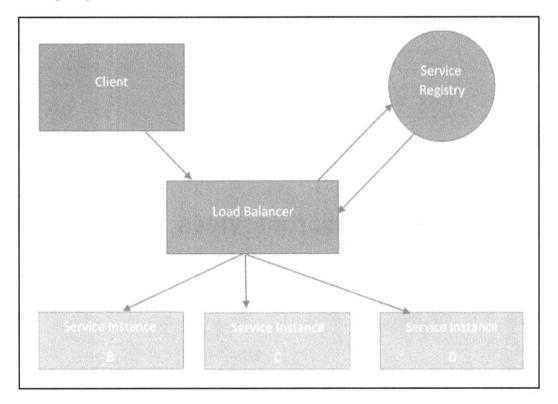

This diagram shows the following process:

1. The **Client** makes a request for an API endpoint
2. The **Load Balancer** intercepts the request and queries the **Service Registry** to resolve the network address for the appropriate service
3. The **Load Balancer** then sends the request to the appropriate network service to handle the request

The advantage of this pattern comes in the form of a reduction of code duplication by the removal of service discovery logic from the clients and better load balancing because the service registry is not taking up the load of the load-balancing algorithms.

Now that we know how service discovery happens inside a microservices architecture, let's focus our efforts on understanding another interesting concept inside microservices.

Imagine that you are building an application that is supposed to handle multiple devices and the functionality provided to every device differs based on certain aspects such as mobile devices will not have feature for allowing to send a direct message to other users. In this case, every device will require a different API endpoint that it can call to access its specific set of services. However, making the clients aware of every single API endpoint can become an issue during the maintenance phases of the application, or when some of the APIs change. To handle these kinds of scenarios, we need to have something that can act as an intermediate layer for our communication.

Fortunately, inside the microservices architecture, we have something to help us with this problem. Let's take a look at what we have at our disposal.

API gateways in microservices

When building a microservices architecture, we have a lot of choices, and we are mostly free to choose a technology stack that is best suited for implementing a microservice. Along with this, we always have an option to render different features for different devices by rolling out a different microservice that is specific to them. But when we do this, we also add complexity to the client, which now has to handle all these different scenarios.

So, let's first take a look at the challenges we may face on the client side, as shown in the following diagram:

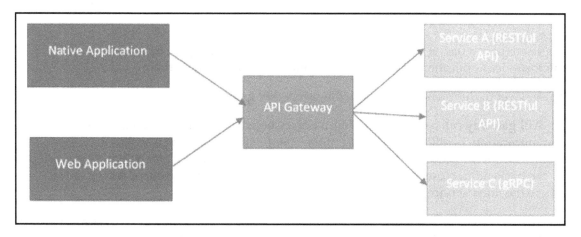

The preceding diagram shows the challenges that we face, as shown in the following list:

- **Handling different APIs:** When every device has a specific microservice that provides the set of features that it requires, the client for that device needs to know about the API endpoints related to that specific service. This adds complexity because now the team that is responsible for handling the development of the clients needs to be aware of the microservice-specific endpoints that may slow down the process of client development.
- **Changing API endpoints:** Over a period of time, we may modify how a specific API endpoint inside a microservice works. This will require us to update all the clients that utilize the service provided by the microservice in order to reflect these changes. This is a cumbersome process, and could also introduce bugs or break existing functionality.
- **Poor protocol support:** With the microservices architecture, we have the power to control the technology stack we use to build a microservice. Sometimes, a microservice may be powered by a protocol that is usually not supported on other platforms or has poor implementation on them. For example, most of the platforms on which the client runs may not support something like AMQP, which will make the development of the client a hard job, because now the developers have to build the logic to handle AMQP protocol inside every client. This kind of requirement may not only be challenging, but may also be impossible to complete if the platform has no support for handling the excess load of the processing required.

- **Security:** If we need to embed the details of the individual network locations of the microservices powering every client, we may also open up security vulnerabilities in our infrastructure if even one of these microservices is not configured properly for security.

These are only a few of the challenges that we may face during the development of microservice applications. But can we do something to overcome them?

The answer to this question lies with the use of API gateways.

An **API gateway** can be seen as an intermediary between the client and application communication, handling the routing of the client requests and the translation of those requests from the protocol that is supported by the client to the protocol that is supported by the backend microservice. It does all of this without making the client worry about where the microservice may be running.

In a microservices-architecture-based application utilizing API gateways, the flow of a request from the client to the application may be described as follows:

1. The client has a common set of endpoints that it knows about to access a certain set of functionalities.
2. The client sends a request to the API endpoint, along with any data that needs to be passed for the request to be completed.
3. The API gateway intercepts the request made to the API endpoint by the client.
4. The API gateway determines the client type and the capabilities that are supported by the client.
5. The API gateway then determines the individual microservices that need to be called for the request to complete.
6. The API gateway then forwards the requests to the specific microservices running in the backend. In case the protocol accepted by the microservice is different from the one in which the client made the request, the API gateway translates the request from the client protocol to the one supported by the microservice and then forwards the request.
7. Once the microservices have finished generating the response, the API gateway collects the response and sends a collective response back to the requesting client.

This kind of process has several advantages; let's take a look at a few of them:

- **Simple clients:** With the API gateways in place, the clients need not be aware of the individual microservices that they might need to call. The clients here make a call to a common endpoint for a particular functionality, and the API gateway is then responsible for figuring out which service needs to be called to complete the request. This greatly reduces the complexity of the clients being developed and makes their maintenance easy.

- **Ease of changing API endpoints:** When there is a change in an implementation of a particular API in the backend microservice, the API gateway can handle the compatibility for the older clients that have not been updated. This can be done by making the API gateway either return a degraded response or automatically update the request it has received to the newer API compatibility layer, if this is possible.

- **Simpler protocol support:** With the API gateway in place to handle any kind of conversion of the protocol that might be required by a microservice, the client does not need to worry about how to handle the protocols that it cannot support, greatly reducing the complexity and the issues that may arise by introducing the support for protocol that are not supported by the platform.

- **Improved security:** With the API gateway, the clients need not be aware of the individual network locations of where a particular microservice is running. All they need to know is where the API gateway is listening to the requests to make a successful API call. Once the call has been made, the API gateway is then responsible for determining where the individual microservices serving that API are running and then forwarding the request to them.

- **Improved failure handling:** An API gateway can also prove to be of help if a particular backend service is experiencing a failure. In this case, if the backend microservice was a non-essential microservice, the API gateway can return a degraded response back to the client, whereas if there was a failure in an essential backend service, the API gateway can immediately return an error response without letting the requests queue up, increasing the load on the servers.

As we can see, the benefits of using an API gateway are enormous and greatly simplify the development of the clients in the microservices application. Also, by utilizing an API gateway, interservice communication can be easily established.

To have the services communicate with each other, all they have to do is make the call to the appropriate endpoint that the API gateway is aware of, and from there the API gateway is responsible for determining the appropriate microservice and its network address to complete the request that has been made to it.

The preceding approach is really good, but there is a drawback: everything here is serialized and synchronous in nature. A call is made and then the calling client/service waits until a response is generated back. If the load on the services is high, these responses may take a long time to arrive, which may either cause a large number of requests to queue up on the infrastructure, increasing the load even further on the infrastructure, or it may cause a lot of requests to time out. This can greatly reduce the throughput of the application, and may even take the whole infrastructure down if the number of queued requests becomes really large.

Is there an asynchronous method of communication between these services through which they can interact with each other, without making API calls again and again? Let's take a look at one such method.

Asynchronous communication in microservices

Inside a microservices architecture, every service does one job and does it well. To achieve any meaningful response for a business application, these services need to communicate with each other. All of this communication happens over the network.

Here, a service makes a request to another service and then waits for the response to come back. But there is a catch. What if the other service takes a long time to process the request, or the service is down? What happens then?

Most of the time, the request will time out. But if this service was a critical service, then the number of requests that might be arriving at it may be huge and can keep on getting queued up. If the service is slow, this will make the response times even worse, and will result in more and more requests experiencing timeouts.

But what if the requesting client could just make a request and then register a callback when a response is ready? This would greatly simplify the whole process, and will also help in reducing the timeouts for a request.

Fortunately, the microservices architecture allows us to build the asynchronous capabilities inside the microservices, through which we can make the whole interservice communication an asynchronous operation. So, let's take a look at how we can make our microservices communicate asynchronously.

Message queues for microservices communication

Message queues are a fairly old mechanism for establishing communication between a lot of different components inside an application. This old method is even good for our current use cases of the microservices architecture. But before we take a dive into how we can use message queues for making microservice communication asynchronous, let's first take a look at some of the jargon that is used when dealing with this method of communication:

- **Message:** A message is a kind of package that a particular service generates to communicate about what it wants to achieve to another service.
- **Queue:** A queue is a kind of topic under which a particular message may come. For any practical application there could be a number of queues, each representing a specific topic of communication.
- **Producer:** A producer is a service that generates a message and sends it to a specific topic.
- **Consumer:** A consumer is a service that listens to a specific topic and processes any messages that may come to it.
- **Router:** A router is a component inside the message queues that is responsible for routing the messages for a particular topic to the appropriate queue.

Now that we know the jargon, we can move on to look at how message queues can help us in establishing communication between the microservices.

When the microservices utilize something like a message queue, they interact over asynchronous protocols. For example, AMQP is one of the more famous protocols for asynchronous communication.

With asynchronous communication, the communication between microservices will take place as follows:

1. A message broker is set up, which will provide the functionality for the management of the message queues and the routing of the messages to the appropriate queue.
2. A new service comes up and registers the topic it wants to listen to or send the messages to. The message broker creates an appropriate queue for the topic and adds the requesting service as either a consumer or a producer for that queue. This process also continues for other services.
3. Now, a service that wants to achieve a particular goal sends a message to the topic, let's say *Topic Authenticate*.

4. A consumer listening to *Topic Authenticate* is notified about a new message and consumes it.

5. The consumer processes the message it has consumed and puts a response back on another topic, *Topic Auth_Response*.

6. The producer of the original message is the consumer for *Topic Auth_Response*, and is notified about a new message.

7. The original requesting client then reads this message and completes the request–response cycle.

Now, we know what communication inside a microservices architecture that is powered by asynchronous message queues looks like. But is there any other benefit to this method other than asynchronous communication?

It turns out that there are a number of benefits that we may see from such a communication pattern. The following list shows some of the benefits that we may experience:

- **Better distribution of requests:** Since there could be a number of consumers that may be listening to a particular topic, the messages can be processed in parallel, and load balancing can be automatically taken care of by the equal distribution of messages among the consumers.

- **Better error resilience:** In the case where a particular microservice goes down, the messages that need to be processed by that microservice can be queued up inside the message queue for a certain time, and can then be processed by the service once it comes up, reducing possible data loss.

- **Reduction in duplicate responses:** Since a message is delivered only once to a single consumer and is dequeued as soon as it is consumed, there is a very small chance that there could be duplicate responses for a single request.

- **Increased tolerance:** During a time when the different microservices inside an infrastructure are experiencing high loads, the message queue system provides an asynchronous request–response cycle, thereby reducing the chance of request queue-ups.

With this, we now have an idea of how we can establish asynchronous communication between the microservices and make our infrastructure evolve over time without having to worry about how to handle the addition of new API endpoints for interservice communication.

Summary

In this chapter, we took a look at how we can work with the microservices architecture and how it differs from the traditional monolithic way of developing enterprise applications. We then took a look at the advantages that come as we move toward the microservice development approach and learned about the guidelines that we can follow to make our journey toward microservices smoother.

Once we had an idea about the basics of microservices, we went on to take a look at how SLAs guarantee us a certain desired set of functionalities between the services and how they act as a contract so as to support a smooth service by the application. We then moved on to a hands-on exercise by writing a simple to-do list management application utilizing microservices.

Once we completed the development of our sample application, we looked at how the manual way of maintaining configuration files to discover services may not work with a microservices architecture, so we took a deep dive into the topics of service discovery and how it can help us in the microservices world of application development. We then moved on to learn about the API gateways and how they can prove to be of use when deploying microservices in production. Finally, we learned how to establish asynchronous communication between these microservices.

With the whole application now divided into small microservices, we now need to understand how these services can be tested and how we can trace the flow of the calls inside these small services that run on our infrastructure in order to analyze how things are working and find out where things are going wrong. The next chapter takes us through the process of testing and tracing in a microservice architecture.

Questions

1. How does a service-oriented architecture differ from a microservice architecture?
2. How can we ensure high uptime for microservice-based applications?
3. What kind of guarantees are provided by a SLA?
4. Can we make API gateways communicate directly with the service registry?
5. What are the tools that we can use to implement asynchronous communication between microservices?

Further reading

Want to learn more about microservices? Take a look at *Practical Microservices* by *Umesh Ram Sharma* from *Packt Publishing*.

12

Testing and Tracing in Microservices

Up until now, we have got to see how microservices can help us change the way that we build and deliver our application to production. Be it faster rollouts for new features, or keeping the teams small, microservices enable that for us. But with this architecture, where every single component is a small service in its own, we have got some challenges to solve. These challenges involve how we can aim to ship a stable and bug free application into production while following the microservices approach.

Inside the Monolithic architecture, we had only a small number of moving components that required testing. We could write unit tests to test the individual methods of the Monolithic application, and then move on to integration testing to verify if these components operate correctly with each other. But now, with the advent of microservices, we have got more and more moving components in the picture. Inside the microservices, we have different features where each feature is described as its own microservice.

Over the course of this chapter, we will take a look at how the testing of microservices differ from that of the Monolithic applications, where we now need to account not only for the correct functioning of an individual microservice, but also have to make sure that these services communicate with each other in a well-defined manner to produce the correct results for the business needs.

Also, since the information in a microservices-based application flows from one service to another, it becomes important for us to understand the flow of this information when a client makes a request to when the response is generated. By doing this, we can accurately find and fix any of the issues that may generate an incorrect response or cause a bottleneck in the application performance.

As a reader, by the end of this chapter, you can expect to learn about the following:

- The difference between the testing of Monolithic applications and microservices-based applications
- Approaching the testing of microservices
- Implementing distributed tracing inside microservices

Technical requirements

The code listings in this book can be found under `chapter12` directory at `https://github.com/PacktPublishing/Hands-On-Enterprise-Application-Development-with-Python`.

The code samples can be cloned by running the following command:

```
git clone
https://github.com/PacktPublishing/Hands-On-Enterprise-Application-Developm
ent-with-Python
```

The requirements for the Python-based application can be installed by executing the following command on your Terminal:

```
pip install -r requirements.txt
```

Beyond the usual Python-based requirements, the code samples in this chapter need to have the following additional dependencies to work correctly:

- **Docker**: The docker client is required to run some of the tools that we will be using inside the repository. The installation instructions for docker related to your platform can be found at `https://docs.docker.com/install/`.

- **Jaeger all-in-one image**: For our distributed tracing examples, we will be utilizing Jaeger, which provides us with an Opentracing compatible library. For the demo, we can utilize the Jaeger all-in-one image that utilizes docker to run the Jaeger server, agent, and client to gather the tracing data and provide visualizations for the same. The Jaeger all-in-one image can be set up by running the following command:

    ```
    docker run -d -e COLLECTOR_ZIPKIN_HTTP_PORT=9411 -
    p5775:5775/udp -p6831:6831/udp -p6832:6832/udp \
     -p5778:5778 -p16686:16686 -p14268:14268 -p9411:9411
    jaegertracing/all-in-one:latest
    ```

Once the Jaeger all-in-one package is set up, make sure to visit `http://localhost:16686` to verify if the Jaeger UI opens up correctly.

Testing in the microservices world

As we move away from the Monolithic architecture, we need to understand that the processes that used to work for us in the Monolithic application development also need to move along. During the development of the Monolithic application, we used to work with the testing strategies such as unit testing, which aimed to cover the functionality of the individual methods inside an application, followed by integration testing, which is used to cover the fact that these methods operate correctly with each other.

Inside the microservices architecture, things get a little bit complicated. We now have small services where each service is supposed to perform a specific functionality. These services indeed need to interact with each other over the network to produce any meaningful output for the business use case that might be there. But things do not end here. Each of these microservices are composed of several individual methods and interfaces that it needs to work correctly. This makes the case of testing the microservices an interesting one, because now, we not only need to perform the unit testing of the individual components of the microservices and the interaction between them, but we also need to test if the microservices are able to operate correctly with each other.

This asks for a more elaborate testing of the application, with several different techniques. Let's take a look at these techniques to understand them better.

Unit testing in microservices

Unit testing inside microservices follows the same principles as in the testing of the Monolithic applications. We work on writing the unit tests for the individual methods inside a microservice and run those tests either manually or through automation so as to validate if those components are producing the expected result or not.

Functionality testing in microservices

Once we are sure that the individual methods inside a microservice work properly, we need to make sure that a microservice, in its complete independence, is able to function without any kind of issues. This happens because most of the microservices are a complete package in themselves. They come with their own set of dependencies, as well as the data sources through which they can manage their data.

As a developer, it is important for us to make sure that the microservice is able to interact properly with its dependencies. For this, we work on implementing the functionality testing for the microservices.

Also, during the functionality testing, we need to take care of certain things. Since each API endpoint inside a microservice may need to interact with some other microservice to produce the correct result, we might need to mock the presence of some microservices for the functionality testing to complete successfully.

Integration testing in microservices

Once we are sure that our microservices work correctly with their dependencies, it's time for us to make sure that they have the same checkboxes ticked when they are interacting with each other. This is important due to the fact that these services, no matter what, need to interact with each other to produce any meaningful business outcome.

During the integration tests, we usually aim to test the request response cycle by introducing both the correct and incorrect parameters to an API endpoint so as to verify that the microservices are able to handle both the use cases and do not fail. This ensures that the communication interfaces between two external services are robust enough for the varied inputs that they may be provided with.

End-to-end testing in microservices

Once we have assured that the different microservices are able to operate seamlessly with each other to generate a meaningful result, it's time to validate if the whole system, consisting of the different microservices and their dependencies, work without any problems. This kind of testing aims to cover the request-response cycle through the whole system, validating the outputs produced in the intermediate stages, as well as the final stages. This is known as **end-to-end** testing.

This kind of testing ensures that the system as a whole behaves in a well-defined manner and does not produce any surprises when an input that is beyond the domain of the system is provided to the system.

Scalability testing

Every microservice inside the infrastructure is made to handle a certain set of requests. As the number of requests to the application increases, some of the microservices may see an increased load on them in comparison to the other services.

Imagine there is an e-commerce website that is based upon the microservices architecture. There is a flash sale going on, and a lot of customers are trying to checkout and pay for their purchase at the same time. If the services that handle the checkout and payment for the customers does not scale up during the increased load, the customers may face increased response times or timeouts, creating chaos for the e-commerce company, whose customer care might now be busy in dealing with the angry customers.

The scalability testing of microservices aims to test that a service is able to scale up and scale down as the load varies, so as to keep the response times adequate, and to properly handle the varied loads during its life cycle.

Now, we have the knowledge of the different kinds of testing that needs to happen for a microservices based application. But what are some the challenges that make this testing a challenging task to achieve? Let's try to go through the challenges one by one and see if there is something we can do about them.

Challenges in microservices testing

The microservice architecture raises quite some challenges when it comes to testing. These challenges sometimes happen as a side effect of the architecture, the poor testing strategy, or the inexperience with the microservices architecture. The following are some of the challenges that make microservices testing a complex procedure:

- **Incomplete knowledge of the microservices**: For integration testing and debugging of issues inside an application built over microservices architecture, the tester responsible for writing the tests for the application needs to have complete knowledge about the infrastructure and the individual microservices. Without this knowledge, the tester is unable to write tests that can cover all the possible request flows inside an application that may result in some of the bugs escaping during the testing phase.
- **Poor coordination**: In the development of microservices, there are multiple teams that own their set of microservices, and are usually working on their pace. This may cause an issue in the coordination and can delay the testing of the application in case a microservice, on which there are certain dependencies, has still not come out of the development phase.

- **Increased complexity**: For an application that has only a small number of microservices, the testing is usually easy. But this testing becomes more and more cumbersome as the number of microservices powering an application increases. This is because now, the testers are supposed to write tests for the increased number of request flows, and also to make sure that the different API endpoints function as intended.
- **High flexibility**: Microservices allow for increased flexibility. As a developer, we are free to choose a technology stack that is going to power a particular microservice. The same thing adds to the increased issues for the testing of the application because now, the tests need to take into account the different types of components that are being used to power a particular microservice.

The preceding points are a few challenges that make the work of testing the microservices a challenging task. However, every problem comes with a solution, and so do these challenges. Let's take a look at the possible workarounds we have to overcome these challenges, outlined as follows:

- **Implement release schedules**: The teams responsible for building an application can commit to a schedule for the release of application in terms of Milestone. At every stage in the Milestone, some of the services are made available for testing based on the priority of the service to be deployed. This helps in improving the team's coordination.
- **Standardize the API endpoints:** Every service needs to expose a set of APIs that it uses for taking in a request and generating a response. Standardizing the APIs and defining what parameters a particular API endpoint may require helps a lot during the testing phase, where the testers can now mock a service easily, even if the service is not yet available for testing.
- **Standardize development practices**: Although every team that is responsible for the development of a particular microservice is free to use any set of tools for the development of microservice, it is usually a good practice to standardize the set of tools and technologies that may be used by a team so as to avoid unnecessary complexity inside the infrastructure.
- **Integration of DevOps practices**: As the shift to microservices architecture happens, the DevOps practices should also be adopted, which aims to make the teams responsible for the complete life cycle of the microservice they are developing. This not only helps in speeding up the development process, but also allows for thorough testing of the microservices before they are deployed in production.

Now, we are aware of what kind of changes the process requires for the testing of the microservices architecture. This allows us to plan our strategy ahead, and make sure that the services are well-tested before they are deployed into the production environment.

With the knowledge of testing in place, it's now time to understand a very important concept in the area of microservices that allows us to understand how the individual services are behaving in production. This also allows us to figure out where exactly a particular request inside a microservices-based application is failing. So, let's take a deep dive into this concept.

Tracing requests inside microservices

Inside any application, a request may flow through several components before a final response for the request is generated. All of these components may do some processing that might be required on the process before they hand the request off to another component.

The tracing of a request allows us to visualize a rich amount of detail about the flow of a particular request. With the complete picture of the flow of the request, we can now work on finding out the places that may be causing a bottleneck in the performance of the request-response cycle, or figure out the components that may be causing the generation of an incorrect result.

Today, in the application development world, any serious application that runs on a large scale has one or another kind of tracing solution implemented into it so as to trace the flow of the requests inside the application. Currently, there are a huge number of tools and services that allow for enabling tracing inside the application.

For the purpose of this chapter, we are going to utilize one of the tracing tools that is available in the open source community, which adheres to the OpenTracing standard, allowing us to trace the flow of the requests in our microservices. This tool, known as Jaeger, provides a complete framework for the end-to-end distributed tracing of a request inside an application. But what exactly is OpenTracing? Let's take a look.

The OpenTracing standard

Currently, there are a number of solutions out there in the wild that provide the functionality of implementing tracing for applications. Some of these solutions are proprietary, while the others are open source in nature.

As a developer, you are free to choose any of them based on the requirements of the application, and what facilities are provided by the solution you have chosen. But the problem is, what happens if you want to move to a different tracing solution because the solution provides better features and more control over the environment? Now you are stuck because you might need to change a lot of things in your infrastructure and the application code to get the new tracing solution to work. That's a lot of trouble.

The OpenTracing standard provides a common set of vendor neutral APIs and instrumentation for implementing distributed tracing inside the applications. Any tracing solution that implements this set of standard APIs is compatible with the OpenTracing standard, and can interoperate with the other tools that follow the same standard.

Our choice of Jaeger as a tracing tool for our demo applications is also an OpenTracing compliant tool. Now, without spending any more time, let's get our hands dirty by implementing tracing inside the application we built in the previous chapter.

Implementing tracing inside ToDo manager

In the previous chapter, we worked on building a simple application that allows us to manage ToDo lists. It's time for us to implement request tracing inside this application. For the first example, we will work on implementing tracing of the requests inside our user service.

For the tracing to work, we will need to have a few requirements in place. If you followed the *Technical requirements* section of this book, you are in a good place to start working with the tutorial. But, before we dive into implementing the tracing, let's take a look at the following components that we will require:

- **Jaeger all-in-one image:** The Jaeger all-in-one image provides us with the Jaeger server, the agent, and a UI that will help us collect the tracing data that is being reported by the application, and will also allow us to visualize the same data
- **Jaeger-client:** The `jaeger_client` allows us to use Jaeger for the collection of the tracing data from the application
- **Flask-opentracing:** This module provides the functionality for implementing tracing and instrumentation in our application through the use of the OpenTracing standard

With the requirements, setup complete, it's time for us to implement the tracing inside our application. For this, fire up the `user_service.py` file inside the code editor of your choice and follow the proceeding steps:

- **Importing the** `jaeger_client` **and** `flask_opentracing`: Before we can implement the tracing inside our application, we first need to import the required libraries for helping us set up the tracing. The following snippet of code needs to be added to the start of the file to allow us to import the necessary libraries:

```
from jaeger_client import Config
from flask_opentracing import FlaskTracer
```

- **Initialize the tracer:** Once we have the required libraries imported into our service, it's time to initialize the tracer inside the application. The following code snippet defines a new method inside our application, which initializes the tracing of the application:

```
def init_tracer():
    """Initialize tracing for the application.
    """
    config = Config(
        config = {
            'sampler': {'type': 'const', 'param': 1}
        },
        service_name='user_service')
    return config.initialize_tracer()

# Setup Flask Tracer
flask_tracer = FlaskTracer(init_tracer, True, app)
```

With the tracer implemented, we can now see a trace of the requests that come to our user service inside the Jaeger UI. To do this, let's make a simple POST request to the `/auth/register` endpoint of the service and see what shows up in the Jaeger UI running at `http://localhost:16686`.

Once this is done, we will see the following output on the Jaeger UI:

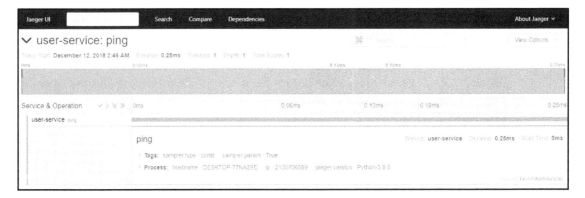

With this, we have successfully implemented the tracing inside the user service.

Now, with this done, we can move on to implementing tracing of the requests between the microservices. So, let's take a look at how we can do this.

Distributed tracing

Inside the microservices world, the requests may travel from one service to another before a final response is generated. Even our simple example of a `todo` list management application shows this behavior, where the `todo` manager service frequently makes a request to the user service to implement user authentication, and to gather the details about the user, thus creating a new `todo` list.

The distributed tracing system aims to enable the tracing of the requests while they travel from one microservice to another.

To achieve this, the tracing systems utilize a number of mechanisms, the easiest of which is to embed a unique tracing key into the HTTP headers of every request that is being made. The tracing system is then able to differentiate and aggregate a particular request as it flows from one service to another by reading the request identifier that is present in the HTTP headers.

Now, it's time for us to see the distributed tracing in action. For this, we will make a few changes to enable tracing inside our `todo` manager service.

The following snippet of code showcases the changes required to enable distributed tracing inside the `todo` manager service:

```
from flask import Flask, request, jsonify
from flask_sqlalchemy import SQLAlchemy
from jaeger_client import Config
from flask_opentracing import FlaskTracer
from opentracing_instrumentation.client_hooks import install_all_patches
import datetime
import requests

app = Flask(__name__, instance_relative_config=True)
app.config.from_object('config')

def init_tracer():
    """Initialize the tracing system."""

    config = Config(
        config={ # usually read from some yaml config
            'enabled': True,
            'sampler': {
                'type': 'const',
                'param': 1,
            },
            'logging': True,
        },
        service_name='todo-service',
        validate=True,
    )
    return config.initialize_tracer()

install_all_patches()

flask_tracer = FlaskTracer(init_tracer, True, app)
```

With the preceding code in place inside the `todo_service.py` file, we have the distributed tracing enabled. But before we see this in action, there are a few things that we need to take a look at. In the preceding code snippet, we imported one extra method named `install_all_patches()` from the `opentracing_instrumentation` library which is shown as follows:

```
from opentracing_instrumentation.client_hooks import install_all_patches
```

This method is responsible for enabling the tracing of the actions that takes place inside the SQL library or through the `python_requests` library.

Once this library was imported along with the `jaeger_client` and `flask_opentracing`, we moved on to configure and enable the tracing for the application inside the `init_tracer` method.

Now, with the tracing configured, let's restart our application and then make a request to `http://localhost:5001/list/new` by passing the appropriate parameters to the API endpoint for creating a new `todo` list.

Once this action succeeds, we can navigate back to our Jaeger UI running at `http://localhost:16686` to see that the Jaeger UI shows the trace for the API call we just made. The following screenshot shows a sample of how the screen may look:

As we can see from the preceding screenshot, the Jaeger UI does not only show the request trace for the todo manager API service endpoint, but also goes further into displaying the endpoint that was called inside the user service, while providing the details of how much time was spent in each of the API endpoints before the response was generated back to the client application.

With this, we now have an idea of how the distributed tracing inside microservices looks. But what are the possible use cases that can see a benefit from having this kind of tracing in place? Let's find out.

Benefits of distributed tracing

With distributed tracing in place inside our application based on microservices architecture, we have enabled a lot of power to tackle quite some use cases, such as the following:

- **Understanding the flow of the application**: With distributed tracing, we can now visualize how an incoming request from the client flows inside our application from one service to another. This kind of information is really useful in figuring out how the application works and to enable better testing of the application.
- **Narrowing down the bugs**: With the idea of how the request goes from one service to another, we can quickly isolate the services that may be causing the request to produce an incorrect response by analysing what steps were taken by which service to process the request before a response was generated.
- **Finding performance bottlenecks**: With timing visualization in place for how long a particular step took in the request-response cycle, we can now quickly analyse which part of the application is causing a performance bottleneck in the request-response cycle, hence allowing us to solve the issue with ease.

With all of this knowledge, we can now efficiently build, test, and deploy our applications based upon the microservices architecture, while also allowing for a more matured process to manage the infrastructure that powers our application.

Summary

Over the course of this chapter, we got to learn about how the move to microservices architecture affects the processes inside our application development life cycle. We got to learn about how the testing inside microservices-based applications differ from that of the Monolithic applications, and what kind of testing phases are usually required when dealing with the microservices architecture. We then learned about the challenges that arise in the testing phases, due to the move toward a microservices-based approach, and how we can overcome them.

The second part of this chapter took us through the journey of distributed tracing inside the application, where we did a hands-on to enable us to trace the flow of requests in the ToDo manager application we developed in the previous chapter. During this, we got to learn about how the tracing works, and how distributed tracing differs from the normal methods of tracing. We also learned about how the OpenTracing standard is helping provide a vendor neutral API for enabling distributed tracing inside microservices-based applications.

Now, with all of this knowledge, let's move on to take a look at another approach of developing our enterprise applications where instead of building services or components, we will build functions that execute on the occurrence of a certain event. The next chapter takes us through this serverless approach of application development.

Questions

- How can we write integration tests for microservices?
- How does tracing a Monolithic application differ from that of microservices-based applications?
- What other tools are available except Jaeger for enabling distributed tracing?
- How can we instrument a specific part of code using Jaeger?

13
Going Serverless

As we have explored so far, Microservices offer a great alternative architecture with which we can approach the application development scenario. With the advantages of having faster release cycles, easy-to-launch new features and high scalability, the Microservices are a compelling choice for developers. But all of these Microservices still run in a server-based environment.

Running in a server-based environment is useful in terms of the response times of the applications because there is always a service that is ready to accept an incoming request. But there is one disadvantage: If there are no users, the applications keep on consuming system resources.

Recently, application developers have started to make a move toward a new approach of application development. This approach of development focuses on the applications being event-driven and launches an action based on the occurrence of some event. These kinds of applications are known as serverless applications because they do not keep on running when there is no user and an instance of them launches only when there has been some event that has occurred.

As we move through this chapter, we will take a look at this serverless approach of application development and how it is changing the development scenario.

As a reader of this chapter, you will get to learn about the following:

- The serverless approach to application development
- The process that powers the serverless architecture
- Building a serverless application
- Benefits of the serverless approach

Technical requirements

The code listings in this book can be found under `chapter13` directory at `https://github.com/PacktPublishing/Hands-On-Enterprise-Application-Development-with-Python`.

The code samples can be cloned by running the following command:

```
git clone
https://github.com/PacktPublishing/Hands-On-Enterprise-Application-Developm
ent-with-Python
```

Additionally, for the code to execute successfully, some additional software will be required:

- **Docker**: Docker is required as a dependency to run the OpenWhisk software platform for the deployment of the serverless applications. To install `docker` on your platform, please take a look at `https://docs.docker.com/install/`.

- **Apache OpenWhisk**: Apache OpenWhisk provides an open source platform for running serverless applications. For our examples, we are going to use the OpenWhisk project to provide us with a mechanism for running the code examples. To set up OpenWhisk on the system, please perform the following steps:

1. Clone the Project installer from GitHub by executing the following command:

```
git clone https://github.com/apache/incubator-OpenWhisk-devtools.git
```

2. `cd` into the `docker-compose` directory inside the project by running the following command:

```
cd incubator-OpenWhisk-devtools/docker-compose
```

3. Execute the following command:

```
make quick-start
```

These steps will help you get the OpenWhisk project set up and running along with the required tools to interact with the OpenWhisk.

The serverless approach to application development

In recent years, as developers, we have grown accustomed to the traditional ways of building applications and handling their deployments on the production infrastructure. In this traditional architecture, we developed applications where the application takes in a request from the **Client**, checks whether the **Client** is authorized to perform that action, and then moves on to executing that action.

Once the application was developed, we deployed it over a platform that would be compatible with our application. This involves the choice of the operating system, the kind of the infrastructure where this platform will be running, for example a bare-metal server, a VM, or a container, and then we maintained the infrastructure by handling its scalability and fixing any issues that may arise. For example, a simple system that manages employee payroll inside an organization will look like this:

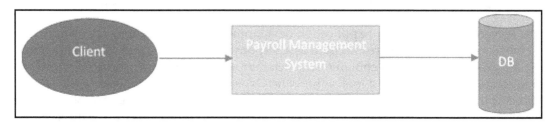

In this case, the application keeps running on a server, waiting for the requests to come, and acting on them as they arrive.

This kind of approach, though highly useful, usually pulls the developers from their main task of writing the logic to achieve a particular outcome from the system, and makes them focus on a lot of areas that involve tasks related to the infrastructure management and scalability.

Now imagine an architecture that would allow developers to focus on just writing the logic behind a particular business process without worrying about where that logic will be executed and how it will scale.

The serverless approach to building applications provides these features. The way this works in serverless is through the introduction of two new techniques to application development:

- **Backend as a service** (**BaaS**): BaaS is a new cloud computing offering that provides the application developers with the functionality of linking their applications with the backend services through the use of APIs, so as to provide some common feature sets, such as user authentication and data storage. It differs from the general architecture of application development in that these services provided by the backend may not need to be developed by the application developers themselves, but access to these services is enabled through the use of APIs exposed by these services.
- **Function as a service** (**FaaS**): FaaS is another category of cloud computing that allows developers to focus on writing the application logic without worrying about where this logic will execute. In FaaS, the applications run in a stateless and ephemeral manner where the infrastructure they might be executing in may be valid only for a few invocations, which may be as little as a single invocation.

In the serverless architecture of application development, the applications are usually developed as functions that are executed as a response to a certain event. These functions execute in their own stateless containers, which may exist in the infrastructure for only a few invocations. We will take a look at how the serverless applications work in the later sections of this chapter. For a quick reference, if we had to implement the Payroll system as a serverless application; the following diagram shows how the architecture of the system would look:

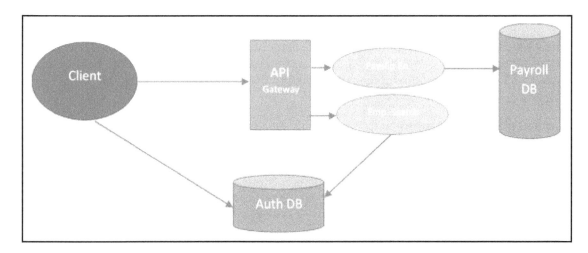

As we can see, our serverless payroll application contains both the features of a BaaS offering where the **Client** directly interacts with the **Auth DB** through the APIs exposed by the **Auth DB** and the **Payslip** generation, and employee search runs in a FaaS offering where they are stored as functions and executed only when a particular event happens.

Both of these functions do not maintain any kind of state, such that they can run in ephemeral containers that may only last for a short amount of time.

So now, let's take a look at the components that power the serverless architecture and how the serverless architecture works to have a better understanding of how we can develop applications that best utilize the serverless architecture.

Components of serverless architecture

As we have seen, the serverless architecture provides us a way to develop applications where we are only responsible for writing the logic behind the applications, and relieves us of the worry of how the infrastructure will be managed for running the application and how the application will scale up and down based on the number of requests.

But what powers this architecture? Let's try to spend some time taking a look at how the different components inside the architecture work to provide a serverless development approach toward application development.

As discussed earlier, the serverless approach to application development is made possible through the use of two technologies that have came into existence recently in the cloud-computing landscape. These technologies, BaaS and FaaS, provide the foundations for building serverless applications. Let's take a look at them.

Backend as a service

Most of the applications that we develop share a common set of functionalities. These functionalities may include the implementation of a user authentication database, providing a way for storage and retrieval of files, or sending notifications either through the use of emails or push notifications.

Most of the time, these functionalities are built into the application by introducing new components inside the application with which the other components can interact. The same is true for the Microservices-based applications, where these features are implemented, as different Microservices and the other Microservices interact with these services to achieve a certain outcome.

In the BaaS approach, we decouple these functionalities from the application by integrating these functionalities through the use of third-party cloud providers. When this happens, our applications usually integrate these functionalities through the use of the APIs that are provided by the third-party providers.

To understand this better, let's take a look at the serverless payroll-management system we introduced earlier. In this system, we have made the user authentication a disjointed part of our application by leveraging the BaaS offering provided by a third-party.

In this approach, our user authentication system and any of the data associated with it is managed by a third-party provider. This provider exposes some of the APIs for the service, which we can use to integrate the service with our application.

In our example, we exposed part of the user authentication service to the client through the use of the APIs exposed by the service. This allows the client to perform the user authentication directly with the service without going through the whole backend of the application. The second place where we used the BaaS offering was when we linked the employee search function with the user authentication service to retrieve a particular employee based on some criteria.

This concept of BaaS provides us with several advantages, such as the following:

- **Reduced development time:** With BaaS, the developers of an application need not worry about the development for the common set of functionalities that they can consume directly from the third-party service providers by using the APIs provided by the service provider.
- **Ease of operations:** Since the service and the infrastructure related to the service is managed by the cloud computing provider only, this reduced the complexity of managing the service and the operations it provides, allowing for reduced operational headaches.
- **Ease of scalability:** The services provided by the cloud computing provider are managed directly by them, allowing for easy scalability, which is now done by the provider only.
- **Flexibility of integration:** The services provided by the provider are usually integrated through the use of APIs. If the necessary API for the service integration is available for a provided platform, the platform can easily integrate with the service without worrying about the complexities behind the integration and hence allowing for support in different kinds of applications.

Function as a service

FaaS is an interesting concept and one of the main technologies that powers the serverless architecture. Inside this approach, we develop the backend code without worrying about how that code will be deployed and where it will be executed.

The applications aimed for FaaS are just like any other application that does not require any kind of special framework for their development and execution. The only difference that comes between an FaaS application and a regular application that is deployed on the servers is the fact that FaaS applications have a severe limitation in terms of maintaining their state and the amount of time they can execute for. So, let's take a deeper dive into these two main aspects of having your application run in an FaaS model.

The restrictions on state management

In the FaaS model, the different parts of the application are built as separate functions where each function is executed on the occurrence of a certain event. When the application is supposed to be deployed, the cloud provider automatically manages the infrastructure where the application will run and how the application will scale up.

In comparison to the traditional applications that, once deployed, start a server process and are ready to accept the incoming connections, the FaaS-based applications are started dynamically as a response to a certain input. Once the event occurs, the function starts and executes, waits for some time, and then the instance in which the function is executing is terminated. Now, this makes the process a bit interesting because the time for which the function is present in the infrastructure is limited and there is no guarantee that the same instance of the function will also handle the next call.

This makes the state management, that is, the management of local data for a currently-executing operation, a challenging task inside FaaS-based offerings, which severely limits what local data we can store inside a function instance while it is executing.

For dealing with such a scenario, we depend upon an external offering that can store the state data for us. This may include the use of an external database or a caching server where the data can be persisted for future reference.

Restrictions on execution times

Once a function starts executing inside an FaaS offering, it has only a limited amount of time in which it needs to complete its execution. Most of the famous cloud service providers have a limit set on their infrastructure for how long a function inside an FaaS offering can execute. For example, if we choose the most renowned FaaS offering by AWS, the AWS Lambda, the maximum duration for which a function can execute is limited to five minutes. This limit may vary marginally on the other providers but won't be too high.

Now this makes an interesting case for us as application developers. If one of the application components that we are trying to implement as a function may take a significantly long time to execute, then we may want to re-evaluate our choice of hosting that component inside an FaaS offering.

Now we have an idea of the kind of restrictions that FaaS offerings implement. But, why do these restrictions happen and where do our functions execute inside an FaaS offering? Let's take a look.

Executing functions inside FaaS

Once we have developed our applications in the form of functions, we need a place to host and run it. This hosting place for the functions is provided by the cloud service provider. Now, once we have successfully hosted these functions and implemented rules when a particular function should execute, it is the duty of the cloud provider to handle the correct execution of these functions.

Now, when these functions have to execute, the cloud provider determines the correct environment that will be required to execute a particular function. Once this environment has been determined, the cloud provider launches an ephemeral container inside which the function code resides. This container provides the function a complete isolation from the other functions that might be executing in the environment. Now, once the container has launched successfully, this function executes, and provides a response back.

The interesting part happens once the function has completed its execution. Once the function has completed execution, the cloud provider can either terminate the container instance in which the function was running or it can keep it alive to handle newer requests. Most of the time, the decision is taken based on the frequency of the requests that are arriving and the kind of policies that have been set by the user.

If a function instance is still running and waiting, a new incoming request might be redirected to that instance only, whereas if there are no ideal instances of a function running, the cloud provider will launch a new instance and redirect the request to that instance.

With this, we have a good idea of how FaaS works inside the serverless architecture and how it enables us to develop serverless applications. But how are these functions actually triggered? This brings us to another important component that comprises the serverless offerings. Let's take a look at what it is.

API gateways in the serverless architecture

In `Chapter 11`, *Taking the Microservices Approach*, when we went through the concept of Microservices, we got introduced to API Gateways and how they help in the development of Microservices. These API gateways also play an important role in the development of the applications based upon the serverless architectures.

The API gateways are nothing but HTTP servers that embed the information about certain API endpoints of an application and associate these endpoints with some handlers. Once a request is made to a certain API endpoint, the handler associated with the API endpoint is called to handle the request.

In the serverless architecture, the handlers that are associated with a particular API endpoint inside the API gateway are the FaaS functions. When the API gateway receives a request at a particular API endpoint, the API gateway triggers an event that will make the FaaS function execute on the request. Any of the parameters that are required by the FaaS function to execute are forwarded by the API gateway to the function and the response generated by the function is then sent back to the requesting client.

Now, here is an important aspect related to the API gateways. These API gateways, which we use in the serverless application development, can usually be configured by us. But these API gateways are mostly hosted on the cloud service provider that is providing the support for serverless application deployment. This makes these API gateways a BaaS offering, which runs on the infrastructure of the provider with the power of configuration available to the user.

Now we have the knowledge of the different components that power the serverless architecture and are ready to take our first steps into the development of our first serverless application. But before we start with the development of our first serverless application, let's look at one last important concept in how a platform handles the execution of a serverless application, which will provide us with a much broader context of the kind of performance we can expect from the serverless applications.

Understanding the execution of a serverless application

So far, we've learned that a serverless application is built in the form of functions that execute based on the occurrence of some event. Also, these functions do not stay alive forever. Instead, these functions are brought into execution as requirements arise. So, how does the provider handle the execution of these functions when a request comes in? Let's take a look.

Cold-starting a function

When the application has been freshly deployed, it is pretty easy to imagine that there will be no instances of the function that will be executing currently. When a new request comes in that asks for the functionality provided by the function we have just deployed on the infrastructure. Now, the cloud provider systems are notified that there are no running instances of the function that can handle the incoming request.

Once the provider system is made aware of the situation, it spawns up a new instance with the function code inside it. This instance now starts to execute the function based on the parameters provided in the request and a response is generated by the function and sent back to the requesting client.

Now, when the function finishes executing, the container holding the function instance is not terminated immediately. Instead, the provider waits for a pre-configured amount of time before it terminates the instance. This is done with the expectation that the same container instance can be used for handling another request, which will save some time which might be required to do a cold launch of the new function instance.

These cold starts increase the response times for clients when no instance is running to handle the incoming requests.

Hot-starting a function

Completely opposite to the cold start, where a new instance of the function needs to be created and brought up to the execution, the hot start of the function utilizes the existing instance of the function that is already running in the infrastructure of the provider. When this happens, an incoming request does not have to spend time waiting for a new instance to spawn up before the request can be handled. This allows for the request to be processed quickly.

There is one thing that needs to be noted here: even in the case of a hot start of a function, the state from the previous execution of the function is not stored.

Now we know about one of the major factors on which the performance of a function may depend. Let's now move forward and build our first serverless application.

Building our first serverless application

With our basic knowledge of the serverless architecture and how it works, it's now time for us to develop our first serverless application. For this tutorial, we are going to use the Apache OpenWhisk project, which will help us run our demo application on our local development system. So, let's take a look at what Apache OpenWhisk has to offer us and how we can utilize the platform for our benefit.

A quick introduction to Apache OpenWhisk

The Apache OpenWhisk platform provides us with the features and functionality that allow us to set up our own platform for running serverless applications. The project provides the functionality for executing functions based on the triggering of certain events in the environment.

The execution of these functions happens inside the docker containers, and the OpenWhisk platform manages the deployment and scaling of these functions inside it.

Here are some of the features provided by the platform:

- **Easy-to-use tools:** The platform provides a number of tools that allow us to easily package and port the application to run on the OpenWhisk platform, with the exception of having the application follow a set of conventions as defined by the platform.

- **Isolation using containers:** The platform isolates the different functions through the use of docker containers, such that every function runs inside its own isolated environment so as to avoid any kind of environmental-dependency conflicts.
- **Support for a wide variety of languages:** The OpenWhisk platform provides us with a number of supported language platforms that we can use to build our serverless application. This also includes the use of binary executables built using Go, C++, and Rust.
- **Built-in API Gateway:** The OpenWhisk package comes with its own built-in API gateway, allowing us to easily integrate the applications through the use of RESTful API endpoints.

All of these functionalities make OpenWhisk a great platform for running the serverless applications, be it on the cloud or in your local development environment.

But, before we start building the application, we need to have OpenWhisk deployed on our system. To deploy the project, please follow the steps in the *Technical requirements* section at the beginning of this chapter.

For the demo, we are going to build an application that queries the GitHub API for us and retrieves the repositories that are associated with our user account.

Setting up the development environment

Before we start writing the code for our application, we need to have some dependencies in place. So, let's build the environment and then move on to writing the code that will power our application.

As a first step, let's create a directory that will contain all the files related to our project. Let's call this folder `github_demo`. The following command gets the folder in place for us:

```
mkdir github_demo
```

Once we have the directory setup done, let's move into the directory and set up a few things:

```
cd github_demo
```

Once this is done, we can now set up our project. Before we start writing the code, let's get the virtual environment setup done, which will help us to keep our project dependencies segregated. The following command creates the virtual environment for us:

```
virtualenv –python=python3 venv
```

The next step is to activate the virtual environment and set up the required dependencies. The following command will get the virtual environment ready for use:

```
source venv/bin/activate
```

Once this is done, let's install our dependency. For our demo application, we will be using the PyGithub library available through pip. To get the dependency installed, all we need to do is execute the next command:

```
pip install pygithub
```

With our dependencies installed, we are now ready to build our application.

Building our configuration file

For the purpose of this application, we are going to use a configuration file to store our user-account-related data, which will allow us to authenticate to the Github API. For this, inside our project directory, create a new file named config.ini with the following contents:

```
[github_auth]
username = '<your github username>'
password = '<your github password>'
```

Once we have the configuration file setup complete, let's move on to writing our application code, which will interact with Github to get our repos.

Integrating with the GitHub API

Now that we're coming to the actual part of our application, let's get started with writing the code. The following code snippet describes the code we use to query the Github API:

```
from github import Github
import configparser

# Provide the location of where the config file exists
CONFIG_FILE = 'config.ini'

def parse_config():
    """Parse the configuration file and setup the required
configuration."""

    config = configparser.ConfigParser()
```

```
        config.read(CONFIG_FILE)
        if 'github_auth' not in config.sections():
            return False
        username = config['github_auth']['username']
        password = config['github_auth']['password']

        return (username, password)

    def get_repos():
        """Retrieve the github repos associated with the user.

        Returns:
            Dict
        """

        response = {}
        config = parse_config()
        if not config:
            response['message'] = "Unable to read configuration"
            return response

        username = config[0]
        passord = config[1]

        # Create the github object to authenticate
        g = Github(username, password)
        repos = []
        for repo in g.get_user().get_repos():
            repos.append(repo.name)
        response['repos'] = repos
        return response
```

Now, we have finished writing the code that will query the Github API for us and provide the results. Let's spend some time going through what this code does.

At the start of the file, we import two of the libraries that we are going to use for our project: configparser, which we are going to use to parse the configuration file we just created, and the GitHub library, which will provide us access to the Github API:

```
from github import Github
import configparser
```

Once this is done, we define a function named parse_config(), which is responsible for parsing the configuration file for us and returns a tuple based on the parsing. If the config file does not contain the correct contents, the function returns a False value indicating that the parsing was not successful.

Once the function is defined, we define another function, which will query the `Github` API for us and return the results from the query. This `get_repos()` function does a few things:

- It calls the `parse_config` function and gets the authentication parameters from the configuration file.
- Once the authentication parameters have been obtained, the function uses those parameters to authenticate to the `Github` API by creating a new instance of the `Github` object provided by the library we imported:

```
g = Github(username, password)
```

Once this object is created, we are now ready to communicate with the `Github` API.

To retrieve the list of `repos` that are associated with our user account, we call the `get_repos()` method of the `Github` object instance, which retrieves the list of `repos` associated with our account:

```
for repo in g.get_user().get_repos():
```

Once we have the list of `repos`, we iterate over the list, collecting the names of the `repos` and adding them to the response dictionary. At the end, the method returns this response dict back.

Once we are done writing the code for our `repo`, we are ready to get it running with OpenWhisk.

Getting the code ready to run with OpenWhisk

With the code ready, it's now time to get it into a format that OpenWhisk can execute.

For any function to execute inside OpenWhisk, the code should be called from the `__main__.py` file. So, let's create the file and add the following contents to it:

```
from github_demo import get_repos

def main(dict):
    repos = get_repos()
    return repos
```

With the code in place, let's try to understand what we did here. First, we imported the `get_repos` function that we created in the `github_demo.py` file, which helps to retrieve the contents from the `Github` API:

```
from github_demo import get_repos
```

Then, we define the `main()` function, which is called by the OpenWhisk, to execute the code. Any code that is present inside the main function is directly executed by the OpenWhisk. So, we use this method to call our `get_repos()` function:

```
def main(dict):
```

Once this is done, we are on the verge of getting our application ready for the deployment.

Taking the final steps toward deployment

We have just a few more steps before we can deploy our application. For the successful installation of the app, let's create a file that stores the dependencies required for running our project. The following command helps us get the dependencies in place:

```
pip freeze > requirements.txt
```

With the requirements packaged, now let's package our project so that it can be deployed to OpenWhisk. For this, running the following command helps in creating a package of different project components:

```
tar -zcvf github_demo.tar.gz github_demo
```

With this, we are now all set to deploy our application to OpenWhisk.

Deploying to OpenWhisk

Once we have the package ready for deployment, we need to run a few commands provided by OpenWhisk to get the package up and running on the platform.

As a first step, we have to execute the following command to get the package uploaded on the OpenWhisk:

```
wsk action create github_demo -kind python:3 github_demo.tar.gz
```

Once this command is executed, the package will be uploaded to the OpenWhisk platform and will be ready to run.

Now, to invoke the application, we can run the following command, which will execute the application in an asynchronous manner:

```
wsk action invoke github_demo
```

Once this is done, our application starts executing in an asynchronous manner. By running asynchronously, we mean that the execution of the command won't wait until the end of the execution of the function, but rather will provide an action activation ID that can be used to track the results of the invocation.

Now, let's take a look at how OpenWhisk handles the execution of this application after the application has been deployed.

Understanding the execution of application Inside Openwhisk

With the demo application in place, it's time for us to understand how the execution of this application works behind the scenes.

Behind the successful execution of the application, there are several steps involved which start from the `wsk action invoke` command that we ran to execute our application. So, let's take a look at the steps that happened behind the scenes:

1. **Making the API call:** Every action that we build to deploy on OpenWhisk is mapped as an API endpoint that will invoke the action. When we run `wsk action invoke`, the command makes a call to the API endpoint that has been mapped for the provided function. This call is then intercepted by Nginx inside OpenWhisk, which acts as a termination point for SSL and then invokes the controller.

2. **Processing by the controller:** The controller, which is an implementation of the REST API, disambiguates what the request is supposed to do based on the HTTP method used for the request. Once the ambiguity of the request has been resolved, the controller then resolves the action that needs to be invoked. Beyond this, the controller has a few more duties to perform:
   - **Validating Authorization:** The controller verifies whether the user is authorized to invoke the action based on their privileges with respect to the action that needs to be invoked.
   - **Fetching the action:** The controller fetches the action from the actions database before the action can be invoked.

3. **Finding the invoker:** The action needs an invoker that can execute the action. For this, the controller queries the service discovery service inside OpenWhisk, which provides it with the list of the invokers that can invoke a provided action. Based on the list, the controller determines a free invoker on which the action can be invoked.

4. **Communicating the Request:** The controller communicates the request to the invoker through the use of Kafka, which is a distributed message platform that handles the processing and delivery of the messages from the producers to consumers. In this case, the type of execution was asynchronous; an action ID is provided to the user as soon as the controller has delivered the message to Kafka.

5. **Invoking the action:** The invoker fetches the message from Kafka and invokes the action by launching a docker-based container inside which the function code executes.

6. **Storing the results:** The results of the invocation needs to be stored somewhere from where they can be queried later. For this, OpenWhisk stores the results in its database, from where they can be queried again using an Action ID.

This is how our serverless code executes behind the scenes with OpenWhisk. Now, with this knowledge, let's take a look at the advantages that a shift to the serverless development approach provides us.

Advantages of going serverless

With an understanding of how serverless applications work, now it's time for us to take a look at the advantages provided by this development approach:

- **Reduced development efforts:** By using the services provided by the third-party cloud providers, we can reduce the development efforts for some of the common functionalities that are found inside an application, such as user authentication, notification, and file storage. All of these functionalities can be implemented through the use of the APIs provided by the cloud providers.

- **Less operational complexity:** The execution and scaling of a serverless application is managed by the cloud service provider, which takes away the operational complexities of managing our own infrastructure to handle the execution of the application.

- **High availability:** The applications built in the serverless manner provide high availability due to the fact that the infrastructure is managed by the cloud provider, which can have the application run in different data centers across the world, hence reducing the chance that the application's uptime will be affected in case one of the data centers is experiencing some issues.

- **Optimized resource allocation:** Since a function is executed only when a certain event occurs, the allocation of resources happens only when a particular function is being executed, which optimizes the usage of resources across the infrastructure.

- **Choice of programming languages:** Most of the serverless solutions provide a wide support for the different types of programming languages that are available, which allows us to implement our solutions with the best-possible technology stack that will work with the application.

With this, we now have enough points that can convince us to choose the serverless development approach in case our needs align with the development methodology that needs to be followed for building a serverless application.

Summary

As we moved through this chapter, we took a look at how the serverless architecture is becoming the new trend in the development of the applications, and how this architecture works. We covered the different components of the serverless architecture and went through the concepts of Backend as a Service and Function as a Service, which power the serverless architecture. We then looked at the role of API Gateways in the architecture and how the API Gateway in serverless applications differs from the one we used in Microservices.

After that, we took a tour of building our first serverless application and ran it through Apache OpenWhisk, which provides an open source platform for running serverless applications. Here, we also took a deep dive into how the different components inside the OpenWhisk project work together to get the final results to us.

We concluded the chapter by exploring the different advantages that the move to the serverless application development approach provides us.

With this, we can now move on and start to think about the deployment strategy that we may want to use for the deployment of our applications. The next chapter takes us through the different deployment strategies in the cloud, and how to decide which kind of cloud to use based on the needs of the organization.

Questions

1. What are the advantages provided by the serverless architecture?
2. How does BaaS help is the development of applications?
3. How does an API Gateway help in the execution of serverless applications?
4. What are some of the things that make it hard to port an application into a serverless format?

Further reading

Did you find the idea of serverless architecture interesting? Take a look at *Building Serverless Applications with Python* by *Jalem Raj Rohit, Packt Publishing*, and dive deeper into the serverless architecture.

14
Deploying to the Cloud

A lot of our focus until now has been spent working on the development of the applications, be it in the form of a big monolithic application or in the form of a microservices-based application where a lot of services are present. For these applications to be made available to the users, the applications need to be deployed somewhere where general users can interact with the application.

In the modern world of DevOps, the deployment strategies and where the deployment of the application is going to happen play an important role in defining how the application is going to work and be made accessible to the user. The decisions taken about the deployment of the applications can influence a lot of things inside the infrastructure, such as the complexity of infrastructure that will be required to run a particular application or how the new features inside the application will be rolled out.

Over the course of this chapter, we will take a look at how to create deployments for the monolithic applications as well as microservices-based applications, and how we can work on implementing the deployment strategies that prioritize the stability of the application when it has been deployed over the infrastructure. We will also take a look at differentiating the modern ways of deploying an application using the containers and making a choice between the private, public, and hybrid cloud deployments.

As a reader of this chapter, you will get to learn about the following:

- The need for deployment strategies
- Containerizing applications for deployment
- Integrating testing as a part of the deployment strategy
- Deployment on a private cloud
- Deployment on a public cloud
- The shift toward the hybrid cloud

Technical requirements

For understanding this chapter, a fair knowledge of containerization using Docker and knowledge about how to use the CLI from at least one of the cloud providers will be of use.

Deploying enterprise applications

Over the course of this book, we have seen how to develop an enterprise application using different principles, be it a monolithic way of application development or through the use of small microservices for developing the application. But these things converge at a common point. For our applications to be made available for general use, they need to be deployed at some place outside the development environment that is accessible to the general users.

This infrastructure and the type of deployment chosen for a particular application need to offer a certain set of features for the deployment to be successful:

- **High uptime:** Any infrastructure where an application is deployed needs to provide high uptime so as to provide a near interruption free service of the application to its users. If the infrastructure is vulnerable to frequent downtimes, then it might cause severe downtimes in the availability of the application, and can cause the processes that are dependent upon the application to come to a halt until the infrastructure on which the application is running comes back online.
- **Low latency:** The latency of the infrastructure serving the application should be low so as to enable adequate response times to the users. If the infrastructure latency is high, the users may keep waiting to interact with the application, or the response to be generated by the application may severely impact their productivity.
- **Fault tolerance:** The deployment infrastructure should be fault tolerant and should be able to recover from an occasional failure of a few nodes. In case of the absence of fault tolerance, even a single issue inside the infrastructure will be enough to bring the whole application down, causing severe reliability issues for the users of the application.

These are just a basic set of requirements that need to be present for an infrastructure to be considered for the deployment of the application. There could be additional requirements that might get imposed as a result of the choice of a particular deployment strategy for the infrastructure, but the discussion of those requirements is beyond the scope of this book.

Untill now, we have heard the words *Deployment strategies* a lot, but what exactly do we mean when we say we need to choose an appropriate deployment strategy for the application? Let's spend some time exploring this.

Making a choice about the deployment strategy

Once we have figured out that we are now ready for taking our application into production, we are now tasked with the work of figuring out the application deployment strategy that we are going to use.

The deployment strategy for the application will usually lay out the rules for how the application will be rolled out, depending upon the kind of application we have. These deployment strategies cover the information about the kind of steps that are required to have the application available in production, and may also cover some other important areas about how the new features are rolled out in the application.

So, let's spend some time discussing the different kinds of deployment strategies available and the benefits associated with choosing one deployment strategy over the other.

The different deployment strategies

Inside the software development world, there is no one solution fits all, and this is true even when making a choice for the type of deployment strategy that we are going to follow for the deployment of our application.

Every deployment strategy we choose will have certain advantages and disadvantages associated with it. Some of the deployment strategies do not provide a lot of flexibility but are simple to implement, whereas the other deployment strategies are very flexible but can become a pain while implementing it in the process. As developers, the choices depend upon how we want to approach the deployment of the application. Majorly, there are six deployment strategies that we are going to cover over the course of this chapter, namely:

- Recreated deployments
- Rolling deployments
- Blue/green deployments

- Canary deployments
- A/B deployments
- Shadow deployments

So, let's spend some time getting familiar with each of them.

Recreated deployments

This is the most traditional approach to the deployment of the applications. In this strategy of deployment, we simply destroy the old version of the application and introduce a new version of the application, and, route all the user requests to the new version of the application. The following diagram shows a representation of the Recreate deployment strategy:

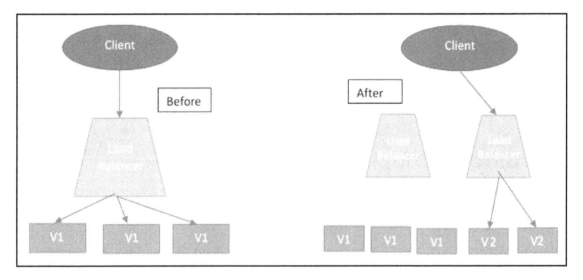

This kind of strategy is really useful for the deployment of an application that follows the monolithic development approach, because for every new feature or upgrade, the whole application needs to be redeployed.

The advantages of going with the recreate deployment strategy are as follows:

- **Simple:** The strategy is very simple to implement; every time we have a new release, we replace the existing instance of the application with the new one and route all the traffic to the new instances.

- **Simple Infrastructure:** In implementing this strategy, the infrastructure is simple since we do not need to embed any kind of logic defining what request will be sent to which instance. A simple **Load Balancer** just balances the requests.

One of the major drawbacks of this deployment strategy is the fact that the downtimes associated with the upgrades can be high, because to make the change from version 1 of the application to version 2, we need to bring down the complete version 1 first and then launch version 2 of the application. In the time period between these launches, there will be no application instance that will be available for processing the incoming requests.

Rolling deployments

In the rolling deployments model of deploying an application, we do not abruptly take down all the instances of the older version of the application to replace them with the newer version. Instead, we take a gradual approach of rolling out the new application version across the infrastructure.

In this process, we first launch a new instance of the upgraded application behind the **Load Balancer**, and once it is ready to accept the traffic, we remove the equivalent instance of the older version of the application. This process continues until all the older instances of the application have been replaced with the newer instances. The following diagram shows a representation of the Rolling deployments strategy:

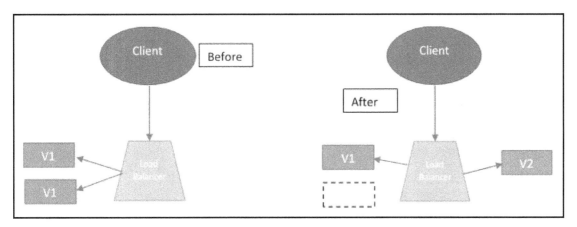

This kind of deployment strategy is also a good choice for monolithic applications in case we want to achieve low downtimes with the application upgrades, because the application is rolled out gradually inside the infrastructure.

The rolling deployments provide several benefits, such as the following:

- **Easy to revert faulty upgrades:** In case an upgraded version of the application introduces some bug or fault, we can easily roll back the upgrade in the mid phase. This is possible because the new version is rolled out gradually inside the infrastructure.
- **Easy to set up:** With the knowledge of the infrastructure on which the application is running, this deployment strategy is easy to set up and automate, where the different parts of the infrastructure are updated one by one.

Blue/green deployments

The blue/green deployment strategy is an interesting strategy. This strategy implements a mix of techniques there are used for testing the application and launching it in production.

Inside the blue/green approach to deployments, the updated application is introduced inside the infrastructure with the equivalent number of instances as that of the older version of the application. Once this is done, the new version of the application is tested inside the infrastructure. Once the version is found to be stable, the traffic is then switched from the older version to the newer version of the application and the older version of the application is decommissioned. The following diagram shows a representation of the Blue/Green deployments strategy:

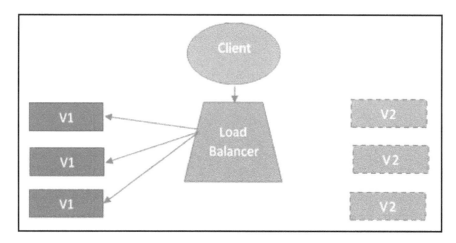

This kind of deployment strategy is highly effective in both monolithic applications as well as the applications based on `microservices` architecture.

This kind of deployment provides a certain set of benefits that are not present inside the recreate deployments and rolling deployments:

- **Quick state changes:** Since the application introduces the new application version as a whole, the traffic inside the production infrastructure is switched from the old version to the new version in one go without any kind of downtime taking place.
- **Instant rollback:** In case the newly introduced application shows some anomaly in the behavior, the requests can be immediately switched back to the older version without any hassle, essentially rolling back the upgraded application. An interesting question that may come up with such a deployment regarding the rollback of the databases if the two versions have incompatible database schemas. In this case, a small rollback helper program might be required to successfully move the data between the incompatible schemas.

The only cons with this kind of approach is that now we need to maintain a bigger infrastructure that can handle two copies of the application, where one is old and the other one is new, and provide an easy way of switching between those instances.

Canary deployments

In this approach of deployment, we follow the same strategy as in the blue/green deployments but with a minor change. Inside the blue/green deployments, the testing was carried out internally, and once the new version of the application was marked stable, all of the requests were used to switch to the new version in one go.

Inside the canary deployment approach, the testing happens based on the actual user requests. The **Load Balancer** is configured to redirect a certain percentage of the requests to the canary version that has been deployed in the infrastructure to see how the new version performs in the presence of the actual requests.

The following diagram shows a representation of the Canary deployments strategy:

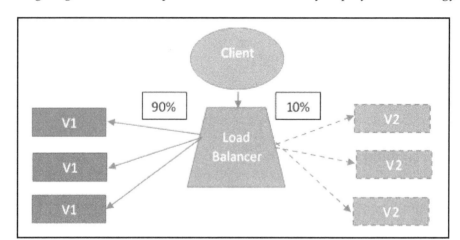

This kind of deployment approach is usually used for microservices-based applications when the internal testing of the application is deemed not to be enough, and there is a doubt about the stability of the infrastructure on which the application is running.

This testing approach provides the advantage of testing the application in the production use case, while allowing for easy rollback in case the application does not meet the expected results.

The drawback to using this kind of approach for deployment is the added complexity inside the infrastructure, which now needs to be intelligent to route a part of the incoming requests to the canary versions of the applications.

A/B deployments

The A/B deployment approach shares a lot of similarities with the canary deployment approach, where a new version of the application is introduced into the production infrastructure and a certain number of incoming requests are redirected toward the canary version.

In the A/B deployments, the upgraded version of the application (version B) is introduced into the production infrastructure, and the load balancer is then configured to redirect a certain set of requests to the upgraded version based on some predefined criteria.

This kind of deployment approach is required when we are not sure how an upgraded version will affect a certain subset of users. For example, how will the users using a smartphone be affected by an upgraded version of the application?

If the functionality for the use cases seems to meet the expectations, version A is decommissioned and version B acts as a production version, handling all the incoming requests to the application.

The advantages of utilizing A/B deployments provide us with the following:

- **Control over request distribution:** With the A/B deployments in place, we are in control of how the requests are distributed across the different versions of the application that are deployed in production.
- **The Ability to evaluate the functionality for a subset of users:** In this approach, if there is some kind of doubt about how a particular update to the application will affect the subset of users meeting a certain criterion, we can specifically test the new version of the application with those users by introducing request redirection rules for the users inside the load balancer.

Shadow deployments

In the shadow deployment approach, we introduce a new approach. In comparison with canary deployments or A/B deployments, where a certain number of requests are handled by the old version and a certain number of requests are handled by the new version of the application, we have two versions of the applications inside the production infrastructure. These are the old version and the new version, which contain the latest updates.

Inside the shadow deployments, the updated version of the application sees the exact same requests that are being sent to the old stable version of the application, with the catch that any processing done by the new version of the application instances does not affect the response for the request that is handled only by the stable instances inside production. The following diagram shows a representation of the shadow deployments strategy:

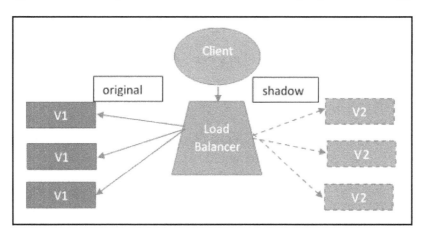

This kind of deployment approach is usually preferred for microservices-based applications, and is used when developers want to test the application for its behavior when the load on the application varies.

This kind of deployment is also employed to check if the application behaves correctly in real-world use cases, which cannot be tested in internal environments.

The only con to taking this kind of approach is the fact that the infrastructure costs are increased for these kinds of deployments because we need to run both the older version and the newer version at full scale.

Now, with this, we are accustomed to the different kind of deployment strategies that are present to help us decide how we want to deploy our application in production. While some of these deployment strategies focus on the simplicity of the process, others focus on making sure that the newer versions being deployed are stable enough and provide the best possible results.

Which deployment strategy to choose for the deployment of your application is greatly dependent upon several factors, which include the cost of infrastructure you can take up, the amount of time that can be spent in the maintenance of the infrastructure, and the type of application that you plan to deploy. Another important factor that limits the choice of the deployment strategy that can be utilized is the fact of having the APIs between the applications changed. Usually, these kinds of changes are governed by the use of SLAs, and if they take place, the deployment strategy might need to be updated to accommodate for the changes made.

At the time of writing this book, a lot of organizations are moving to the cloud as their preferred choice of infrastructure to deploy their applications in production. So, let's spend some time understanding the various kinds of cloud infrastructures that are present, and how can we decide upon which one to use for our deployments.

Making a choice of infrastructure

An application needs an infrastructure over which it can run. Depending on the type of application that is there, the infrastructure that's required may be changed. The choice of which infrastructure to choose for the deployment of the application is greatly influenced by the type of the application that is being deployed, the complexity of the application, and the kind of use cases the application is going to support.

Another important factor while choosing the infrastructure for the deployment of the application is the concern for the scalability of the application, which includes the complexity with which we can scale the application up and the type of scaling we can employ.

First let's take a look at the traditional ways of deploying the applications and understand the issues that happened that provided a push for the move toward cloud-based deployments.

The traditional infrastructure

In the past, when the applications used large monoliths to perform a number of business processes, the developers and the organizations used to resort to an infrastructure that was composed of large mainframes or virtual machines running over beefy servers to provide the adequate amount of resources required to run the applications.

These bare metal machines or virtual machines were provisioned with all the requirements that are essential for running the application, and then the application was deployed on these machines and made available to users for general use.

This kind of infrastructure choice worked well and even allowed multiple applications to exist on the same beefy bare metal server, isolated through the use of virtual machines, abstracting away the hardware of the server.

However, this approach was plagued by a number of issues, such as the following:

- **High cost of infrastructure**: For deployments that utilized bare metal systems or virtual machines, the cost of infrastructure was high. The organizations either needed to purchase those beefy servers that were capable of running these applications, or had to resort to dedicated hosting providers, which used to cost a lot.
- **Increased overhead**: For any application that was running inside a virtual machine, the overhead incurred by running a full-fledged virtualized operating system that supported the application was very high, greatly reducing the number of applications that could coexist on the same hardware.
- **High start up times**: As the load increased, new instances of the application needed to be spawned up to handle the increased number of incoming requests. However, starting the complete virtual machines with the application instances running inside them was a slow procedure due to the whole process that needed to be carried out for a virtual machine to boot up.

- **Difficulty in scaling**: In the traditional infrastructure, the amount of horizontal scaling that could be done was very limited, and usually the only choice left for scaling the applications up was through the use of vertical scaling, where the resources dedicated to the application were increased based on the needs.

These drawbacks made the developers think about the alternatives to the traditional way of deploying applications.

Another major reason that fueled this move away from using the traditional infrastructure was the move toward the containerized approach to application packaging. Let's take a look at what this is.

Containerized approach toward application packaging

With the advent of modern hardware and progress in software engineering, some operating systems introduced a light-weight alternative to heavy virtual machines. This alternative came in the form of containers, which promised not only a lower overhead approach to application segregation but also the fact that they were also fast enough to spawn up due to the fact that they did not abstract the underlying hardware at all.

As the development of the applications moved toward the use of microservices architecture, the containerized approach to application packaging became more and more mainstream. In this approach, every microservice used to be packaged as a separate container that could be deployed within an infrastructure. This container used to package all the dependencies that were required for a particular microservice to run and also kept the microservice isolated from the other microservices or applications that were running on the same hardware.

Now, when a particular application used to see a higher load, the scaling up of the application took place by the virtue of launching new replicas of the containers of the specific microservices. This process was blazing fast in comparison to launching new virtual machines consisting of the application instances due to the fact that containers were a very light-weight processes that did not require an initialization of a complete operating system inside them to start an application.

With this, the cost of maintaining the infrastructure also got reduced and now more applications could co-exist on the same hardware, in comparison to what was the case when virtual machines or bare metal servers were being used.

All these developments led to the eventual rise of cloud service providers and fueled the process of cloud-based deployments for applications.

The move toward the cloud

In the last decade, a number of cloud providers have come into existence to help provide support in regards application deployment. Each of these cloud providers offers a distinguished set of features to make their service stand out from the competition when it comes to luring the organizations and developers to use their platform for the deployment of their applications.

The shift toward the cloud deployment model provides various kinds of advantages for the developers/organizations that are responsible for the development of the applications, including the following:

- **Reduced cost of infrastructure maintenance**: As the application deployments move to the cloud, the costs of maintaining the infrastructure are reducing. This is happening due to the fact that the cloud providers are now responsible for maintaining the hardware on which the applications are running, and the individual developers and organizations do not need to purchase this hardware and handle any kind of issues that may happen with it.
- **High uptimes**: Most of the cloud providers guarantee a high uptime for their infrastructure, which is made possible due to the high amount of infrastructure replication done on their end. The end beneficiaries of this are the developers who are maintaining a particular application in the cloud, because now they can provide a high uptime to their application users without worrying about the productivity losses that may happen if the infrastructure goes down.
- **Low latency**: Inside the cloud deployment approach, the developers can aim to provide low latency to the application for the users. This is made possible by replicating the application instances across the different geographical data centers of the cloud service provider. Once the application is replicated, the cloud service provider then re-routes the requests to the application servers, which are in close proximity of the client so as to facilitate low latency responses.

- **Easy scaling**: As the load on the application increases, new application instances might need to be spawned up to handle the increased load. The cloud service providers usually provide the facility of dynamically scaling up the application as the load on it increases and scaling down of the instances as the load subsides. This provides a high throughput, low cost solution to handle the peak loads without worrying about the manual intervention that is usually required in the traditional infrastructure. Also, the response times associated with this scaling are usually low in comparison with what is present in the case of traditional infrastructures.

All of the preceding points make a compelling argument for the shift to cloud-based deployments for the applications. But based on the needs of an organization, they may or may not want their application to be deployed on a third-party server where the organization barely has any control. To handle such scenarios, the organizations may decide to move toward their own private clouds that run on their infrastructure and handle the deployments of all the applications inside the organization. So, let's spend some time understanding the various models of cloud deployments that are out there.

The different types of cloud deployments

When it comes to enterprises, they are highly sensitive about where their applications are running. This happens because of the fact that the enterprises deal with a wide variety of data that may contain a lot of sensitive information, and any kind of breach may threaten their business. As a developer who is building an enterprise application, it is our responsibility to suggest and decide which kind of cloud deployment should be used for the deployment of the application. Mainly, the type of clouds that exist currently are categorized into two main categories:

- Public clouds
- Private clouds

Recently, a third kind of category is also on the rise, known as hybrid cloud. So, let's take a look at what differentiates these clouds from each other, and which one should we use.

Private clouds

A private cloud is a set of computing resources that are tightly governed by an enterprise. These clouds run inside the corporate intranet and are usually located either in the data centers owned by the organization or are maintained by the third parties.

These clouds implement a very strict security policy that defines how the applications running on them can be accessed and who can access them.

Usually, an enterprise chooses a private cloud due to the following points:

- The enterprise already has a data center of its own and it doesn't want to reinvest in a third-party cloud
- The kind of application that is being run by the enterprise is highly security sensitive and the security policies implemented by a public cloud provider cannot be trusted or are not enough for the required use case

The private clouds offer a certain set of advantages:

- **More flexibility:** Since the organization is in control of deciding what compute resources will be present inside the private cloud, the organization maintains the flexibility to take decisions that will be in their best interests
- **Improved security:** The organization is free to run their cloud infrastructure behind a corporate firewall or an internal network with tightened security policies that may not be possible when using a public cloud

For any enterprise that is dealing with security sensitive data and does not have the barriers of cost, a private cloud makes a good choice for deploying and running applications.

Public clouds

In a public cloud, the compute resources are owned and managed by a third-party cloud service provider. As an enterprise, the application deployed by you shares the same hardware resources with a number of other applications, which may be developed by you or some other organization.

The organization usually resorts to a public cloud when their applications are not dealing with some kind of security conscious data that may require strict security policies to prevent any kind of incidents, or to run the applications that are of common use, such as their email servers.

The advantages offered by a public cloud could are vast. Some of them are as follows:

- **Lower costs:** Since the infrastructure provided by a public cloud provider is shared across multiple applications, the organization usually pays less for running their application on the shared infrastructure.

- **Reduced maintenance:** Since the cloud provider owns the resources for running the applications, they are also responsible for the maintenance of the hardware. This reduces the headache for the organization to take care of the hardware resources.

- **High failure resilience:** The cloud service provider owns a number of nodes that can be used to run the application in case one of the nodes fails. This translates to improved capability of handling the failures.

- **Increased scalability:** The cloud providers make the resources available on demand. This can be used to dynamically scale up the application to a near unlimited level as the load on the application increases.

As an enterprise, if your application does not deal with any kind of security sensitive data and you want to keep the costs required to run the application low while also maintaining the ability to scale up the application as the demand sores, you can go ahead and choose the public cloud model of deployment.

Hybrid clouds

The hybrid cloud deployment model provides the best of both worlds of the private cloud and public cloud approach. Here, the compute resources from the private cloud and the public cloud are pooled, and the applications can move from the private cloud to the public cloud as and when required.

The enterprises usually employ this kind of deployment model to run some of their less security sensitive applications on the public cloud while running the security sensitive applications inside the private cloud.

Another approach that is usually taken is to deploy the application in the private cloud first and then when the number of requests increase, the resources from the public cloud are pooled in to scale the application up by launching more processes inside the public cloud.

The benefits associated with the hybrid cloud approach are as follows:

- **Control**: The organization can take control over running the security sensitive applications inside their private clouds while running the less security sensitive application on the public cloud

- **Flexibility**: As and when the need arises, the organizations can pool in the resources from the public cloud to handle higher loads

- **Cost effectiveness**: Since the resources from the public cloud are only pooled when the demand for the application is high, the organization can save upon the costs of the public cloud by using the public cloud resources only when required

For applications that can easily transition from one place to another, or any that may require the facility of dynamic scaling up while also keeping security in check, the hybrid cloud deployment approach provides a good choice for infrastructure.

Summary

During our journey through this chapter, we took a look at how we can make decisions related to the deployment of enterprise applications. We explored the different deployment strategies that are there and how they can affect the way our application runs inside the production. Moving on, we learned about six different deployment strategies that can be used for the deployment of monolithic and microservices-based applications, and saw what advantages and disadvantages they offer.

Once accustomed to the deployment strategies, we took a deep dive into the infrastructure choices on which the applications are deployed and got to know about how the move to a microservices-based development approach has fueled a transition from traditional deployment approaches using virtual machines and bare metal servers to cloud-based deployments.

We ended this chapter by taking a look at the advantages that are offered by cloud-based deployments and the different types of cloud deployments that can be chosen by an organization to deploy their application.

In the next part of this book, we will turn our focus to a very important topic that covers the integration of the applications we are developing with the other applications that are running inside the organization, and how we can facilitate that kind of integration without introducing unnecessary complexity inside the infrastructure of the organization.

Questions

1. What are the benefits of having a blue/green deployment approach?
2. How does a canary deployment help in testing the applications before the application goes into production?
3. What are the issues that we may face if we run microservices-based applications using the approach of virtual machines?
4. How can we handle deployments in the hybrid cloud model?

15
Enterprise Application Integration and its Patterns

During the course of this book, we've covered how to implement enterprise applications. These have been either large monoliths that implemented a lot of components in order to provide a certain set of functionality or microservice-based applications where the application consisted of several small services, all of which worked to provide a certain feature and provide output based on the business's needs by interacting with each other over the network.

But, in any enterprise, there's seldom a case that the application we have developed will be the only application that might be present. Rather, most of the time, the enterprise infrastructure will consist of a number of applications that have been deployed by the enterprise to achieve one or another business need that the enterprise might have. This may include applications facilitating employee record management and customer support management. All of these applications that are present may have been developed internally by the enterprise or could have been taken from a third-party solution provider. To have all of these applications work effectively, there's a requirement for these applications to communicate with each other.

Over the course of this chapter, we'll take a look at how we can achieve this integration between the different applications that exist in the infrastructure, so as to achieve the business needs of the organization.

As a reader of this chapter, you'll get to learn about the following:

- The need for enterprise integration
- Challenges in enterprise integration
- Utilizing middleware for achieving enterprise integration
- The patterns in **Enterprise Application Integration (EAI)**

Technical requirements

The follow up for this chapter does not require any special tools or presence of a particular software on the development system. But some knowledge about the functionality of middleware and enterprise service bus solutions will help in understanding the context of this chapter.

The need for EAI

In any large enterprise, there're a number of applications that may exist to solve a particular problem domain. Each of these systems works to solve only one set of problems. Often, this kind of approach is desirable for building applications inside an enterprise, because now the applications can use the best available technology stack for solving the problems of their domain.

But to have any useful business impact come out of these applications, its often the case that these applications need to talk to each other through one way or another, so as to facilitate the exchange of data that may be present in one application and required by another.

But this integration of different applications is a challenging task due to a number of factors:

- **Incompatibility across the infrastructure:** When the applications are deployed in the infrastructure, the individual applications may be running on different platforms, which may involve varying operating systems. They may have their own way of representing data and facilitating communication between the different components of the infrastructure. This makes the task of integrating these applications with each other difficult.
- **Integration of data:** Each of the applications that we introduce into our infrastructure may introduce its own data source that it'll use to store and retrieve its data. For the successful integration of these distributed systems and applications with each other, we need to make sure that the data being held by these applications is integrated properly and is consistent across the different data sources.
- **Robustness of the integration:** Most of the integrations are made possible through the use of glue layers between different applications. These layers, which facilitate the integration of the applications, should be robust enough and should be able to scale well so as to accommodate the growing needs of the enterprise.

To overcome these challenges, we have a number of options. One of the traditional ways of achieving this was through the use of point-to-point integration between the different applications. So, let's take a look at what this approach provides us.

Point-to-point integration

One of the approaches to solve the problem is to enable point-to-point integration between the applications. By this, we mean that each application has a set of connectors that allows it to talk to another application. For every pair of applications that need to talk to each other, there needs to exist a separate connector that facilitates communication between the applications.

This approach is completely fine when the number of applications that need to talk to each other is small. But as the enterprise grows, its needs also grow, which means commissioning new applications into the infrastructure. Now, as the number of applications grow, the number of connectors that are required to facilitate the communication between the different applications will also start growing, reaching a level at which the infrastructure will become just too complex to manage and maintain.

To enable the integration of a large set of applications inside the enterprise, which may grow over the time, we may require something that is more flexible and that can help us to standardize the way these applications communicate with each other. The move to EAI is just the kind of architecture that we are looking at, as it aims to help us achieve these objectives. So, let's take a look now at what EAI has in store for us.

Moving towards EAI

When we aim to standardize the way in which the different applications running in our infrastructure will communicate with each other, and how they will store the data, the EAI approach really provides us with an option that is not only flexible in nature but also scalable, without introducing unnecessary complexities into the infrastructure.

The EAI pattern provide us with a framework that consist of tools and technologies that help us standardize the way the communication between the different applications takes place. An EAI framework usually comes with the components that facilitate the exchange of data between the applications and their transformation from one format to another and act as a glue layer between the different applications.

With this approach, every application does not need to have an understanding for how to communicate with another application directly. Usually the integration between the applications is achieved through the applications talking to a centralized EAI arbitrator, which acts as an intermediate between the cross-application communication and translates the requests of one application for another application and propagates back the response.

All of these components that come as a part of the EAI framework are collectively known as middleware frameworks.

So, how does EAI work? Let's try to take a look at the different ways in which EAI was used to be achieved and how it's changing with the technologies moving forward.

The traditional approach to EAI

In the early days of EAI, the applications needed to interact with each other in various formats, which may include communicating some information or exchanging data. To facilitate this exchange, the organizations came up with a hub and spoke model for EAI.

In this hub and spoke model, there's a router-based middleware component and a concept of events. Whenever there was some change in the state of one of the applications, the application used to generate an event. The other applications subscribed to the event stream they were interested in.

Now, whenever a new event was generated, the router was responsible for the delivery of the event to the interested applications handling the conversion of data from one format into another, so that the applications could communicate with each other. In this kind of approach, the router became the central point of facilitating the integration between the different applications.

The router provided a lot of features, such as the following:

- **Adapters and SDK:** For the applications to communicate with the router to raise events, they need to have some kind of glue that facilitates the connection between the application and router. The adapters provided by the router middleware used to provide this necessary glue layer. In case there was no supported adapter for an application, the router middleware provided an SDK to facilitate the development of an adapter.

- **Message transformation:** When a new event has been generated, the router, based on a set of some pre-defined rules, used to translate the messages associated with an event into a format that can then be consumed by another application. This kind of functionality was important to facilitate communication between two different applications, each of which have their own data storage formats and communications styles.
- **Intelligent routing:** For the applications to work seamlessly with each other, there needs to be a guarantee that the correct event is reaching the correct target audience. The router middleware used to implement intelligent routing based on which application generated the event and which applications are interested in listening to that event, so that the messages generated as a part of an event are delivered to the correct recipients.

This kind of approach provided a nice mechanism to remove the unneeded complexity from the enterprise infrastructure that would have been developed if every application had to communicate with other applications directly, managing their own connector, and handling data consistency. Whereas, with this approach, the router facilitates the communication between the different applications.

But, as good as this approach was with all of the benefits, it suffered from some of the following serious drawbacks:

- **Single point of failure:** The broker model to the EAI proved to be a single point of failure. In case the router middleware goes down, all communication between the different applications will come to a halt.
- **Centralized logic:** The logic for the transformation of the data, along with the routing of the data, was all centrally located inside a single router. This caused the broker to become a complex component making the operations and maintenance of the broker a difficult task.
- **Poor scalability:** When the load on the router increases, the handling of the messages by the router can take a hit. This results in an inconsistent state of data between the different applications. Also, having a single, centrally located router becomes a hurdle in the geographical scalability of the router if the applications that are trying to connect to each other are located in the different geographies around the world.
- **Proprietary solutions:** In the earlier days, when the router-based hub and spoke approach of integrating enterprise applications was there, most of the solutions used to be proprietary in nature and supporting only a subset of vendors. To get some application from an unsupported vendor integration, it was a huge problem for the developers, who would then need to write and maintain their own adapters based on the provided SDK.

All of these issues called for a better approach to be implemented that does not suffer the same issues as the router-based approach had. Eventually, the enterprises started to shift to a **service oriented architecture** (**SOA**) model and introduced the use of an **Enterprise Service Bus** (**ESB**) for integrating these different services inside the SOA. So, let's take a look at how the ESB changed the way EAI happens.

The introduction of the ESB

As the times moved forward, enterprises shifted to a new model of application development. This model used to model the applications as a service, where each service used to provide a certain set of business capabilities. So, for example, in an enterprise there will be a payroll service, which will provide all of the necessary functionality related to the management of the employee payroll, such as handling the data for the new employees, keeping a record of how much salary they have got and generating the monthly payslips.

Now, these services needed to be integrated with each other so that the exchange of data between these services could be facilitated. At this point in time, the enterprises needed something that would allow these services to communicate with each other over the network without the bottleneck of handling the different data formats that each service maintains.

The solution to this came in the form of the introduction of the ESB. The ESB model of service-based integration focused on the message oriented style of service communication. When the services have to communicate with each other, they will do it through the use of messages.

Let's take a look at some of the features of the ESB and how it allows for a better integration model:

- **Decoupling of applications:** The ESB provides the decoupling between the different applications by introducing an arbitrator bus between the applications. The applications now need not talk to each other directly, but rather talk to the bus, which is responsible for facilitating communication between the applications.
- **Standardized data format:** All of the messages that flow inside a bus usually follow a standard format, such as XML. Every application that needs to communicate with another application now only has to deal with one data format, except for their own, greatly simplifying the process of integration.
- **Orchestration:** The ESB is responsible for the orchestration of the message flow and making sure that the messages are being delivered to the correct recipients.

- **Ability to scale:** The ESBs are usually easier to scale, because they do not have any centrally located business logic built inside them that will need to be replicated. The scalability is usually achieved through either vertical scaling, by dedicating more resources to the ESB, or through the use of horizontal scaling, by introducing more instances of the ESB into the infrastructure.

This makes the ESB a great choice for the integration of the applications inside the enterprise while also allowing the flexibility in the integration process.

Now we have an idea about the different approaches to the EAI. So, now it's time for us to move on and understand the different patterns of EAI.

Patterns in EAI

EAI is an approach that has several patterns associated with it that govern how the applications are integrated. Which pattern to use usually depends upon the type of applications that are present in the enterprise infrastructure, and what kind of challenges there are in the integration.

So, let's take a look at these patterns and see how they are usually implemented.

Integration patterns

During the EAI, the integration patterns define how the applications will be integrated with each other. This may define how the different applications will communicate with each other and how these applications will transform the data. So, let's take a look at two broad ways in which the applications are integrated with each other.

Mediation pattern

In the mediation pattern of EAI, there's a central component that is responsible for the propagation of the events. For example, in the broker-based middleware model, whenever one of the applications generates an event, the event is handled by the middleware broker, which is then responsible for the propagation of the event to the other applications that are interested in that event.

In this type of integration pattern, usually the applications directly interact with each other, facilitated by the middleware broker who relays the events that happen, and after which the event handlers for the other application are responsible.

Another integration approach that usually implements the mediation pattern is the message bus approach, where the message bus acts as a mediator between the different applications delivering messages to each other to facilitate the communication between them.

Federation pattern

The federation pattern is the complete opposite of the mediation pattern in terms of functionality. While the mediation pattern focuses on direct communication between applications without providing any kind of barrier between them, the federation pattern usually restricts free communication between applications.

Inside the federation pattern, there's middleware that exposes a standard set of endpoints through which the other applications can communicate with it. Once the application makes a request to an API of the federation middleware, the federation middleware is then responsible for translating and passing that request to the backend application. Once the backend application processes the request, the federation middleware then responds back to the requesting application with the response.

The use of gateways inside an EAI usually utilize this kind of pattern, where the gateways restrict what functionality is exposed by the backend applications and how those functionalities will be exposed to the third-party applications.

Access patterns

Access patterns define how the access to the data happens within the applications inside the enterprise infrastructure.

Usually there are two kinds of access patterns that are followed: asynchronous and synchronous access patterns. Let's take a look at what these patterns aim at.

Asynchronous access patterns

The asynchronous access pattern follows the fire-and-forget approach to data access. In this case, once the middleware forwards the request, it doesn't wait for the response for that request to arrive back and moves on the handling of the newer requests that it's receiving.

The asynchronous access pattern is usually followed in the mediation approach, where the router middleware, once notified about the occurrence of a certain event, propagates the event forward and forgets about the event without waiting for its reply.

The same is the case with the message bus model; the message bus, once it has delivered a message, does not care about the response for the message being generated, hence making the process an asynchronous process.

Synchronous access patterns

The synchronous access pattern works in the opposite manner to the asynchronous pattern. Instead of forwarding the request and forgetting about the response, the synchronous access pattern makes a request and then waits for the response to be generated by the other application.

This kind of pattern is usually followed in the case of federated integration, where the middleware acts as a intermediate, handling the access to the backend applications it's managing.

For example, inside a gateway-based pattern, the middleware usually takes up the request, forwards the request to the backend application, and then waits for the response to arrive, before moving on to the next request.

These were just a few basic patterns that govern the process of EAI. There are close to 65 EAI patterns that are still in use that facilitate the concept of EAI.

Now, let's take a look at some of the common issues that prevent a successful integration between the different enterprise applications.

Issues in EAI

The successful integration of enterprise applications is usually affected by a number of factors; let's take a look:

- **Proprietary data formats:** Some of the applications use their own proprietary data formats with very little documentation on how to integrate with them, preventing integration between the applications or causing the application integration to be of poor quality, and therefore resulting in a number of issues.
- **Data consistency issues:** Maintaining data consistency can turn out to be a problem for EAI. When every application maintains their own data source, the consistency of data across the different data sources can turn out to be problematic, especially if the middleware is experiencing heavy loads, resulting in different versions of the same data to persist across the infrastructure.

- **Performance implications:** Inside EAI, a middleware is responsible for providing a glue between the different applications. This glue layer facilitates the transformation and transportation of data from one application to another. When a lot of applications are trying to communicate with each other concurrently, this middleware may see high loads impacting the performance of its routing and data transformation processes, causing an overall impact on the application infrastructure that might result in some slowdowns until the load on the middleware is reduced.
- **Security issues:** Since the different applications communicate through the use of a middleware, the middleware needs to make sure that the transportation of the data is secured from end to end. If even one endpoint is left unsecured, the whole application may see a security compromise.

Summary

Over the course of this chapter, we took a look at why EAI is necessary for the proper functioning of enterprise business processes. Once we understood the necessity of EAI, we then moved on to understand the approach toward EAI, where we explored the point-to-point integration of application, and why the process of point-to-point integration is problematic. We then explored the traditional way of implementing EAI through the use of a broker middleware model, before continuing the discussion about how the model transformed as SOA came into place, and how the ESB took the place of the broker-based model.

We then moved on to understanding the different patterns that are in EAI and learned about the mediation and federation integration patterns of connecting the different applications, followed by understanding how the different access patterns, such as asynchronous and synchronous access, work in the transportation of information from one application to another. We concluded this chapter by exploring some of the issues that plague the successful integration of applications in an enterprise.

As we move to the next chapter, we'll learn about how the introduction of microservices has changed the EAI landscape and has ousted the use of the ESB, and how it's now being replaced by distributed message brokers and API gateways.

Questions

1. What are the issues that are usually faced during point-to-point integration?
2. How does an ESB connect the different types of applications together?
3. What are the different types of EAI patterns that exist facilitating the approach of application integration?

16
Microservices and Enterprise Application Integration

The introduction of microservices architecture has completely transformed the way in which enterprise applications are viewed. These applications are no longer large monoliths or big services providing the functionality to solve the problems of a specific domain. Instead, we now have small microservices, each providing a specific set of functionalities.

These small microservices communicate with each other over the network to provide a certain output corresponding to the business needs of the organization.

As we move through this chapter, we will see how the traditional approach of doing **Enterprise Application Integration (EAI)** is being made obsolete by the move towards the use of microservices that have introduced new integration patterns consisting of small, stateless message brokers instead of a large and complex Enterprise Service Bus.

The communication between the clients has now been replaced by the use of API gateways that provide a federation between the clients and the backend microservices.

As a reader of this chapter, you will get to learn about the following:

- Microservices and the change in the EAI landscape
- The transformation of the Enterprise Service Bus
- Thinking EAI in terms of microservices architecture

Technical requirements

This chapter builds upon the contents of `Chapter 11`, *Taking the Microservices Approach*, and `Chapter 15`, *Enterprise Application Integration and their Patterns*. As such, no special set of hardware or software is required to understand the contents presented in this chapter, but some knowledge of distributed message brokers and asynchronous messaging systems will help provide a broader context as you go through this chapter.

Microservices and the changing EAI landscape

Recently, organizations have started to move toward a new approach for the development of their applications. This approach focuses on the development of the application when composed of several small services that are good at providing a single functionality and providing it well. These small services are known as microservices.

These microservices model the functionality of a subset of an enterprise domain. For example, there could be a service in the infrastructure that is responsible for handling the user credential and authentication, another service that could be handling the functionality of emails, and yet another service that processes the paychecks of the employees.

All of these services communicate over the network by the mechanism of passing messages or through making API calls from one service to another service through the use of APIs exposed by the service so as to achieve a particular use case.

Now, in contrast to traditional applications that were large and required middleware that could handle the transformation of the data from the format supported by one application to the one supported by another application and then transporting that data securely, microservices require either an API through which one service can directly talk to the other or a small message broker through which the data can be transported from one microservice to another in the form of messages.

This has changed how Enterprise Application Integration used to happen, because now, there are no complex middleware solutions present in the infrastructure providing the glue layer to connect the different applications inside the infrastructure.

So, let's take a look at why the traditional approaches do not work in the microservices architecture and try to understand the new alternatives that have come up to facilitate the integration of application in the enterprise.

Challenges of traditional EAI in microservices

In applications that have been developed by the modern practices of developing small microservices, hosting them over the enterprise infrastructure, and then integrating them together to talk to each other, we can no longer use the traditional approaches we were familiar with during the times of running and maintaining large monolithic applications or services. Let's first take some time to understand why point-to-point integration might not work in the case of microservices.

Point-to-point integration of microservices

In the point to point integration approach for microservices, we make the microservices interact with each other directly through the APIs exposed by them. For this to happen, each microservice needs to have the knowledge about the endpoints exposed by the other service. This is perfectly fine, but what happens if the microservice has to do some operation that depends on interaction with five other microservices?

At this point, we have to embed the endpoints of five different microservices into our microservice. As a one-off task, this is a completely OK solution. But, pertaining to the nature of microservices, they keep on evolving over time. This now causes us to keep on updating our microservice again and again to reflect the updated APIs.

This is just one of the challenges. Usually, applications based upon microservice architecture grow over a period of time to have more than 100 hundred services that are operating in the infrastructure, making it really hard to achieve point to point integration between the different microservices.

So, we now have an idea about how the microservices cannot be integrated through the use of point to point integration, can we use the good old Enterprise Service Bus? Let's take a look.

Integrating microservices using the ESB

The Enterprise Service Bus usually provides an intermediate bus through which two applications can communicate with each other by the mechanism of message passing. This ESB also has a standard format in which the messages can be encoded before they are sent.

Now, we can possibly hook our microservices to the ESB and then these services can communicate with each other by passing messages. This approach is absolutely fine and works. But the real problem starts to happen as the number of microservices start to grow in the infrastructure. Once this happens, then the ESB starts to see a heavy load due to the huge number of messages that are being transported by it.

Another reason why the ESB fails to scale well is the fact that the microservices can be running anywhere inside the infrastructure distributed across geographies. Having to scale a resource-heavy ESB, along with the possible replication required for the different microservices to work properly, can pose a challenge in the integration of microservices through the use of ESBs.

So, let's briefly examine what challenges are posed in the integration of microservices as a result of utilizing the traditional EAI approach:

- **Complexity of the application:** An application may consist of a huge number of small microservices. If these services are to be integrated directly with each other, it can create a very complex infrastructure that could be really hard to manage and maintain as the application evolves over a period of time.
- **Difficulty in communication:** Inside the microservices approach to application development, every microservice is free to use the set of tools and technologies that are best suited for it to achieve its purpose. This makes a really difficult case to support the integration of microservices with each other directly because of the different data formats and tooling supported by individual microservices.
- **Performance issues:** If microservices are integrated through the use of middleware, integration can frequently run into performance issues due to the excess load that the microservices architecture can generate on the infrastructure.
- **Scalability concerns:** The applications built on top of a microservices architecture can really have a large number of microservices running that could be distributed across the geographies. Reliably scaling up the middleware and providing replication across the geographies can turn out to be a really hard task to achieve.

So, let's now see how the microservices architecture replaces the traditional integration approaches with the modern ones.

Utilizing API gateways for the integration of microservices

The use of API gateways in a microservices architecture provides a really interesting way of approaching the microservices integration problem, while also following one of the patterns of application integration through the use of federated gateways. So, let's take a look at how the API gateways help us in the process of microservices integration.

An API gateway inside the microservices-based application acts as central point through which the microservices can interact with the other microservices present in the infrastructure. This API gateway provides the following characteristics:

- **Restricted exposure of APIs:** The API gateway provides the functionality of exposing only a restricted set of APIs from the backend microservices, hence limiting what functionality is exposed. Along with this, the API gateway can also introduce new API endpoints in the infrastructure, where each API endpoint can map to multiple API endpoints of the backend microservices.
- **Federated access:** An API gateway implements federated access for the integration of the microservices. This happens because of the fact that, if any two services want to interact with each other, a call needs to be made to the API gateway, which will indeed make the request to the other microservice and provides the result from the microservice.
- **Transformation of request:** The API gateway is also responsible for the transformation of the request between the microservices if both of them use a different mechanism of representing the data. For this kind of transformation to take place, the API gateway usually implements a common data format that every service can use to handle the communication with the API gateway, a concept which was usually implemented by the ESBs.

For microservices integrated through the use of API gateways, the process of communication between the different microservices looks as follows:

- Imagine that there are two microservices, *A* and *B*
- The microservice *A* wants to notify the microservice *B* of some event that has taken place as a result of some call or any other outside event
- The microservice *A* makes an API call to an endpoint of microservice *B* exposed by the API gateway
- The API gateway takes up the request, performs any kind of transformation on the request, and forwards the call to the microservice *B*

- The API gateway now waits for the response to be returned from the microservice *B*
- Once the response is returned, the API gateway transforms the response into the format supported by microservice *A* and returns the response back completing the cycle

This kind of process is usually followed with the other services as well.

The use of API gateways for the integration of the microservices provides a number of advantages over the traditional approaches, as in the following examples:

- **Improved security:** Since the API gateway restricts the exposed backend APIs, the API gateway provides better security between the different microservices. This security can also be increased by implementing simple end-to-end encryption between the communications happening between the different microservices and API gateway.
- **Better scalability:** An API gateway provides better scalability than traditional middleware-based approaches by allowing for dynamic scaling through the use of a load balancer. Multiple API gateway processes can run behind a load balancer, eventually distributing the requests coming to them.
- **Easier maintenance:** Applications integrated with the use of API gateways are usually easier to maintain due to the reduced amount of API endpoints that they need to manage individually.

Those are some great benefits and it seems like a good approach for integration of microservices-based applications. So, do we not require an ESB anymore? Has the ESB gone?

The answer to this is no. Rather, it has transformed with the advent of microservices. Let's take a look at how this transformation looks.

Transformation of the ESB

With the advent of the microservices revolution, the Enterprise Service Bus has also seen a change, where it has now been replaced by some similar solutions, but with the advantages of far better scalability and the removal of single point of failure.

The ESB in application integration used to play the role of a central bus, which acted as an intermediary between the applications that wanted to communicate with each other. The ESB facilitated this communication by introducing common data formats and providing adapters through which the applications could talk to the ESB.

But the ESB still suffered two major drawbacks:

- **Scalability:** The ESB was a heavy piece of middleware that required a specialization to work with. The scalability of the ESB was hard due to the sheer amount of resources required to scale the bus, and this was even harder when the bus had to be scaled to support applications located in different geographies.
- **Single point of failure:** The ESB proved to be a single point of failure. Since all of the applications used to communicate through the use of a single central bus, if the bus fails, all of the applications will come to a halt. One question that may come here is, why can't we have more than one instances of the ESB deployed to provide high availability? The answer to this is that although we can have a highly available setup of an ESB available, it might be too costly in terms of the resource utilization and maintenance.

These two issues are really major concerns in the microservices architecture, where the services are distributed in nature and need to talk to each other to provide meaningful business outcomes. The ESB needs a transformation here.

To deal with asynchronous communication, the microservices architecture introduced the use of stateless message brokers. These message brokers were very lightweight in nature and overcame the challenges that were present in the ESB, while supporting most of the essential features from the ESB.

The use of these message brokers provided the following set of functionalities:

- **Asynchronous communication through messages:** These message brokers provide the facility for implementing asynchronous communication between the different microservices through the use of messages and asynchronous message communication protocols such as **Asynchronous Message Queuing Protocol (AMQP)**.
- **Support for common data formats:** The message brokers support the use of common data formats in which the messages can be transformed.
- **Easy scalability:** These message brokers are very easy to scale by simply launching more instances of the broker and support replication across the multiple geographies.

- **Removal of central point of failure:** With the use of these stateless brokers, there is no single point of failure. If one of the message brokers goes down, the services can start routing the messages to the other brokers inside the infrastructure. Also, the messages that have been previously sent are not lost due to the presence of the replication functionality. This replication happens through the use of a message queue replication mechanism when we run the message broker in a master-replica configuration, where there is a master node and one or more replication nodes. When a message arrives, it is first written to the message queue on the master node, and then it is replicated across the mirror nodes. In case the master node fails, these connections are routed to one of the mirror nodes, which can then take on the responsibility of the master node.

This makes a very strong point in the use of message brokers for the integration of microservices-based application, and providing asynchronous communication between them.

Rethinking EAI in microservices

With microservices in the picture, with their own set of tools and different requirements, we now have to rethink the approach of EAI in the enterprise infrastructure. So, let's take a look at few of the points that we need to take care of when considering the application integration in microservices-based infrastructures:

- **Planning for expansion:** The applications inside the microservices infrastructure are evolving continuously, and their integration needs to be planned in the same manner. While thinking about the integration strategy, we need to make sure that it will be able to support the future scale of our applications and the type of communication that our application may warrant.
- **Defining the APIs:** The APIs exposed by the microservices play an important role in the integration of the different applications. Before the development of a microservice is started, its APIs should be planned well and documented, so as to allow for smoother integration with other services.
- **Keeping the data formats standard:** The data formats in which the different microservices manage their data should be standardized to have only a few sets of formats, so as to enable an easy integration and reduced complexity in the infrastructure.

Summary

Over the course of this chapter, we took a look at how the introduction of microservices as a development approach to enterprise applications has completely changed the way applications inside an enterprise used to integrate.

We took a look at how the traditional approaches to Enterprise Application Integration fail when applied to the microservices architecture, and then we took a look at how the transformation of EAI has happened with the introduction of API gateways and distributed message routers.

At the conclusion of this chapter, we took a look at how the planning for the Enterprise Application Integration has changed as we have moved to a microservices-based approach.

From here, we now have an idea about the different aspects of the development of enterprise applications and their complete cycle inside the organization, from development to deployment. Further, you can now dive deeper into the specific areas that you, as a reader, found out to be interesting.

Questions

1. What are the bottlenecks of point to point integration in microservices applications?
2. How has the Enterprise Service Bus changed with the advent of microservices?
3. How do the message brokers inside microservices architecture provide high availability?

Assessment

Chapter 1

Answer 1

Concatenation of a `byte` type, which is an immutable type, and a `str` type isn't permissible in the Python 3 standard; any attempt to concatenate these two types will raise `TypeError`.

Answer 2

The type-hinting support introduced in Python 3 is only intended to provide greater clarity in documenting the methods and the parameters and doesn't enforce any standards on the operations.

Answer 3

Beyond the functional and nonfunctional requirements, a software requirements specification document also specifies other requirements, such as UI, performance, business, and market requirements.

Answer 4

The various kinds of requirements are categorized as follows:

- **Must-have requirements:** These are requirements that must be present inside a system. If any are missing, their absence will affect a critical functionality in the system.
- **Should-have requirements:** These are requirements that, if present, will enhance the functionality of the application.
- **Could-have requirements:** These are requirements that are noncritical in nature. If they are missing, they won't have any impact on the application's functionality.
- **Requirements wish list:** These are requirements that the stakeholders might want to see in future updates of the application.

Answer 5

Once the software requirements specification document has been generated, the next steps in the process include the design phase of the software. In the design phase, the structure of the software application is decided upon and decisions are made regarding the possible technology stacks that might be used to build the software.

Chapter 2

Answer 1

The chain of responsibility pattern inside Python allows us to build an application with loose coupling in mind. This is achieved by passing a received request through a chain of objects inside the software.

The following code snippet shows the implementation of the chain of responsibility pattern inside Python:

```python
import abc

class Handler(metaclass=abc.ABCMeta):
    """Handler provides an interface to build handlers."""

    def __init__(self, handler=None):
        """Initialize the handler.

        Keyword arguments:
        handler -- The next handler object to be called
        """

        self._next_handler = handler

    @abc.abstractmethod
    def handler(self, data):
        """The handler abstract method.

        Keyword arguments:
        data -- The data to be processed by the handler
        """

        pass

class StringHandler(Handler):
    """String type object handler."""
```

```
    def handler(self, data):
        if type(data) is str:
            print("Stringt type data found.")
        elif self._next_handler is not None:
            self._next_handler.handler(data)
        else:
            raise Exception("Unable to find a suitable handler for data.")

class IntegerHandler(Handler):
    """Integer type object handler."""

    def handler(self, data):
        if type(data) is int:
            print("Integer type data found")
        elif self._next_handler is not None:
            self._next_handler.handler(data)
        else:
            raise Exception("Unable to find a suitable handler for data.")

if __name__ == '__main__':
    int_handler = IntegerHandler()
    str_handler = StringHandler(int_handler)
    str_handler.handler(2)
```

Answer 2

The __new__ method is the first method that's called when a new instance of an object needs to be created, whereas the __init__ method is run only when the newly created instance of the object needs to be initialized. In the normal flow of class instance creation, the __new__ method will always be executed first and should only be overridden when the developer wants to gain control over the creation of new instances. This method should then be followed by a call to the __init__ method, which will be called once the instance has been created and will need to be initialized.

Answer 3

It's quite easy to define a new abstract class using the ABC metaclass. The following code snippet shows an example of achieving this kind of behavior:

```
import abc

class Handler(metaclass=abc.ABCMeta):
    """Handler provides an interface to build handlers."""

    def __init__(self, handler=None):
```

```
    """Initialize the handler.

    Keyword arguments:
    handler -- The next handler object to be called
    """

    self._next_handler = handler

@abc.abstractmethod
def handler(self, data):
    """The handler abstract method.

    Keyword arguments:
    data -- The data to be processed by the handler
    """

    pass
```

Chapter 3

Answer 1

The normalization of the schema inside a DBMS provides a number of benefits, such as the following:

- Improved overall organization of the relationships
- Reduction in storage of redundant data
- Improved consistency of the data inside the database
- Better indexing of the data, which improves access to the data

Answer 2

The lazy loading in SQLAlchemy provides the developer with an option to use the *select* or *joined* modes, in which the lazy loading can be performed. When the developer goes with the *select* mode of loading the data, the loading of the datasets happens through the emission of SQL SELECT statements, which load the data on a per-requirement basis.

When using *joined*, the related datasets are loaded all at once through the emission of SQL JOIN statements. This technique is also known as joined eager loading.

Answer 3

There are multiple ways through which we can maintain the integrity of data as we perform data updates. One of the easiest methods for this that we can implement is through the use of transactions, which allow us to make a number of updates in an atomic transaction, where either all of the updates in the transaction are applied or none are applied.

In the case that one of the updates inside the transaction fails, the previously applied updates inside the transaction are rolled back as well, thereby maintaining a consistent state of relations across the database.

Answer 4

The different levels of caching that can be implemented with a database are as follows:

- **Caching at database level:** When we cache at the database level, we usually utilize the built-in functionality of the database, which caches the datasets that are being frequently used by maintaining the query caches.
- **Caching at block level:** Caching at the block level happens at the application level, where we cache the data fetched by the ORM layer into a memory-based data store so as to avoid running a database query every time a certain result is asked for.
- **Caching at the user level:** When caching at the user level, the non-security-critical data is cached at the client side through the use of session cookies or local storage.

Chapter 4

Answer 1

Python has two different ways in which it allows us to build applications that can process requests concurrently. These are listed as follows:

- **Multiprocessing:** The Python multiprocessing module allows the developer to launch multiple processes to handle the workloads in parallel
- **Multithreading:** The Python multithreading module allows the developer to execute multiple threads, which can be used to handle the concurrent workloads

Answer 2

When the thread that has acquired a lock terminates abruptly, there are multiple possible scenarios based on how the lock was acquired.

If the lock was acquired through the use of a `with` statement in Python, then the lock will be released as soon as the thread terminates.

If the lock was acquired inside the `try-except-final` approach, then the lock will be freed as the exception propagates to the final statement.

If the lock was acquired without any kind of safety procedure, an abrupt termination of the thread will cause a deadlock because the lock has not been freed.

Answer 3

Usually, when the main program receives a termination signal, the signal is also propagated to its threads; otherwise, a thread can be marked as a daemon thread so that its execution is terminated with the main program.

Another way to achieve this is through the use of flags, which a thread can check at regular intervals. If the flag is set, then the thread starts with the termination.

Answer 4

The sharing of state between different processes can be achieved through the use of pipes, which can help the processes communicate with each other.

Answer 5

In Python, we have multiple ways of creating process pools for the distribution of the tasks. We can create these pools manually—as shown in the example in the *Synchronization of processes* section in this chapter—or we can utilize the provided `ProcessPoolExecutor` from the `concurrent.futures` library.

Chapter 5

Answer 1

For handling requests through the use of multiple application instances, we use the concept of horizontal scaling, where we launch more than one instance of the same application behind a load balancer. The load balancer is then responsible for distributing the incoming requests across this pool of application instances.

Answer 2

The process pools can be implemented through the use of `ProcessPoolExecutor` from the `concurrent.futures` library in Python. An example of how to use `ProcessPoolExecutor` to distribute the requests over a pool can be seen in the *Using thread pools for handling incoming connections* section of this chapter.

Answer 3

It is completely possible to have a program that combines the use of multiprocessing and multithreading. The following snippet of code shows this implementation:

```
import threading
import multiprocessing

def say_hello():
    print("Hello")

def start_threads():
    thread_pool = []
    for _ in range(5):
        thread = threading.Thread(target=say_hello)
        thread_pool.append(thread)
    for thread in thread_pool:
        thread.start()
    for thread in thread_pool:
        thread.join()

def start_process():
    process_pool = []
    for _ in range(3):
        process = multiprocessing.Process(target=start_threads)
        process_pool.append(process)
    for process in process_pool:
```

```
        process.start()
    for process in process_pool:
        process.join()

if __name__ == '__main__':
    start_process()
```

The preceding way of achieving this is valid and can be easily implemented without any issues, though you might find that it has a limited number of use cases, and its use will be limited by the implementation of the GIL.

Answer 4

A simple example of implementing a socket server is shown in the *Implementing a simple socket server with AsyncIO* section of this chapter. Another way is to implement a fully functional web server through the use of AsyncIO is by using the `aiohttp` framework, which provides an AIO-based HTTP server.

Chapter 6

Answer 1

In addition to the generic `View` class that we saw during this chapter, Flask also provides another prebuilt pluggable view class known as `MethodView`.

Answer 2

Yes, it's possible for us to remove the foreign key constraint for the role table from the user table and keep the relationship there. But whenever we need to store the data, we will need to manually insert the required object for the role object inside the user table.

Answer 3

There are a number of alternatives to Gunicorn to serve a Flask-based Python application, such as the following:

- uWSGI
- Twisted web
- `mod_wsgi`
- Gevent

Answer 4

Increasing the number of Gunicorn workers is very simple. All we need to do is to add the `-w <worker count>` parameter in the command to set the number of Gunicorn workers, as shown in the following example:

```
gunicorn -w 8 --bind 0.0.0.0:8000 wsgi:app
```

Chapter 7

Answer 1

The use of CDN does improve the loading performance of a web page. This is because of the way the browser caches the content from a given URL. Sometimes, we can gain the following benefits when we use an existing CDN to serve some of the content:

- For some of the frontend libraries that are common, there is a chance that the libraries are already cached by the user's browser while they visited some other website, which include the content from the CDN. This helps us to avoid redownloading those libraries and reduces the bandwidth usage and improves the loading speed of the page.
- CDNs can also route the request to the servers based on the user geography so that the content is downloaded with the least possible latency, thereby improving the loading speed of the page.

Answer 2

To make the browser use the existing connections, we can utilize a concept called `KeepAlive`. When the `KeepAlive` headers are set in a request, the connection that is used to make the request is kept open by the server for a fixed amount of time in the hope that the same connection can be used for working on another request, avoiding the cost of the initial connection setup for every other request.

Answer 3

The JavaScript API provides a very handy method known as `removeKey(key)`, which can be used to remove a particular key from the local/session storage of the browser.

Chapter 8

Answer 1

The major difference between a unit test and a functional test is the scope of testing, as described in the following:

- **Unit test:** A unit test usually focuses on the testing of individual components in a software that could be factored to a single function or a method of a class
- **Functional test:** Functional tests are also known as integration tests and usually test a specific functionality of the system that may encompass the interaction of multiple components with each other, along with their interaction with the external environment, such as database systems.

Answer 2

A test suite is a collection of test cases that needs to be run on a specific program. Writing a test suite using Python's `unittest` library is quite easy to achieve. For example, if you've written a few test cases, such as `TestTextInput`, `TestTextUppercase`, and `TestTextEncode`, we can combine them into a test suite by using the following code snippet:

```
import texttest # Module containing our text related test cases
import unittest

# Create a test loader
loader = unittest.TestLoader()

# Create a test suite
suite = unittest.TestSuite()

# Add tests to a suite
suite.addTests(loader.loadTestsFromModule(texttests)
```

Answer 3

The purpose of fixtures inside Pytest is to provide a fixed and stable environment over which the tests cases can execute. These fixtures are responsible for initializing the environment by setting up the required variables or interfaces that may be required for a test to execute.

Another advantage of using a fixture is its reusability, which allows the same fixture to be used for multiple tests without any issue.

Answer 4

The fixture scopes in Pytest describe how often a fixture will be called. The fixtures have a lot of different scopes that can be applied to them, as shown in the following:

- **Function scope:** Fixture is run once per test
- **Class scope:** Fixture is run once per class
- **Module scope:** Fixture is run once per module
- **Session scope:** Fixture is run once per test session

Chapter 9

Answer 1

There are multiple factors that can be a cause of performance bottlenecks inside an application, including the following:

- Inadequate planning of hardware resources required to run an application
- Poor choice of algorithms for implementing a functionality in the application
- Improperly implemented database relations with a lot of redundancy
- Not implementing proper caching for frequently accessed data

Answer 2

Time profiling on a method in Python helps us to understand how much time was taken by the method to execute. Based on the requirements, there are several different ways through which we can run a time profile on a method, as shown in the following lost:

- **Using the `timeit` module:** The `timeit` module provides us with a functionality that we can use to find out the time it takes for a script or a method to execute.
- **Using the `time` module:** We can also use the `time` module to help us measure the runtime of a method in Python. We can do this through the creation of decorators, which can help in the profiling of the method runtime.
- **Using the `cProfile` module:** The `cProfile` module allows us to profile the runtime of the different steps inside a Python program.

Answer 3

Although Python is a garbage-collected language with no direct access to memory pointers, the typical memory leaks possible through illegal pointer operations can hardly happen. But there's another way through which the Python program can continue to consume more and more memory without releasing it. When the program forgets to dereference the objects once they're no longer in use, this may cause new objects to be allocated without the garbage collection of objects that are no longer in use taking place.

Answer 4

The API response from an application can be profiled by measuring the average time taken for an API to return a response over a fixed set of executions. This can be measured in multiple ways that may involve the use of the `timeit` or `time` modules from the Python standard library.

Answer 5

The design patterns can have an important role in the performance of the application, and an incorrect design pattern can have a performance penalty on the application performance. For example, consider the allocation of an object that may be used implement logging throughout an application. If this logger object allocation needs to happen separately for every individual module or class, then we might be wasting quite a lot of resources to allocate an object when it could have been shared across the different modules.

Chapter 10

Answer 1

There are a number of issues that make security an application hard these days. These issues include the following:

- The rise in sophisticated attacks that are hard to mitigate
- The increase in the rise of 0-day vulnerabilities that have not been patched
- More and more state-sponsored attacks that target multiple vulnerabilities of a system and are usually hard to trace
- An ever-increasing number of devices coming online without proper security in place, making them vulnerable to being used in DDoS attacks

Answer 2

An XSS—or cross-site scripting—attack is when an attacker injects a malicious script inside a trusted website. When the page with the malicious script is loaded, it causes the client system to be compromised by the attacker.

Answer 3

A DoS—or denial of service—attack is used by an attacker to make a service or resource unavailable to its users by flooding the system with superfluous requests, which causes the system to queue up those requests causing a disruption in the service.

The attack can be mitigated through the use of different techniques, implemented at different levels, such as the following:

- Adding a firewall rule to deny traffic from a given untrusted source
- Using services from the cloud security providers, who can analyze the incoming traffic and block it before it reaches the application infrastructure, helping to mitigate the DoS attack
- Configuring the infrastructure to sink the traffic to a node where there is no application running, or by rerouting the traffic to a nonexistent network interface by using DNS rules

Answer 4

There are lot of possible mistakes that can compromise the security of the application, such as the following:

- Using insecure third-party libraries inside an application, which may contain security vulnerabilities
- Not filtering the user-provided input to the application
- Storing security-sensitive data unencrypted inside an application
- Not implementing proper restrictions to control access to the internal infrastructure

Chapter 11

Answer 1

The major difference between service-oriented architecture and microservices architecture is the fact that, in a service-oriented architecture, the application consists of different services, each providing the functionality to work on one of the business domains of an organization. These services communicate with each other through the use of the enterprise service bus, which routes the messages from one service to another while also providing a common format for message exchange.

In the case of microservices, the application will consist of a number of small microservices, where each microservice is responsible for providing only a single functionality that may not map to a complete domain of an organization and may just be a subset of larger problem domain. These microservices communicate with each other through the use of APIs exposed by the individual microservices or through the use of stateless message routers that allow the delivery of messages from one service to another.

Answer 2

To ensure that a microservice-based application has a high uptime, we can make use of the following techniques:

- Not using a single storage for all of the microservices
- Running multiple instances of the same microservice behind the load balancer
- Using API gateways to provide graceful degradation in a service where the client still receives a response when a critical service has failed

Answer 3

The use of service-level agreements—or SLAs—provides a number of guarantees, such as the following:

- A guarantee about the API stability of a service
- A guarantee about the uptime of a service
- A guarantee of the expected response times of a service
- A guarantee of the request rate limitation implemented by a service

Answer 4

The API gateways can communicate directly with the service registry through the use of the SDK provided by the service registry or through the use of the APIs exposed by the service registry. This allows the API gateway to automatically fetch the correct location for a given service from the service registry.

Answer 5

Asynchronous communication inside microservices can be implemented through the use of stateless message brokers. To implement asynchronous communication, some microservices act as producers and send a message to the message-broker queue. Then, other microservices may consume that message, process it, and send a response back to the microservice that sent the message. The response is then processed by the callback that was set by the requesting microservice. This is how the asynchronous communication between the microservices is established.

Chapter 12

Answer 1

The integration tests for microservices are written in mostly the same way as those for monolithic applications, with the following few differences:

- If the microservice needs to communicate with some another external microservice, then the integration test might need to have the external service set up so as to properly execute the test case
- The components that comprise the individual service should be set up for all of the microservices in place in the infrastructure—for example, a database that accompanies a particular microservice that is needed for testing purposes

Answer 2

The tracing of a monolithic application differs from that of a microservice-based application in the way that the tracing of a monolithic application involves understanding the flow of the request from one component to another inside the application. In contrast, tracing a microservices-based application involves understanding how the request flows not only inside a particular microservice, but also from one microservice to another.

Answer 3

There are multiple tools that are available for tracing within the microservice architecture, as shown in the following list:

- Jaeger
- Zipkin
- Appdash

Answer 4

For tracing the individual components inside a microservice, we can utilize one of the functionalities provided by Jaeger known as spans. An example of how to use spans can be seen at `https://github.com/jaegertracing/jaeger-client-python`.

Chapter 13

Answer 1

There are a number of advantages that are provided by a move to serverless architecture, such as the following:

- Reduced development effort through the integration of third-party services
- Less operational complexity, because now the organization doesn't need to take care of the infrastructure
- Improved security, since the individual functions execute in their own separate containers, which helps us to keep the different functions from interfering with each other
- Improved scalability of the application

Answer 2

The use of **Backend as a Service** (**BaaS**) helps in the creation of applications by providing common set of functionality through the integration of the APIs. These services are hosted by a third-party provider,thereby reducing the effort that the application developers will have to expend in rebuilding them in their application from scratch.

Answer 3

The API gateway in a serverless architecture maps the API endpoints to a function in the backend. These API endpoints can then be called by the clients when a particular event occurs, invoking the backend function.

Answer 4

There are certain reasons why an application cannot be ported successfully to a serverless architecture. These reasons are as follows:

- The use of a technology stack that may not be supported by the serverless infrastructure provider
- Applications that need to store the state of the request processing to generate correct results
- A tightly coupled code base that makes it hard to define individual methods
- Some components of the application taking an extremely long time to execute

Chapter 14

Answer 1

The use of blue–green deployments provides us with the following set of benefits:

- The ability to switch the application from one version to another instantly
- The ability to easily roll back the application from a newer version to an older version in case the new version experiences some critical functionality bugs
- A reduction in downtime related to application upgrades

Answer 2

Using a canary deployment can help in the testing of an application in the following ways:

- The application is tested with a small sample of real-world requests, which may help expose any unidentified bugs in the application
- Canary deployment gives us the ability to run the new version of the application along with the older version so as to compare the responses provided by the APIs

Answer 3

Using virtual machines for running microservices-based applications can cause increased overhead for running the microservice instances because of the higher requirements incurred by a virtual machine. In addition, the use of virtual machines limits the number of services that can coexist on the same infrastructure because a virtual machine is comparably heavier to run than containers, which utilize operating-system functionality to keep the programs isolated.

Answer 4

The deployments in the hybrid cloud model can be handled in the same way that they are handled in the public or private clouds. The difference arises when the application needs to be scaled. In this case, when using the hybrid cloud approach, an organization can pool the resources from the public cloud based on the scaling necessity and can then run some parts of their application in the public cloud and the others in the private cloud.

Chapter 15

Answer 1

The point-to-point integration of the enterprise applications requires a connector to be built for every pair of applications that needs to integrate. This creates a complex infrastructure that can be hard to manage as well as scale if new applications are introduced into the environment.

Answer 2

The enterprise service bus is responsible for helping different services inside an infrastructure connect to each other through the use of message-passing mechanisms. The ESB provides connectors for the applications through which the applications can connect to the ESB and send messages to the ESB.

The ESB then assumes responsibility for routing these messages to the correct service that they are intended for, thereby promoting communication between the two services inside an infrastructure.

Answer 3

The different types of patterns that facilitate the approach of EAI are as follows:

- Mediation pattern
- Federation pattern

Chapter 16

Answer 1

The point-to-point integration of different microservices is hard to achieve because of the different technology stacks that may be used by a particular microservice that is present in the infrastructure. This may cause individual connectors to be built for every pair of microservices in order to translate the data format of one microservice to another.

Another bottleneck happens because of the scalability of these services, since now the connectors have to connect every single instance of the deployed microservice.

Answer 2

The enterprise service bus has been replaced with stateless message routers with the advent of microservice architecture, where these routers can be scaled up individually and implement message routing for the wide number of microservices that might be running inside an infrastructure.

Answer 3

The message brokers inside a microservice architecture provide high availability by replicating message queues between the multiple instances of the message broker that might be running. This allows the routers to take the place of a failing router and keep communication inside the infrastructure intact.

Other Books You May Enjoy

If you enjoyed this book, you may be interested in these other books by Packt:

Hands-On Software Engineering with Python
Brian Allbee

ISBN: 978-1-78862-201-1

- Understand what happens over the course of a system's life (SDLC)
- Establish what to expect from the pre-development life cycle steps
- Find out how the development-specific phases of the SDLC affect development
- Uncover what a real-world development process might be like, in an Agile way
- Find out how to do more than just write the code
- Identify the existence of project-independent best practices and how to use them
- Find out how to design and implement a high-performance computing process

Clean Code in Python
Mariano Anaya

ISBN: 978-1-78883-583-1

- Set up tools to effectively work in a development environment
- Explore how the magic methods of Python can help us write better code
- Examine the traits of Python to create advanced object-oriented design
- Understand removal of duplicated code using decorators and descriptors
- Effectively refactor code with the help of unit tests
- Learn to implement the SOLID principles in Python

Leave a review – let other readers know what you think

Please share your thoughts on this book with others by leaving a review on the site that you bought it from. If you purchased the book from Amazon, please leave us an honest review on this book's Amazon page. This is vital so that other potential readers can see and use your unbiased opinion to make purchasing decisions, we can understand what our customers think about our products, and our authors can see your feedback on the title that they have worked with Packt to create. It will only take a few minutes of your time, but is valuable to other potential customers, our authors, and Packt. Thank you!

Index

C

caching
  at block level 71, 72
  at database level 71
  user level caching, using 72, 73
  utilizing 70
canary deployments 295, 296
client-side caching
  application-wide cache control, setting 164
  benefits 163
  request level cache control, setting 165
  utilizing 163
client-side service discovery 244, 245
cloud deployment
  hybrid cloud 304, 305
  private cloud 302, 303
  public cloud 303, 304
  type 302
cloud
  about 301, 302
  advantages 301, 302
component-level performance analysis
  executing 199
  memory usage, profiling with memory-profiler 203, 204, 205, 206
  profiling, with cProfile 201, 202, 203
  slow operations, measuring with timeit 199, 200, 201
composition 30
concurrency
  in enterprise applications 77, 78
  in GUI applications 76, 77
  need for 76
  problems, of accommodating 100
  scaling up 101
concurrent access
  communication, establishing between Nginx and Gunicorn 152
  deploying for 150
  Gunicorn, setting up 150
  Nginx, setting up as reverse proxy 151
concurrent programming
  Global Interpreter Lock (GIL) 91, 92
  with multiprocessing 92
  with multithreading 79, 80, 81, 82

with Python 78, 79
cProfile
  for profiling 201, 202, 203
credential theft 218
Cross-Site Request Forgery (CSRF) 218
Cross-Site Scripting Attack (XSS) 217

D

data loading
  advantages 69
  optimizing 69, 70
database consistency
  maintaining 60, 61
  transaction, utilizing 61, 62, 63
database models
  developing 138, 139, 140, 141
  migrating 142
database
  about 50
  SQLAlchemy, setting up 52
deadlocks
  about 89
  avoiding 90
Denial of Service (DoS) 218
deployment strategy
  A/B deployments 296, 297
  about 291, 292
  blue/green deployment 294, 295
  canary deployments 295, 296
  recreated deployments 292, 293
  rolling deployments 293, 294
  selecting 291
  shadow deployments 297, 298
design pattern, classification
  behavioral patterns 27
  creational patterns 27
  structural patterns 27
design pattern
  about 25, 26
  choice, defining 28
  consequences 27
  problem statement 26
  solution 26
development environment
  database, setting up 128, 129

SQLAlchemy
  setting up 52
synchronous access pattern 315

T

test-driven development (TDD) 179
testing, microservices
  about 257
  challenges 259
  end-to-end testing 258
  functionality testing 257
  integration testing 258
  scalability testing 259
  unit testing 257
  workarounds 260, 261
testing
  benefits 173
  importance 172, 173
  integration testing 175, 176
  types 173
  unit testing 174
thread pools
  incoming connections, handling 106, 108, 109
thread synchronization
  about 82, 83
  condition variables 85, 87
  re-entrant locks 84, 85
timeit
  slow operations, measuring 199, 200, 201
to-do manager service
  about 238
  implementing 238, 239, 241, 242
tracing
  distributed tracing 264, 265, 266
  implementing, in ToDo manager 262, 263, 264
  of requests 261
  OpenTracing standard 261
traditional infrastructure
  about 299
  issues 299, 300
transaction

consistency, maintaining 61, 62, 63
type hinting 12, 13

U

Unicode 10, 11
unit testing
  about 174
  features 174
  in microservices 257
unit tests
  writing 180
  writing, with pytest 183, 184
  writing, with Python unittest 180, 181, 183
user level caching
  using 72, 73
user microservice
  /auth/login API 236
  /auth/register API 236
  /auth/validate API 236
  about 234
  functionalities 234
  implementing 236, 237
  token database model 235
  user database model 235
users
  management 19
  workforce 19

V

vertical scaling 101
views
  building 143
  index view, developing 143, 145
  index view, getting to render 145
  user registration view, building 146, 149

W

web storage
  local web storage, using 167
  session storage, using 168
  utilizing 166, 167

www.ingramcontent.com/pod-product-compliance
Lightning Source LLC
Chambersburg PA
CBHW080613060326
40690CB00021B/4675